YOU'VE NOT COME HERE TO ENJOY YOURSELF

YOU'VE NOT COME HERE TO ENJOY YOURSELF

The astonishing story of the soldier who walked around the world

DAVID FAIRS

First paperback edition 2023

ISBNs:

978-1-80541-257-1 (paperback)
978-1-80541-259-5 (hardback)
978-1-80541-258-8 (ebook)

Marcus Fairs

27th November 1967 – 30th June 2022

Beloved son

CONTENTS

FOREWORD

I met David for the first time when, as young Army officers, we served together at the Headquarters of 3 Commando Brigade, based in Singapore, but also for much of the time separately engaged in the Confrontation with Indonesia in Borneo. It was a strange war but the Defence Secretary at the time said 'it was one of the most successful uses of military forces in the history of the world'. Not many Defence Secretaries have been able to say that.

We had both recently completed the Commando course at Lympstone at the Royal Marines Commando Training School, receiving our green berets, and together, shared many escapades on active service in Sarawak and Sabah. There, our paths separated for a while as David was based in Kuching with Brigade Headquarters looking after the logistics operations and I was having a less comfortable time attending to the Intelligence operations.

On return to Singapore, we shared a flat together and life could not have been more ideal with both of us finding a taste for non-military accommodation for the first time in those tranquil days before Singapore gained its independence.

We lost touch for a couple of years when I left the Army to study Classical Arabic at Oxford while David stayed on to attend the Canadian Armed Forces Staff college in Kingston, Ontario. We met up again on his return and I was delighted to be invited to Marcus and Rupinder's wedding and, later, our relationship was further strengthened when he asked me to be Marcus's godfather.

We have maintained contact over the years and it gives me so much pleasure to write the Foreword to an extraordinary man who has drawn so much from life, whether it was navigating the cataracts of the Nile or receiving the Freedom of the City of Duisburg after a traumatic start or becoming the proud member of the Parachute Brigade with its red beret and his 80 jumps from low-flying aircraft.

His planning has always been outstanding, backed by his ability to resolve problems even as they arise. While his Army training remains deep within him, it runs hand in hand with his humour. I can see both of these traits reflected throughout the pages of this book. Meanwhile, David will continue to stretch his clients minds or expand their goals, or both. I wish him every success in the future.

Sir Geoffrey Tantum, CMG OBE MA MCIL

– former member of the British Intelligence Services

Some of Those Who Helped Me

I would like to say a huge thank you to the following for their help and cooperation in so many different ways and their contribution in putting this book together. It is greatly appreciated.

Marcus Fairs – My son, for his valuable help and guidance in how to approach writing the book, based on his own collection of publications and for recalling the early days of Langdale Walking Holidays when he was a Partner and Tour Leader.

Lieutenant Colonel Philip Bulpin – Tough Airborne Officer who has remained a friend throughout thick and thin and a captivating speaker at dinner parties on Langdale Walking Holidays.

Malcolm 'Nipper' Taylor – For his recollections of our early days together in Gower and some of the exploits we got up to.

Jim Dalziel – His meticulous collection of notes, far superior to mine, of our trip down the Nile and for identifying all the places we visited. All his grandchildren used our expedition as school projects and received 'A' stars for such original and detailed descriptions.

Sarah Medwell – Sarah, my niece, spent a considerable amount of time checking and re-checking the manuscript.

Steve Bavin – For taking the time and trouble in vetting some of the early chapters of the book.

Sir Geoffrey Tantum – It was a great pleasure sharing several weekends with Geoff going over some of the events of our days together when, as young Army officers, we were seconded to 3 Commando Brigade Royal Marines in the Far East. We each remembered events, some of which one or the other of us had forgotten. A great reunion of minds.

Dan Visser, Director of Langdale Leisure Ltd. – Dan sent me some excellent images of the lodges and hotel on the Langdale Estate and kindly allowed me to see some of the notes associated with the 'buyout' of the Estate from Scottish and Newcastle plc.

Howard and Lorna Jones – In drawing my attention to our camping expedition in Wadi Rum, Jordan, and still struggling to forgive me for not providing electricity for her hair dryer in the desert.

Elwyn and Jill Jones – For their strong support, friendship in connection with Langdale Walking Holidays over many years and bringing our group back safely from Peru and Bolivia when faced with civil disturbances and rioting in Peru.

Geoff Buck – Geoff is a formidable photographer and, as well as sharing some of these with me for the book, he also provided comprehensive reminders of some of his trips when he was tour leader.

John and Chris Williams – My Welsh history and Welsh language advisors for help in planning our Welsh destinations, particularly the visit to the Falcondale Hotel in Mid Wales which included a recital by the Cwman Male Voice Choir and a Harpist for our evening entertainment.

John Harris – For his comprehensive and much valued reviews after every Langdale Walking Holiday and developing significant friendships with many clients over the years.

Sheila Crouch – Great help in contributing to the many shared experiences of events that took place on The Langdale Estate.

John and Rosanne Levy – As a top London lawyer, John prepared the legal requirements for Langdale Walking Holidays Booking Conditions and kept us on the straight and narrow over the years. Generously without fees, apart from dinner in a local hostelry and a glass of wine on the next get-together. Also, wonderful friends and provider of remarkable hospitality.

Denise Fairs – Last but not least, to my wife, Denise, for making allowances over nearly 12 months when I was hunkered down writing the book, sometimes to the exclusion of all else, particularly when there were chores to be done and the ever important garden to look after.

Others will come to mind and I apologise for any omissions here, but need, at least, to thank them here as well.

OVERTURE

'Touch and Go'

It was a warm, sunny day. The training jump was straight down the line. Standard. It should have been just as I had been taught. Wait for the light and jump. It was not something the everyday businessman would have thought of doing, of course, but I was in the Paras where getting out of planes quickly and efficiently was something I did for a living. My issue, and the reason for writing this now was I found myself, this time, upside down and tied up with cords like a trussed-up chicken ready to roast.

RAF Abingdon was the venue for low altitude jump training and 800 feet doesn't give much space to make corrections if things go wrong. Something was going wrong in a big way when I realised my chute had deployed inside-out, damaging many of the nylon panels causing my descent to be too rapid. The word 'bugger' did cross my mind. But I knew there was always my reserve chute. I pulled the release cord pretty darn quickly. However, this only caused the chute to become entangled with my boots but, as luck would have it, with an enormous 'whoosh' it disentangled itself, though leaving me in a state of upside down-ness.

Meanwhile my main chute had, by this time, managed to become entangled with my kit and collapsed over my head.

I was told, later, 'helpful information' was being relayed to me by a loud hailer courtesy of the instructor who had his feet firmly on the grass. Me?. I heard nothing at all. Further 'help' meanwhile, was being deployed in the form of a stand-by ambulance roaring and clanging its way to my anticipated impact point which was coming ever nearer at a rate of knots.

Holding my nerve, I grasped each of the rigging lines in turn, disentangling each one from my boots until the last one was freed with just five seconds to go. It was a count-down I was happy not to have to experience again.

This most 'interesting' experience did not put me off. I was immensely proud, eventually, to join the ranks of Airborne Forces and collect my wings and Red Beret.

– PART ONE –

THE IRRESPONSIBLE YEARS

'I live in that solitude which is painful in youth, but delicious in the years of maturity....'

CHAPTER 1

Early Days

"Let us remember, one book, one pen, one child and one teacher can change the world." Malala Yousafzai

I had the good fortune to be born in Mumbles, residing in a prominent position on the Gower Peninsula – that's South Wales – and up until the age of eighteen enjoyed an idyllic childhood with my two sisters, June and Elizabeth who were permitted (at times) to join in my adventures. Later, when my father was called up for military service in the Second World War, we moved to be close to my grandmother and aunts in an area known as The Uplands. We were guided and guarded, directed and driven by Edie Lewis, our sort of, nanny. When the family could no longer afford to employ her, she remained a firm family friend and provided the support and advice as might a second mother do for me.

My father was a dental technician by profession, though his greatest love was, undoubtedly, the Army. He was in the Territorial Army with the rank of Company Quartermaster Sergeant (regrettably, this is the first of many mouthfuls). As soon as war was declared, he became one of the first to enlist and was called up for active service. He was posted to France with the British Expeditionary Force and took part in the evacuation from Dunkirk in May 1940. We have all watched TV documentaries of the beaches teeming with queuing men, attacked by constant artillery shelling on the ground and strafing from the air. Our men had been ordered to destroy as much equipment as possible to prevent it falling into the hands of the enemy, and told to make their way to the beaches and piers carrying only their personal weapons. Some were lining up on those jetties waiting for the rescue ships, while others waded out from the beaches with the water up to their necks.

Safely back in England, exhausted but alive, my father was given a forty-eight hour leave and a rail warrant to get home. Approaching Port Talbot in his train, the sky ahead lit up. The Luftwaffe was yet again attempting to destroy Swansea Docks. It failed to do so in its mission, succeeding in missing the docks but, at the same time, managed to flatten Swansea town centre. Everyone was told to get off the train as, understandably it was not going any further. My father had to walk all night to get home, draining his strength further and within a few hours he had to return to his unit, with most of his leave taken up with travelling. Shortly after that, he was posted to the Canal Zone in Egypt.

He never came home.

One day, at the age of ten in 1944, there came a ring on the door bell as I was about to go to school. It was a telegram from the War Office. My mother read it, saying nothing, and told me to take it to my grandmother on the way to school with firm instructions not to open it. But, I knew perfectly well it was to confirm his death. The telegram remains in my possession today.

Father was buried in the Commonwealth Cemetery in Matruh in Egypt where my sister, Elizabeth, and I paid a visit many years later. Having contacted the military attaché in Cairo he arranged the whole day with great professionalism. The Cemetery lay in a military zone and required permission to enter. When we arrived, we were greeted by a friendly Egyptian Army officer who gave us a conducted tour before allowing us time, on our own, to reflect on our father's comparably short life. We were asked to sign the visitors book and were saddened to see we were the first visitors in six years to sign; it was right and good we had taken the trouble to find my father's final resting place.

Now, very much on her own, my mother brought up my two sisters and I on a small War Pension and little else. It was a hard change to our lives, but we managed. We never went on holiday because we could not afford it, but there was no real need, because all our leisure time was spent either at Langland Bay or exploring the Gower.

One of the things we greatly appreciated, were regular food parcels from the Canadian Government. They contained all sorts of treats, food we would never have bought ourselves, even if we could have found it in a shop. Peaches for goodness sake, tins of fish…and butter…in a tin! Much of it was as rare as hens' teeth and we were lucky to have such a caring mother who always put us first.

My school years highlighted, well, put a searchlight on my academic inability, if this is the correct phrase to use, preferring the teaching that outdoors brought to me. My life revolved around sport and adventure. To try and counter this lack of application, Vera, one of my aunts, a teacher, spent night after night giving me additional tutoring, but the 11 Plus still eluded me, barring me from entry into a Grammar School. This meant ending up in a Secondary Modern School where I, regrettably, drifted until Edie, my still faithful nanny of years past, paid the fees for me to go to Clarke's College in Swansea. It was a private school, way ahead in its ability to provide first-class education. She opened a window and gave me a chance. In those days only about ten percent of students managed to pass into grammar schools, the remaining ninety percent ended up either in a technical college or a Secondary Modern school. The system was, of course, unfair, but, in my case, I was considered to be a "late developer" (that is a kind way of saying I was lower than average) but, by virtue of hard work and determination, managed, eventually, to climb on top of life's many obstacles.

By this time, Edie had joined the Land Army based in Carmarthen and for several years I would travel by bus to see her. She had been appointed Manager, responsible for allocating the Land Girls to different farms every day. One of them was in a small holding in a village called Whitemill. Edie became friendly with the owner and I was invited to stay for a summer holiday. That year, I spent an amazing time learning the rudiments of farming, helping out with milking, feeding the hens and being more than useful with haymaking. Shortly after the war, Edie went to Liverpool University to study social science. After graduation she spent the rest of her life finding homes for children born out of wedlock, something considered a sin in those days. She never had any children of her own. She was, truly, a very good woman, and someone I shall never forget.

As an indicator perhaps of the future, my first venture into tourism took place at Clark's College at the age of 14, when I hired a private coach for a visit to Llandrindod Wells. It included lunch in a local hotel and an hour's rowing boat hire on the lake. It poured with rain all day and we became as wet as the lake itself in a short time. We had hired the boats for an hour, but sitting on a wet thwart soaked to the skin, with cold water running down one's neck is no fun at all. We had had more than enough, and were ready to quit. However, one of the tighter fisted boys in our boat, insisted, stupidly, on getting his money's worth by sticking it out for the full hour. It was something akin to sitting in one's car in a car park until one had used up the full hour paid for parking, even though you had completed your shopping well before time. The word prat was, and is, designed for individuals such as this clot.

Attending the gymnastic club at the Swansea YMCA allowed me, as a result of many differing strengthening exercises, to gain increased body strength. It prepared me, unwittingly for the Army. It allowed me, later in life, to pass both the parachute course and commando course, thus earning my wings, red beret and commando green beret. Bouncing about in the gym all those years earlier, I had no idea how valuable it was going to be.

An old bike belonging to Peter Fairs, my cousin, was passed on down to me.. It was ancient and much too big for me as I could only reach the pedals by standing up. It did, though, get me out and about. On the way to school I remember gazing lovingly at a Raleigh Super Sports, drop handlebar bike on display in the window at Halfords. Just before Christmas I noticed it was no longer there, and pondered long and hard on who had the money to buy such a wonderful bike. It was thus, to leave me dumbfounded and delighted when, on waking up Christmas morning to be told to go and look in the hall. There was the bike, the same bike from the window. This wonderful woman, Edie, had bought it for me. It became my pride and joy and always kept it in tip top condition. It received the same sort of loving care as if I had had a puppy.

Inevitable, in time, a sports car finally replaced the bike and became part of my life. I have to admit to enjoying, pressing the accelerator to the floor to see what she would do each day. This led, as sure as eggs is eggs, one day to being booked for speeding along the Mumbles Road. The traffic policeman, in the process of taking down my details with laborious licking of his indelible pencil and seeing my surname, asked if l was related to Peter Fairs.

When I replied: 'Yes,' he said: 'We used to play rugby together.' After a friendly chat as if I was chatting to Dixon of Dock Green, he wished me a pleasant journey and no further action was taken. Peter ended up emigrating to Australia where he became the Assistant Headmaster at one of the country's most prestigious boarding schools. He lived well into his 90's and was awarded the Medal of Australia for services to the community. Ability was in his family. Peter's father, Arthur, my uncle, was commissioned into the infantry and later transferred to the RAF where he was awarded the Military Cross for gallantry, and the Croix de Guerre during the Second World War.

Although Peter had emigrated to Australia, he never forgot his roots and came back regularly to Swansea accompanied by his wife, Barbara, and it was always a fascinating experience listening to his stories. One was about the rotten old bike he had given me. He told me, one day, he left it outside Woolworths in Swansea, only to find someone had stolen it. He saw the thief peddling like mad in the distance and gave chase until losing him in the crowd. A year later Peter recognized his bike leaning against a shop window again in Swansea. It hadn't gone far. A policeman was passing by, so Peter told him how it had been stolen. The policeman said: "Just take it then mate". Peter returned the bike home.

My father's youngest brother was a bit of a lad with the girls. As a teenager, one night, he did not get back home when expected. These were the days when one was expected to return to the fold by a time written in blood – well, almost. Granny Fairs went searching for him and chased him all the way home with a frying pan, so the story goes, probably with much embellishment over the years, but I don't expect she managed to land one on him as he was a Physical Training Instructor in the RAF during the war and later Head of Physical Training at Lymm Grammar School.

More uncles. Another one being a strong swimmer, saved my father's life when he was swimming off Limeslade Bay. My father found he was being pulled under by a strong current; My uncle went to his rescue, regardless of his own safety. He brought him ashore, exhausted but alive. He went on to enlist into the Royal New Zealand Navy and had risen to the rank of Chief Petty Officer when torpedoed twice in the Pacific during the war. As their ship was sinking, he, along with several members of the crew, climbed on to a life raft. After several days adrift, they ran out of water and food, but there was hope as they spotted an island on the horizon. Worried about drifting past, Ted decided to swim for it. He was never seen again and was believed to have been eaten by sharks. The others in the lifeboat managed to make it ashore and lived to tell the tale.

Life in Mumbles included being a member of the local Mumbles Rowing Club entering into all the local regattas. No pots were ever achieved but I was able to catch my first "crab" when practising a racing start before the line-up at the Hereford Regatta. The crab caused me to fly gracefully – not sure if this is the right word – up into the air, and from there, down into the water. Soggily attempting to climb back into the boat, the rest of the crew, fearful the boat might capsize, beat me off with their paddles as if I was an enraged hippo somewhere on the Limpopo. It took a lot of living down.

Better success was achieved some years later when the Army took me on for Inter-Services regattas and in Hong Kong, the Inter-port regattas between Hong Kong, Singapore and the Philippines. So? Where else does one row?

•••

There were six of us in our gleeful band of brothers – Nipper, Geoff, Terry, Peter, Jas and myself. We carried out some ridiculous, eccentric and bizarre events but all geared, we earnestly believed, towards having a bloody good time.

In 1952 at the age of eighteen we all began to feel the tug of the wide world; Nipper joined the Royal Navy, Terry the Royal Air Force, Peter, Geoff, Jas and I the Army. We wanted to see if it was all true, that what we had read in books and newspapers was as good as it appeared. Geoff alone, lived in Nigeria worked for an oil company for most of his life and later, in retirement, came back to live in the area. No-one else returned to Mumbles, which is an indignity to the town, because we all had come to appreciate Gower as a great place to live and to bring up a family. Some of us, however, did manage to return for reunions and stuff ourselves at Geoff's famous barbeques.

'Band of Reprobates' might have been a better title than 'Brothers' for the gang developed a skill at Scrumping, as I believe it is termed. Nicking apples that is. We would plan it as if it were one of my early military operations. It was not so much the desire to munch free apples, more to enjoy the thrill of avoiding being caught, a sort of "escape and evasion" exercise. After a discreet reconnaissance of the garden to be raided, we would work out timings, agree our route, post look outs and allocate rucksacks to pickers. Only once were we nearly caught. We had taken a fancy to something more exotic, grapes. At our level, one didn't eat grapes. Posh you see? Right in the middle of this operation, being in the greenhouse itself, the owner arrived, red-faced – as were we – and, not unsurprisingly, shouted at us in pure Anglo-Saxon. We managed to dodge around the loaded vines as he gave chase, and, being young and quick-witted, left him gasping in impotent rage. On the debrief, we concluded that, anyway, the grapes were not yet ripe. We, sensibly, decided not to make a repeat raid when they were expected to have ripened. Besides, none of us knew how to make wine.

After closing time at our favourite pub one Saturday night, someone had the bright idea of taking a cruise around Swansea Bay in a friend's converted Motor Torpedo Boat, that's an MTB once fitted with two torpedo tubes. Shortly after every one had clambered aboard and we were underway, Geoff mentioned there was a bottle of whisky in the dingy we were towing, and offered to retrieve it. We became concerned some time later when we discovered the dinghy with Geoff still supposedly in it, was no longer attached to the transom. Panic ensued. It was pitch black by this time with no sighting of Geoff or dinghy. We carried out a full search of the area, but still no sign of him, or, for that matter, the bottle of whisky. We later discovered he had been swept under the Mumbles Pier by the fast-flowing, ebbing tide, then drifted towards the Mixon Sound, where turbulent, dangerous sandbanks having a history of much tragedy, covering treacherous rocks was renowned as a graveyard for many ships. The MTB's owner saw a merchant vessel anchored in the Bay so sought permission to come aboard. Having explained what had happened, it enabled the radio officer to alert the Mumbles Lifeboat Station. Up went the maroons, (rockets) to call out the volunteer crew and a full-scale search was about to get under way. - three rockets for a real emergency. Meanwhile, Geoff had managed to land at Limeslade Bay a small, sheltered cove and when he saw and heard the bang of the maroon he suspected it might have something to do with him, so made his way to the Mumbles Lifeboat Station. The crew were just about to launch the lifeboat down the slipway and were not at all amused. Better to have stayed in bed. We had a few things to say to him the following morning when we all met at the Rowing Club.

The whisky? No idea what happened to it!

•••

For several years I was a choir boy at St Paul's Church in Sketty, a suburb of Swansea, which involved choir practice once a week to ensure we would be word and tone perfect, ready for morning and evening services on Sundays. We were paid a penny for each service. So, big deal for us choir boys! Soon, I mused, there could be need for my own bank account.

One warm Sunday in August, while I was setting off for church, the gang was heading for Langland Bay waking me up to the realization of what I was missing. The cassock came off first, then the surplice and I never went back again.

Stupid events! They just continued as we worked our way through our teenage years.

In the woods in Mumbles one day, we found a group of younger boys playing on a swing with a rope they had thrown over a branch of a tree which grew out over a quarry. When it was time to go home they could not retrieve their rope. This was a challenge, so I climbed the tree and edged my way along the branch until the rope came within reach. To save climbing back down the tree, I had the bright (?) idea of climbing down on the rope, so I asked the guys below to hold on tightly to one end of the rope, while I lowered myself down on the other end. I slipped, grabbing the wrong end of the rope and down I went…quite quickly. It was rather like sitting on the wrong side of a branch when you saw it off! The fall took my breath away and, accompanied by chest pains, slowly, well, very slowly, cycled home. I discovered the next day I had broken three ribs. Could have done better was a phrase which came to mind… and still does. Confined to bed, as one did in those days, my mates called to see me after school each day. It was painful to laugh, sneeze or cough, so my mother told them not to get me excited as my injury caused considerable hilarity when they retold, ad nauseam to other friends, how the broken ribs had been achieved. It was a time when I was pleased to see my pals leave.

Pwlldu Bay, on the South Gower peninsular, was a great place to visit because access is only by foot which discouraged most walkers from going there and one was more than likely to have the small beach to oneself. It contained a gully with the menacing label of Grave's End. Once a thriving little port, where limestone was quarried from the cliffs and transported across to Devon, now long abandoned, we learned there remained some interesting caves and diggings. Geoff, Nipper and I set out to explore one day and entered one of the caves, which was a challenge owing to the low headroom. After crawling a good distance, and banging one's head like a football into a net during practice, Geoff, who was leading the way, suddenly had a panic attack of claustrophobia. I was close behind him and Nipper behind me. Geoff started yelling and kicking me in the head, which led to me repeating the action to Nipper in our haste to get out. We beat a hasty retreat. Geoff's claustrophobia was set much earlier at a party at his house. During a game of hide and seek, he had hidden in a large chest and accidentally locked himself in. We heard his muffled screams and released him quickly, but not before the experience had given him a lasting fear of enclosed places.

Caving naturally, followed. The Swansea Caving Club had been fun until one day when we tackled a notorious cave near Glynneath in the Brecon Beacons. There used to be a gunpowder works close by. Along with a guide, we entered by lowering ourselves down a narrow entrance and then manoeuvring on our backs along a very low passage maybe twenty metres long, before emerging into a large cave. Emulating Geoff's issues on enclosed spaces, I immediately began to feel oppressed followed by the onset of claustrophobia, moving towards a state of panic. Controlling myself maybe, but I was much relieved to get out of there. Such an event surfaced years later at a time when I was serving with the Royal Marines. One of the annual tests we had to perform was to escape from a ditched helicopter. We had to climb into a mock-up of a helicopter fuselage with full kit and weapons while being lowered by crane into the deep end of a swimming pool. As we undid our safety belt to slide the door open, claustrophobia began to tickle at my nerves which prompted me to exit as quickly as possible, probably a good lesson to learn in an emergency. This issue, perhaps, could help me in other tricky situations. As the door of the chopper could not be opened until the cabin was full of water, there was always the risk of equipment getting caught up when unfastening the safety belt. As you will realise, the door of the chopper did open at the right time allowing me to be writing here today.

There have been a lot of words about my friends, all male, boys, lads, enjoying themselves. None of us bothered very much with girls, although there were two, Joyce and Hilary who were accepted members of our gang. When we went camping to Crawley Woods near Oxwich Bay, with its two and a half mile long beach and sand dunes, we were surprised when they both turned up, each telling the others' parents they were going to stay with the other. Instead, they hightailed it down to our camp site. The problem occurred over sleeping arrangements. Joyce was interested in Terry so she had a place to sleep but, previously unknown to me, Hilary had a crush on me, but I was oblivious to the unwillingness of my machismo to rise in my pathetic, young body. She found most welcome overnight shelter elsewhere, allowing me to kick myself in the head for a lost opportunity.

Sex, or the thought of it, was temporarily placed on hold as the idea of roast-jacketed potatoes on the campfire, replaced these other desires but we had forgotten to bring any with us. Potatoes that is. We found a field of magnificent Gower potatoes (Gower is famous for its potatoes) and it did not take long to fill the rucksack. All was going well until, as luck would have it, a police car stopped and two rather large policemen walked over to find out what we were doing. How we managed to talk ourselves out of a tricky situation was never to be known, but someone had the initiative to mention we were studying the stars for a Scout badge.

Camping experiences continued. At Three Cliffs Bay in the valley below Pennard Castle's twelfth century works built during the Norman invasion of Wales, we pitched our tents but did not sleep much due to the change of air on our faces. In the middle of the night we saw a ghostly figure walking towards us. He was whistling which was strange as I had never heard of a ghost whistling before, and gave us all a bit of a scare. We had an even bigger shock at first light when we realized we were surrounded by the incoming tide. Sea water was about to surround our tents as effectively as a Comanche raid on a wagon train. We were out of our sleeping bags quite quickly, well…pretty darn quickly in fact, pretty darn fumbling as well in our haste to strike the tents and carry all our camping gear to higher ground. No sooner had we relocated everything than the sea, in its wisdom, and its routine which we had forgotten, started to recede. Better to have stayed in bed. The next night, more learned, and level-headed we were more sensible in our choice of a camp site.

Part of life's rich tapestry?

Peter's home in Mumbles was like a second home to us, and his parents, always made us feel welcome. If the weather was poor, all six of us would make our way to Peter's with never any shortage of sandwiches and hot drinks. This cocktail of delight brought with it a continuous gale of laughter. His dad would wind us up and later, when we had all been called up for National Service, he continued to goad us on. Craftily, he spoke to me confidentially while kicking a ball around at Langland Bay in the winter, that Geoff was going to show me up by beating me to be first in the water to show how tough he was. Unbeknown to me, he then passed on the same information to Geoff. We kept a close eye on each other, until, by taking my sweater off, Geoff took this as a sign I was about to race into the water. He stripped off, followed quickly by me and, like idiots, we both raced into a freezing cold sea. One all, I think, is fair.

Weekly events involved everyone turning up at my house on Monday evenings to listen to the Goon Show with Peter Sellers and Spike Milligan on the wireless. Later, when living in Rye, East Sussex, l met Spike and realized he was not only a comedian, but confirmed to me what many had been saying about him for a long time. Completely off his head.

The coastline continued to hold us, the sea never far away. One jewel in our marine lives was Granny Addis's beach hut at Langland Bay. We could never afford to go on holidays, so the hut became our destination most days during school holidays and weekends, no matter what the weather threw down on us. It was our base for swimming, surfing, crabbing, prawning, canoeing, and, when the tide was out, kicking a rugger ball. Prawning and crabbing were always on the agenda. Food for hungry lads, My grandmother always objected to the smell when we cooked them in the hut, until we offered her some, when she rapidly changed her mind. From then on she was hooked.

When I was eleven years old, my grandmother would often keep an eagle eye open for the delivery of ice cream to the beach café. As soon as the truck arrived, I was dispatched to race over and join the queue. In those days, hard to believe now, it was a rare treat and one not to miss. Cone or wafer became the only decision of the moment. Today, it is chocolate wrapped in silver foil but, somehow, never as good as the original ices locked forever in our minds.

We mixed with a great number of locals also drawn to the sea. One of the most delightful people I had the pleasure to befriend was Arthur Goss, Head Lifeguard at Langland Bay. Listening to his stories, Arthur always took a close interest in what I was up to, particularly when the Army became my choice of career. He had rescued one young girl who had got into difficulties, and who was in great danger of drowning. She was the daughter of a wealthy family and Arthur was saddened he never received a 'thank you', even though he had risked his own life. On another occasion he saved the son of a Welsh coal miner from one of the mining villages near Merthyr Tydfil. Again, surprised, he received no words or letter of thanks, until several weeks later, he received a telephone call asking if he was free on Saturday night to attend a function in the village. Wondering how he would get there as he did not have a car, they said a taxi would be arranged to pick him up together with his wife. They arrived to a packed house in the village hall and were greeted by a loud cheer. He was invited to go up on the stage where he was presented with a wonderful gift in gratitude from the family and the whole village. He was on duty as a life guard until well into his 80's and continued to present a picture of rude health until his death.

We used to play tennis at Langdale Bay, but tennis balls were expensive on our limited pocket money. The courts were situated behind the beach huts. When balls were hit over the surrounding fencing by those not quite as skilled as others, they had a habit of getting stuck, or lost, under the huts raised floors. This was when our crabbing hook came in handy and, as a result, we always had a large stock of balls, some of them better than ours.

The Gower peninsular is, in many ways timeless, and even today, remains exactly as it was in my younger days. This is due to the tireless efforts of the Local Authorities, the National Trust and the Gower Society. As a matter of record, the Gower Peninsula was the first location in Britain to be designated an Area of Outstanding Natural Beauty.

Part of this area is Worm's Head, the mile-long promontory at the far end of the Gower Peninsular. It looks more like a dragon than a worm, and only accessible at low tide. Scrambling over the rocks to reach it and then walking to the end, was always an adventure – 'would we make it back in time…or not', being close to nearly losing out to an incoming tide on several occasions. Like the time when Geoff and I were preoccupied with netting a lobster in a deep rock pool. Always elusive to catch, this big bugger had retreated into deeper water and we knew it was time to give up when a huge wave broke over us. Looking around we discovered we were nearly cut off by the incoming tide just managing to scramble through the filling rock pools to get back before being engulfed in a more serious issue. And no mobile to call the RNLI.

I had long wanted to explore the end of Worms Head. It was where guillemots were supposed to be nesting on the rocky ledges. Setting off on my bike from Swansea on my own and having checked the tides because access is only possible for several hours a day, the ledges finally came into view. Guillemots do not make nests, but produce a shaped egg which prevents them from rolling away. Clever, nature that is. Common sense told me to abandon the idea when l discovered that the ledges where they were nesting was on a vertical rock face with the sea and rocks about 200 ft (that is 61 metres) below. Still, it was worth giving it a try, crabbing myself along a narrow ledge. Then, it went wrong. I fell, only a few feet, admittedly, desperately clutching onto a narrow outcrop though that was all. There was nothing in the way of a foothold beneath my feet. Adrenaline took over and I gathered my strengths before finding a narrow foothold about waist height. Carefully, lifting myself up, there I was, back on the narrow ledge. Two hundred feet down is a long way to fall and I don't believe I would have bounced much. The experience shook me up, as it was a close call, one of several to follow in my life time. I just managed to make it back to the mainland before being cut off by the tide.

One experience which has changed since my childhood is the Mumbles Railway, now converted into a delightful five-mile walking and cycle track, close to the sea shore running from Swansea to Mumbles pier. It had been the first passenger railway in the world in 1807, when it carried its opening passengers in double-decker horse-drawn coaches. It was later electrified, but that grand destroyer of railways, Richard Beeching, did not share the locals' wishes and with much sadness the line closed in 1960. The local authorities have since introduced 'a noddy train' which trundles along part of the same route during the summer. Wacky and weird come to mind, especially to older folk like us who remember the original train with its dirty smoke filling the trees close by with soot and grime.

Penclawdd in North Gower is well known for its cockle industry where the famed cockle-women gathered them together before loading up donkeys with giant bags. They were sold at Swansea market. It was a family outing to go cockling, judging the tide carefully. We would set off across the sands of Burry Estuary with rake, riddle and buckets and it would not take long to fill the buckets. Back home they were cleaned and left to stand in water overnight to enable them to spit out all the sand conveniently for our evening feast. Cockles are now gathered on both sides of the estuary, using tractors and trailers to bring them in. Cockle and lava bread stalls are still thriving at Swansea market which ensures that any return to Swansea necessitates a visit to the market and buying both.

There was, as I say, cockling and climbing, though they did not go together. Nipper and I had an interesting experience climbing the Great Tor near Three Cliffs Bay with its wonderful two and a half miles of beaches below us. Gaining the top, we peered over the edge of the sheer cliff to see a flock of wild goats who promptly disappeared. Investigating their almost magical disappearing act, we climbed up on the opposite side of the cliff where we found a cave. So this is where the blighters had gone! It was full of goats which caused a stand-off as we wanted to go in… and they wanted to get out. The cave was quite narrow, but we decided to make our way in, ignoring the small matter of being butted over the cliff by one or more of the goats. We disturbed a rabbit which scuttled off to the back of the cave; the thought of rabbit stew for dinner spurred us on. After a protracted parley with Head Goat, we reached a compromise with the goats, stepping aside to allow them to make their escape to fresh air. It was a safer place to be than in front of two rather dirty youths. We were not about to give the same rite of passage to the rabbit, which arrived the next day lying rigid below a lightly browned layer of pastry.

•••

Time moved on. I left school at the age of fifteen with no qualifications and began to look for a job to fill the time until I was old enough to join the Army at eighteen, my chosen career. I set my sights on the railways. Swansea was the terminus for two railway companies. Great Western Railways (GWR) which operated through to London and the west country, and London Midland and Scottish (LMS) which ran on lines through Central Wales, the Midlands and Scotland. I applied for a clerical position with GWR but was rejected due to lack of academic qualifications. My grandmother, Granny Addis, suggested I should apply to the LMS where my grandfather was once a Director, although I never knew him as he died before I was born. She gave me the name of the Managing Director who my grandfather had worked for and sent the application direct to him. I was invited to attend an interview and take their entrance examination. I had two hours to complete the exam and, struggling towards the end with several questions unanswered, the Managing Director came in to the room. He looked over my shoulder, made several suggestions which allowed me to complete the paper. Without his help it is unlikely I would have passed.

The old adage is as true now as then. 'It is who you know and not what you know,' which counts.

The railways had been nationalized in 1948 by a Labour Government with the result LMS and GWR were amalgamated and renamed. Bland was to be expected and British Rail resulted. Hey ho!

I was offered a job as Station Clerk at St Thomas's station. My salary was £2.50 a week for working six days a week. Once the ropes had been learnt the Station Master confided in me saying if I studied for the Railway Station Accountancy examination there was no reason why I could not, one day, become a Station Master like him with a salary of £8.00 a week. Crumbs, how could I turn that down? After a year in this buffer of a backwater of a station with very few passengers, British Rail decided to close it down. I was transferred to High Street Station, where I had originally been rejected, and became responsible for passenger train documentation. It was tedious but better than the other work.

By this time I was beginning to have serious regrets at not having any academic qualifications, realizing if I was to get on in life, credentials would be needed to show to prospective employers, so a determined effort was made to do something about it. As well as embarking on a two-year Railway Accountancy Course, it included night school three times a week to study for some GCSEs, then called School Certificates. I chose Geography, Maths and English Language. It was a bit of a struggle but I thought it could help when joining the Army or returning to British Rail on completion of my National Service. It was a very remote idea to me at the time. The Army was fixed in my own firmament.

Outside of my work on the railways, I remained a strong supporter of the Scouting movement and am forever grateful for everything it taught me. One of my proudest moments was when I was selected, as senior sixer of our cub pack at St James Church, to carry the flag at the church service on Armistice Sunday. Two incidents happened to wreck the day. Leaving the house, a seagull, with exceptionally good aim, shat on my neckerchief. The next, when approaching the church altar for the flag to be blessed, I failed to look up and the flag pole became tangled with some low-hanging ornamental metal work at the altar. It was hugely embarrassing at the time for a youth coming to terms with growing up. Later in life when serving with Airborne Forces I nearly came a cropper when my parachute became tangled up with the previous jumper, all because I had failed to look down when my parachute was deploying. The lesson learned the second time (my excuse is I had forgotten about the altar incident when I jumped out of a plane). Be careful to look up or down which ever is appropriate.

Back to Scouting aged seventeen, one more badge was needed to qualify as a Queen's Scout. It was the Venture Badge which involved a 24 hour hike around the Gower Peninsula. Overnight should have been out of doors, but as it was raining I asked at a farm near Llangennith on the western edge of the Gower, if I could sleep in their covered haystack. The farmer's wife said 'Don't be so soft cariad, you can sleep in our caravan'. Before going back to the farm house to get clean sheets. I said "I can't do that because I am meant to sleep in the open. She repeated "Don't be so soft cariad" or, as she put it more succinctly, 'Paid a bôd yn twp cariad'. The icing on this particular cake was the ham and eggs for breakfast. After a comfortable night's sleep, and profound thanks to the farmer's wife, I was in good spirits and ready for the final part of the journey. Strangely, no mention was made in my written report to the District Commissioner, that I had spent a luxurious night in a warm caravan. Plus breakfast. For many years I felt guilty about this. Serving with

Airborne Forces at a Brigade Commander's briefing before an overseas exercise, someone asked if it was permissible to take shelter in a farmhouse if offered a bed by the farmer. His reply 'If given the choice between sleeping in a wet ditch or a warm bed in a farmhouse, you should use your "airborne initiative"'. For the first time I no longer felt guilty and you will find the Brigadier's advice guided and influenced me on many a number of occasions throughout my life and, perhaps regretfully, but meaningfully, to me, I have dotted the phrase throughout this book as confetti to a bride. Ad nauseam is the other phrase I could have used. It proved to be my anchor and get-out-of-jail card, so many times in my life.

In August 1952, I attended the World Scout Jamboree in Haverfordwest and became the first person in Wales to be presented with a Queen's Scout Award, comparable with today's Gold Duke of Edinburgh's Award. The next day, I hitched a lift back to Swansea, and, packing a bag, I took a train to Aldershot to join the Army.

It was the start of a new life and a new world, one I have never regretted.

Denise and author Ibiza 2016. *'Mates.'*

Gower Peninsular 1934 *'I was born not far away from here.'*

'n.b. the tin of Nescafé which puts a certain modernity into this ancient land.'

Second cataract, Nile. 1961.
'Guide used a goat's bladder to float down in front of us.'

Capsizing on the Nile. 1961. *'Told you I saw a rock.'*

Looks as though I am sitting in the Temperate House, Kew Gardens.
note: I swapped berets with a Marine Officer for this photo.

'Honour lost; honour repaired.'

This one opened properly.'

'We had quite a few of these.'

'The start of a million miles.'

Joining the Army – Now life gets a bit more difficult

– PART TWO –

THE RESPONSIBLE YEARS

'Bravery is being the only one who knows you're afraid.' Col. David Hackworth

CHAPTER 2

Joining up, Settling in

"If you hang out with chickens you are going to cluck and if you hang out with eagles you're going to fly." Steve Maraboli

Leaving home in August 1952 to join the Army was the beginning of a twenty-five year career which gave me the solid base for the rest of my life. It is true to say it was the best decision ever taken in my life. A life full of adventure and challenge to look forward to, it was a relief to leave provincial Swansea and only later in life, did I come to appreciate it was such a great place to live. Walking along our street early in the morning to catch the train for Aldershot, I realised how fortunate I was to be leaving whilst all my friends and neighbours were, in my view, going nowhere. Arriving at Ash Vale Station and met by a Sergeant from the training depot at Buller Barracks, life, from that moment changed for ever. Shouted at, ordered, disciplined, regimented and chased from pillar to post was all part of the military psychology of breaking the recruit down so that, eventually, one instinctively obeyed every order given, until we were rebuilt as the Army saw fit. I had chosen the Royal Army Service Corps (RASC), later to become the Royal Logistics Corps, because my father and grandfather were in the same Corps and, at the same time it meant I would learn to drive.

Although my father had been in the Reserve and called up for World War Two, he would have enjoyed being a Regular. Had he survived the war, I suspect he would have been a strong candidate to continue in the Army. My grandfather, on the other hand, left home at the age of 18 to join the Army in Aldershot, just like me. He entered the Commissariat and served throughout the South African war in the rank of Warrant Officer, later to become the Senior Warrant Officer in the Corps before being commissioned. He retired from the Army after a full career in the rank of Captain. Granny Fairs, in relating stories about their life together, only ever recalled his days as the Senior Warrant Officer, Buller Barracks, due to the prestigious position he enjoyed. It was sad I never met him. We would have had a lot to talk about.

During my first year in the Army, unable to go home for Christmas having been detailed for guard duty, the nature of what I was guarding remaining a mystery to me apart from the single essential of providing the Officers Mess with sufficient waiters for their Christmas meal. You may find it unclear as to why there is supposed to be a connection between guarding our base with serving officers at their Christmas parties. I found it muddling as well but regret it will have to remain a mystery. Briefly trained by the Mess Sergeant, we were told always to ask the officer being served what they wanted. Obediently, serving a crusty old Major I asked him if he wanted a dessert. His reply:

'What the bloody hell do you think I'm sitting down here for', did not exactly fill me with the confidence needed to go over the top behind him and his whistle.

There appeared to be an obsessive need to keep everybody busy during basic training, as though we would not know what to do with ourselves if left to our own devices. This was never substantiated, but we believed they put bromide in our tea to calm any sexual urges we may have had. After four weeks of being confined to barracks, we were finally allowed out. Some made the decision to go to the Saturday night dance at the Farnborough Town Hall. We dressed to kill in our drab military uniforms with boots and gaiters, not exactly the most suitable form of dress for dancing. My confidence took a further turn for the worse when, dancing with a delightful young lady, she retired, injured, to the benches in disgust after macerating her feet for the tenth time. Hob-nailed boot, dainty foot equals 'ow!'

During this period of training, I had applied for a Commission and was graded as a Potential Officer

Cadet and qualified to attend the War Office Selection Board, a searching, succession of tests which took place over three days. Having now 'passed out' from basic training, my options available were to go, either to Mons Officer Cadet School for officer training or train to be a Clerk. The selection board, in its wisdom, not shared by me, was to assign me as a Clerk, not considered yet in a position to take charge of men. My company sergeant major pulled me to one side and said that I should not to be too disappointed as I was being considered for promotion to lance corporal ensuring I could add 'Crumbs!' for the second time to my life. All was not lost, however, because my failure was clarified as failed watch, which meant I could try again in six months on the basis I could be a late developer. Posted to Shorncliffe as clerk to the Company Sergeant Major there followed a fairly monotonous few months of mundane office work and guard duty every four or five nights. Guarding what? Hut after hut of Army stores unlikely to be of interest to anyone. From dusk to dawn we wandered around with unloaded rifles, two hours on and two hours off. When off-duty, we had to remain in the guard room with beds without any bedding or mattresses, only the springs, just to make sure one was never comfortable and stay awake and, more importantly, to leap into action in the unlikely event of an emergency. One assumes it was good training, but it was not understood at the time, nor evermore.

•••

This all came to an end when an invitation arrived to attended the Selection Board for a second attempt/try/bid. My life was now to change radically, reporting to the Officer Cadet School for Officer training. In those days anyone with a regional accent, mine was Welsh, cariad, making me feel a subsidiary to life itself. A high percentage were educated in public schools, so my education, and accent combined, were a distinct disadvantage. Most of the cadets advertised their privileged background by sporting expensive cars along with accents which could cut glass like a stained glass window artisan. I was able to offer Welsh, look you, and a bicycle.

During the first week, each of us had to select a subject for a lecturette to be presented to the other cadets, something I had never done before and quite dreaded the prospect due to a distinct lack of confidence. Finally, choosing to talk about Scouting, it came as a pleasant surprise that, despite obvious nervousness, I was congratulated by the instructor on selecting such a suitable subject. He turned out to be a good supporter of the Scouting movement himself. This, not only helped boost my confidence, but enhanced my standing amongst the other cadets. Towards the end of our course, we were eager to learn where we were going to be posted but dismayed to learn that no-one on a National Service Commission would be posted overseas, apart from good old Germany, BAOR in fact. I immediately applied for a three-year Short Service Commission and had the good fortune to be posted to Hong Kong. My future life in travel began at this very moment…my accent gone if not my love of Wales.

Air travel in those days was a tedious, if comfortable affair compared to today. The flight to Hong Kong took several days, with stop-overs in Rome, Basra, Rangoon and Singapore. Experiencing all these exciting places gave me my first taste for travel, and laid the foundation of the rest of my life after I left the Army. A noteworthy experience began on leaving Singapore en route for Hong Kong. Instead of checking into the airport I was driven to the Naval Base embarking almost immediately on the cruiser HMS Sheffield, destination Hong Kong. Nobody mentioned the ship was to be involved in a naval exercise with the Australian, New Zealand and United Stated navies. No cabins were available and my sleeping berth was a fold-up camp bed in one of the corridors. Many of the regular crew made it very clear how unwelcome our presence was by bumping the sides of our cots and generally being a pain in the arse, not that sleeping was much of an option because lights burnt all night. At 06:00 (that's six in the morning) promptly, the tannoy blared out instructions for all companionways to be cleared immediately. Camp beds had to be packed away in a locker and, before breakfast, a quick shave which involved queuing behind about ten others all waiting for the same wash basin. No sooner had I started to shave than the Lieutenant Commander behind me was agitating for us to hurry up. Welcome to the Royal Navy. Eventually, we cruised into the naval base of Hong Kong, lining the decks, where I was one of the first to disembark.

My home for three years was the Sham Shui Po Officers Mess, formerly a Japanese Prisoner of War Camp. The fear and the terror of those dark days was long gone from the woodwork, making life, pleasant, privileged and very comfortable. The idea of returning to Swansea was very difficult to imagine where my job with British Railways was being kept open for me. I applied for a Regular Commission which involved returning to the UK to attend the Regular Commission Board. Not confident of success, I thought it prudent to cast around to see what other opportunities might be open for me in Hong Kong. This resulted in applying for a Trainee Manager's position with British American

Tobacco, but had my feathers ruffled when the job turned out negatively. The reason was, a distinct possibility, being a non-smoker and loathed the idea of burning leaves in my mouth for pleasure! So, not too surprised and not too disappointed.

I rowed for the Royal Hong Kong Yacht Club with a senior manager employed by Jardine Matheson, one of the largest import/export firms in the Far East. Mentioning I was looking for an opportunity to stay in Hong Kong he pointed me in the right direction, and was called for an interview. Repeating my earlier comment: 'it is not what you know rather who you know' is what matters. I was offered a trainee manager's position with an attractive salary and benefits. The very next day, coincidentally, the invitation arrived asking me to return to the UK for the three-day Army Regular Commission Board. This was to include a series of tests, designed to examine one's leadership skills, team work, ability to present problem solving, academic ability, intelligence tests and, incorrectly as it turned out, how you hold your knife and fork at the dinner table. (Useful in wartime perhaps?). We were also given practical team projects such as how best to get across a river or ditch, using rope, timber and 40 gallon oil drums while the instructors observed who was leading, who had the good ideas, and how others responded to your suggestions at problem solving. There appeared to be a sensitive balance between being neither too pushy nor too retiring. For the entire three days we were under constant observation and had been forewarned, observers might be prowling the camp at night to ensure we were wearing suitable pyjamas, not that I had ever thought it necessary to dress up for going to bed. I never did find out if the stripes on my pyjamas were acceptable to the Army.

Having travelled back to the UK from Hong Kong to attend the RCB selection board, I returned home in Swansea to await the result. A week later and still in bed, my mother brought me a letter delivered by the GPO franked 'On her Majesty's Service'. This was the letter. Pausing before opening it to reflect on my future life being hung, as it were, in the balance, expecting the worse, with a life in Swansea working for British Rail, I opened it. There it was, writ large, selecting me for a regular commission in the British Army.

I took my mother and two sisters out for dinner that night, something rare in those days, even though it was only fish and chips. A further enforced period 'being confined to barracks' and missing the companionship of my 'band of brothers' who, now, were all dispersed around the world pursuing their careers, it came as a great relief to receive my travel instructions for the return to Hong Kong'.

Apart from my military duties as a troop commander, a position that carried the responsibility of commanding some thirty non-commissioned officers and drivers, a number of outside interests developed; these included rowing and scouting. I joined the Hong Kong Rowing Club and quickly found myself in training to row for the Club in the forthcoming Inter-Port Regatta. This was an annual event which included Hong Kong, Singapore, Saigon and Manila. The Rowing Club was part of the Royal Hong Kong Yacht Club with a clubhouse on a tiny island near Repulse Bay. After hosting the event on home ground (or waters) we went into training for Manila. The main purpose of the visit should have been the rowing, but there were so many associated social events to attend we hardly had time to train. I was accommodated in the delightful Colonial home of the local Shell Manager. There were so many parties that I can recall little of the visit, including the rowing, though the image of being awakened every morning by a beautiful Filipino girl offering me either fresh mango or coffee. I found making this choice a time-consuming event, to which she replied '*Mr David, you are very naughty*'. Second prize was the mango which I found myself eating with subsequent sticky fingers.

One of the top grammar schools in Hong Kong is the King George V who were looking for a scout master to manage their senior troop. I jumped at the chance and for two years, thoroughly enjoyed the company of thirty or so multi-national students, teaching them skills which I had learnt during my quest to be a Queen Scout. The Army looked upon it as a good PR exercise, supporting their words with camping equipment and transport. What was special was the multi-national and multi-cultural features of the school and the scouts in particular. There were Portuguese, Indian, Pakistani, Chinese and British scouts and one of the Chinese scout's parents had been particularly helpful in providing funds for equipment; wanting to repay them in some small way for all their help. I decided to invite them to lunch in the Officers Mess, but was told by the Mess Committee that Mess Rules only allowed non-Europeans to enter the Mess if they had been previously vetted by the Mess Committee. What an insult and how out of touch they were with the realities of life. I found this unforgivable. Can you imagine asking them to come along to be vetted by a bunch of old farts to see whether they were worthy enough to set foot in the Officers' Mess? It was unbelievable. Although Hong Kong was still a British Colony, these rules were so out of date and disgraceful it cast a deep shadow over our colonial past from my point of view. I experienced more of this attitude when serving in Singapore a few years later.

One morning an urgent instruction to report to the Colonel arrived and wondered what it could be about. The question, without warning, demanded of me: '*Are you a communist sympathiser?'*. I had no idea what he was talking about. It seems that the Royal Military Police had nothing better to do than to check why I had ridden a motorcycle along the border between Communist China and the Hong Kong border during a spin out to the New Territories. Having explained that away, I was then asked why I had a Communist Chinese flag in my room in the Mess. Explaining that my collection of flags included many nationalities I vehemently added, I was no more a communist sympathiser than a Welsh Nationalist.

The issue faded away as the same Colonel invited some of us single subalterns to lunch one Sunday. He had a plan, of course, which was for us to bring gardening forks and spades to do 'a bit of gardening.' We should have declined, but we had our careers to think of. Anyway, digging and shovelling for our lunch could have been worse and the exercise did no harm. Quite why the Colonel wanted us to dig the garden in his married quarters was hard to understand, because all expats and military officers lived a privileged life in Hong Kong with servants dotted around like confetti at a society wedding. Even us single subalterns had a shared Chinese servant who did everything for us, including washing and ironing our clothes, looking after our kit and cleaning our rooms. It might have been a good idea to ask him if he would like to take over the running of my platoon of thirty men for me. Shame We could have spent more time on the beach.

Every British Camp had an Indian contractor who, amongst other things, and at a nominal cost, provided staff to look after the comfort of live-in soldiers by cleaning their kit, making beds and even wake-up calls in the morning with a cup of tea in bed. One began to realise this was going a little too far when, on one occasion, I was inspecting my platoon and pulled up one of the soldiers for the poor condition of his kit. His response was *'Not my fault Sir, it's the guy the Indian contractor employs to look after it. Better tell him off, not me'*.

As well as being keen on inviting young officers for Sunday lunch, accompanied by forks and spades from the company stores to give his garden the once over, the Colonel was keen for us to learn how to ride. A horse, that is. We had a mule transport unit stationed in the New Territories, and twice a week we were dragged out of bed in the middle of the night to arrive at dawn for riding lessons, though, once there we found it enjoyable. Before the arrival of helicopters, the only way to haul ammunition, guns and other heavy equipment across the mountains was by mule, and the unit had several hundreds of them. One day we returned after a bit of a giddy-up over the local hills to witness a drama caused by one mule who refused to be loaded (stubborn as a mule comes to mind surprisingly).

Staff were loading up the mules with ammunition in support of one of the infantry battalions. They were being driven into a pen but this mule was having none of it and was blocking up the whole loading system. Our instructor, who was also the sergeant major with a fierce reputation, stormed off to sort it out. The mule was unmoved by all this attention until the sergeant major stuffed a bundle of hay underneath him and set fire to it. The mule, rapidly reappraised his situation and made the wise move to fall into line with his mates. Issue over. Loading continued. Nobody had heard of Animal Rights in those days, but the sergeant major said mules had a great sense of preservation, just like everyone else and had enough sense to appreciate when the game was up.

Digging slightly deeper into my memory of that time, again associated with Mess Rules dating back to prehistoric practices, involved a bell. It was considered unbecoming to have a bar in the mess and we had got into the habit of asking the mess waiter to get us a drink. But if he was not around, we would give him a shout as he would never be far away. But the Mess Committee decided to install a bell in the ante room. If you wanted a drink one had to ring the bell. No one liked the idea so we got rid of the bell one dark night. This caused a lot of fuss and it was re-installed. Again, it mysteriously disappeared. More fuss was made until we had a record played on Radio Hong Kong. It went: *'Who stole the ding-dong, who stole the bell, somebody knows but nobody tell'.* It was popular at the time. Nothing else was said and the message had got across. The song never made the Top Twenty.

•••

My job as a Troop Commander was to look after Divisional Headquarters transport. This included a number of different types of vehicles – staff cars, motorised offices/caravans, tank transporters, jeeps and four-ton trucks. I got into trouble one day when a senior officer wanted to be picked up from the Star Ferry in Kowloon. The duty NCO tried to explain there were no vehicles available and suggested he got a taxi. That was not good enough for him, so there followed a lively conversation until the duty NCO said the only vehicle available was a tank transporter loaded with a fifty ton tank. The senior officer, clearly having difficulty understanding what the duty NCO with a strong Glasgow accent was saying, nor grasping what a tank transporter was, calmed down when the tank transporter was sent to pick him up. His lack of good humour prevented him seeing the funny side of it.

Exercising in the New Territories, helping other members of my platoon camouflage some of the four ton trucks, I was pulled aside by (the same) crusty old major who pointed out to me it was unbecoming of an officer to be doing such manual work. Later in my career, when serving with Airborne Forces, it was refreshing to discover, officers had to lead by example and "mucking-in" was exactly the right thing to do. Nevertheless, at the time, this out-of-date attitude to leadership was confusing.

•••

Life in Hong Kong had been, not to put too fine a point on it, idyllic, but it was time to move on being posted to a training establishment in the UK. Sailing out of Hong Kong harbour on a troopship called *The Empire Clyde* previously of the Empire line, prompted more emotion than expected, but, back in Bedford reporting to my new unit I found a totally different lifestyle awaited me.

Having enjoyed a privileged life in Hong Kong, there were to be no such luxuries in the UK. After a couple of weeks disembarkation leave, the car was loaded up and drove myself to Bedford. Not that there was much room in the car because my second-hand Austin A30 was not designed to carry much more than a toothbrush and a spare pair of socks. I had saved up over my three years in Hong Kong for this car and, despite its size, it was my very first car and my pride and joy. My dear Great Aunt had left me a few hundred pounds in her will, ensuring my pleasure in the old Austin to evaporate after passing a local garage to see a shiny MG TC sports car with my name written all over it.

The new posting allowed me to join the Bedford Rowing Club where I was accepted into the Town First Eight. Fitting in training six days a week with my military duties was something of a problem, but a very understanding Commanding Officer went out of his way by making allowances so I could prepare for the Henley Royal Regatta. The Head of River was a challenging annual competition attracting hundreds of entries from rowing clubs throughout the country and overseas. There was the promise of other regattas. From my days at the Mumbles Rowing Club, then Hong Kong and now to be rowing for one of the top clubs in the country was indeed, a privilege. We managed to get to the semi-final of the Thames Cup at Henley, but were pipped at the post by a strong American crew, who went on to win the Final.

After twelve months training, the crew was ready for a break. I had parked my car opposite the Little White Hart Inn near the river before joining the crew for a night of celebration. As no alcohol was permitted during training we had fallen somewhat out of practice. We suffered the consequences the following day. One of the repercussions of the night was a total void on where I had parked my car. Scouring the town produced no results until, returning to the Little White Hart, I had a vague recollection of leaving it there, though there was no sign of it. This was, perhaps not surprising. A huge grandstand had been erected overnight for finals day and my MG had disappeared under the scaffolding, where it remained until the regatta was over.

It was at this time I nearly came a cropper during the Lieutenant to Captain promotion examination. I was asked to draw up my plan of attack on an enemy position. I completely forgot to include armour. The examining officer, a Major in the Royal Armoured Corps, with his tank cap badge staring me uncomfortably in the face, was beginning to show his displeasure at my presentation, huffing and puffing with instructions to get on with it; clearly I was about to fail, I recognised my mistake and hopefully, seamlessly even more hopefully, I announced with as much bullshit as possible. *'I now come to the most important part of the plan, and that is the disposition of armour'* The major frisked his not insignificant moustache, calmed down and, glowing with pride, said: *'Well done'*.

My posting turned out to be a unit near Bedford responsible for training the Army Emergency Reserve; each regiment would turn up for two weeks a year. Apart from the training, one of the most important events at the end of the instruction periods were the Regimental Dinner Parties in the Officers Mess. Each Commanding Officer placed considerable importance on these events, attempting to outdo all others with the quality of their cordon bleu menus, the finest wines, the impeccable service. Dignitaries such as Lords Lieutenant and other VIPs were invited, so these events always presented a challenge. Fortunately, we had, on the Establishment, a Specialist Messing Officer from the Army Catering Corps, his name was Graham Kerr who later achieved TV fame in Australia and in Britain as the '*Galloping Gourmet*'. Unfortunately, he decided to leave the Army and was not going to be replaced. The Colonel sent for me and despatched me to the Army School of Catering in Aldershot, where I was given free range to sit in on cookery demonstrations, attend lectures and learn as much as possible before returning to my unit full of ideas for exquisite dishes.

Some months later I attended an officers' course at the Army School of Physical Training. Amongst other things, I was taught how to organise athletic meetings, boxing tournaments and qualified as a boxing judge. I followed this up with basketball, football and hockey as a referee. To achieve all this my routine began with an early morning five-mile run, breakfast in the Mess, followed by a day in Maida Gym attending lectures, gymnastics and learning how to manage different sporting events. Mostly enjoyable, one could not say the same about the assault course over a canal. The course showed up a particular weakness if one's upper body strength was more cranky than the rest. The result: one fell into the canal! Falling into the ice-cold water once was a salutary lesson which was not to be repeated.

There were several officers from a prestigious Iraqi Army regiment attending the course. We became good friends and it was to be deplored when later, we found ourselves at war with them. I often wonder what became of them, though am aware one of them became a General, but of the others, I have no idea if they survived the war. Being Muslims, they sometimes sought guidance on the customs of our country. One such was to ask about the ingredients of a full English breakfast on the menu in the Mess each morning. After the five-mile run and before each day's training, breakfast was a major event of the day, much enjoyed by everyone. I had to explain, quite carefully, that an Army's Full English Breakfast contained both sausages and bacon, both forbidden under Islamic Dietary laws. It meant they would have to stick to eggs and toast which, although nice in its own way did not have quite the zing that a banger produces.

The Army basketball team was based at Maida Gym, enabling me to join in with their training and coaching sessions. At the end of the course, I was flattered when the Commandant asked me to manage the Army Basketball team on their forthcoming tour. It was a great idea and was delighted to have been asked but other plans were afoot.

CHAPTER 3

The Paras: Ready for Anything

'Even more bloody difficult!'

Much to the disappointment of my Commanding Officer, shortly after my stint at the Army School of Catering, I started to get itchy feet and volunteered for service with Airborne Forces. Having played a great deal of basketball and, combined with rowing and other sporting activities, it had brought me to a peak of fitness. Before starting the course, I was due a couple of week's leave. Instead of sunning myself at Langland Bay, my time was taken up running around the cliffs of Gower with half a dozen bricks in my rucksack and doing press-ups on the beach. The locals realised the man on the beach had gone mad, or, possibly something had leaked into the local water supply. It certainly increased my level of fitness, making me even more determined to pass the course, not least because the Parachute Brigade had been deployed to Jordan and nothing was going to stop me getting there. (There was that Travel lust raising its head again).

The Corps had several specialist units within Airborne Forces and on return to my unit I applied to attend the Parachute Selection Course, known as 'P' Company. Historically, only about one out of ten volunteers pass the course and go on to get their wings and the coveted red beret. Even though I was reasonably fit, this would be my biggest challenge so far. Failure to complete any of the confidence tests, physical challenges or aerial apparatus work, resulted in immediate Return to Unit, as unfit for service in Airborne Forces. I was determined not to be sent back to Bedford. One of the tests is called 'milling' which involves boxing with someone your height and body weight and hammering away at each other. Rather like women bringing their knitting to watch executions during the French Revolution, all spectator seats would be filled in the gym with staff coming along to watch the milling, hoping to see some good old-fashioned slugging matches and a bit of blood thrown in for colour. They were not disappointed. It did not matter if you won or lost provided you showed aggression. Facing up to a London barrow boy used to street fighting, it was not long before he landed a beauty to my face. It was a wake-up call to me, re-entering the fray with my nostrils flaring in annoyance at dropping my guard, and continued to battle away at each other, both passing at the end. Some were not so lucky and ended up cowering in a corner after receiving several blows. They were on their way out, packing their bags and returning to their unit the same day – RTU.

The highest rate of failure was caused through upper limb weakness, particularly when attempting the tree-top apparatus which was certainly daunting, particularly when you had to stand erect on parallel bars high up in the trees and shout out your number, rank and name and then leap for a hanging rope almost out of reach and swing into a net before scrambling down to the next obstacle. Passing 'P' Company was an enormous relief and allowed me to move onto RAF Abington for parachute training. This was less of a selection course and more to do with teaching the techniques of parachuting. Refusal to jump is, naturally, an immediate RTU. Eight jumps, had to be completed to qualify for one's 'wings'; I very nearly did not make it. The rule was, that as soon as one's parachute had deployed after free-falling about two hundred metres, one has to carry out "all round observation", checking the chute had deployed properly and, ensuring there was no one else close so as to avoid a mid-air collision. This time, my parachute developed what is called an inversion, (I had another word for it) causing spillage of air resulting in a much faster rate of descent. The drill is to deploy your reserve parachute, a quite sensible plan when you think about it! Attempting to do this, mine refused to fly and became tangled up with the rigging lines of my main parachute with the point of suspension being my right ankle. I was descending upside down.

Not a good idea. This was a serious problem because I was descending at a rate of knots, head first. Trying to lift all 16 rigging lines from around my ankle together proved impossible. I was getting close to the ground and landing head first could be terminal, or at the very least, resulting in a serious accident. Adrenaline kicked in. It became clear, the only course of action was to lift one frigging rigging line at a time. There are sixteen of the buggers and time was running out. I just managed to release the last one when my legs swung down underneath me and I found myself on the ground. Apparently, while I had been in the upside down position my instructor had been bellowing down a megaphone while his own feet were firmly on the ground. Useful to know. Safety crews and ambulances had been on their way and came racing over, but apart from realising it had been a very narrow call, all was well. The experience had no lasting effect and I was able to complete the eight jumps required to pass the course and was proud, and yes, honoured to join the ranks of the Parachute Brigade and be presented with my wings and red beret.

We were known as *'eight-jump wonders'* As a result it allowed us to ditch the ceremonial black 'crap hat' berets. Reflecting back now, it is difficult to recognise how it was a rational thing to throw oneself out of an aircraft travelling at 120 miles per hour, a thousand feet above the ground but, after a few mishaps, and more to follow, I went on to complete over eighty jumps during my time with Airborne Forces and later with the Royal Marines Commando.

It meant I could now fly off to Jordan to join my unit in the desert, but there was a hitch. The Parachute Brigade had been sent to the Hashemite Kingdom of Jordan under a defence agreement between King Hussain and the British Government, to support Jordan if it was attacked. Iraqi armoured units had massed on the Jordanian border, but timely deployment of British Forces, including the Parachute Brigade, was sufficient to suppress Iraqi ambitions. A diplomatic agreement had been negotiated resulting in no additional reinforcements being sent to Jordan.

But, my luck was in. My unit was an officer short, requiring me to assist with the withdrawal of transport via Aqaba to Cyprus and then back to the UK. So there was a chance for more travel. I was on my way after all but not, it turned out, with the RAF, as all their aircraft were allocated to the withdrawal of personnel. Travelling in civilian clothes with uniform, kit and Sterling machine gun wrapped in a towel and all packed away in my suitcase, I left Heathrow on a Middle Eastern Airlines flight to Jerusalem, where I was met by a driver with a Land Rover. Security checks were slack, to say the least in those days. Consider the machine gun packed away in my suitcase!

Instructed to take a convoy of trucks to Aqaba, the Jordanian port on the Red Sea, of T.E. Lawrence (Peter O'Toole) fame, I had to wait for shipping to pick us up and transport us through the Suez Canal to Cyprus. Asking the Officer Commanding how to get there, stupid question really, the reply, snapped back sharply was: 'You have a map and compass, so use your Airborne Initiative'. I never forgot the term, it has remained with me all my life; you will see it occurring here, ad nauseam. Feeling suitably chastised, our convoy set off at dawn and, after an overnight stop, reached Aqaba where we pitched out tents and waited for shipping, which we discovered would not be for several days. Using my *Airborne Initiative*, (you see what I mean) a group of us drove up to Petra to do a bit of exploring. A fort, manned by the Arab Legion, offered us hospitality, providing a base for a couple of interesting days hiking around the antiquities. There were no tourists in those days. Today, Petra receives about 237,000 tourists each year. Quite a change.

Arriving in Cyprus, we were allocated a huge, dusty field to park the vehicles. To our amazement, we found a water tap in the middle of the field standing up as if it were Excalibur's sword. Just the place to pitch our tent and enjoy the luxury of hot and cold running water; hot when turned on and cold when left running for a while.

Waiting to be shipped back to the UK, two incidents arose, neither to be forgotten. This was a time when Cyprus was seeking independence from the United Kingdom and the internal security situation on the island was fragile to say the least, further complicated by the conflict between the Greek and Turkish Communities. It became known as the Cyprus Emergency and was a nasty affair.

A colleague knew one of the nurses at the military hospital and we were invited to a dinner dance at the Garrison Officers Mess. All was fine until it was time to leave when we discovered there was a curfew in place, owing to an incident in a local Greek village. There had been a shooting, followed by an infantry unit carrying out a "cordon and search" of the village (a military tactic to cordon off an area) with several arrests of suspected terrorists along with the discovery of weapons and ammunition. Not surprisingly, there was considerable tension and resentment directed towards the British Forces. Using our *Airborne Initiative*, we crept into the Officers Mess and slept in the lounge. Everything remained peaceful until early the next morning when the cleaners started to scream, seeing us asleep on the settees. Appreciating we had rather over stayed our welcome, we climbed into the Land Rover and drove off, not realising the curfew was still in force. It was very early morning and we had to drive through the village where the cordon and search had taken place the previous day. We were not expecting a welcome committee, but were uneasy when a large mob approached us wielding metal bars and making threatening noises. There was no space to turn the vehicle around and sensing our lives were in danger, we followed a well-established piece of Army doctrine which says the best form of defence is attack. Putting the vehicle into low gear, we revved the engine and drove at speed straight at the motley, but dangerous crowd. Quite sensibly, we thought, the rabble got out of the way and we were relieved to get back to our tent with hot and cold running water.

I mentioned two incidents. The second occurred when we were driving along a seemingly peaceful road. We heard a loud bang as we drove over a culvert. Curious to know what had caused it, we saw a couple of locals scurrying away from their bomb which had failed to explode properly. As I have already stated, we were glad to get back to our tent… with hot and cold running water!

Adjusting to life as a member of Airborne Forces reminds me of a comment made by Field Marshal Lord Montgomery:

"What manner of men are these who wear the maroon beret?

They are firstly all volunteers and are then toughened by hard physical training.

As a result, they have that infectious optimism and that offensive eagerness which comes from physical well-being.

They have jumped from the air and by doing so have conquered fear.

They have the highest standards in all things whether it be skill in battle or smartness in the execution of peacetime duties.

They have shown themselves to be tenacious and determined in defence as they are courageous in attack.

They are in fact, men apart."

Nice one Monty.

Leadership in the Airborne Forces is, quite simply, everything. As an officer, you had to set a good example at all times. There was to be no strutting around because you were an eight jump wonder, and wore a red beret. It was essential to gain the confidence of the soldiers under one's command and could not rest on your laurels, neither could you expect any privileges. No more batman to look after your kit, you took care of yourself. In fact, throughout the rest of my service I was pleased to be allocated a driver when given command of a squadron or regiment, but declined to employ him as a batman. I considered it too demeaning. The advantage of having one's own driver meant one could concentrate on the job in hand and arrive at the destination, fresh and relaxed. This idea of leading could be seen even when jumping out of an aircraft. When jumping, officers always led. There was no prancing around brandishing a pistol; you took your turn with some of the heavy weapons, setting the right example to everyone else. The segregation of ranks into the officers' mess, sergeants' mess and junior ranks was different and everyone was comfortable with this tradition.

As well as commanding a platoon, there was the additional responsibility of overseeing the training and selection of officers and other ranks who had volunteered for Airborne Forces. This involved putting them through their paces in preparation for 'P' Company. Within the Brigade, units gained a lot of credibility if they obtained high success rates, so we were careful not to send anyone forward unless they had a good chance of passing. One officer did not look like making it, so I took a personal interest in him, encouraging him to show more determination. It began with a ten-mile road walk and run but he kept falling behind. Everyone has a point when they believe they cannot carry on, but almost everyone has the capability to continue for much longer than they think. Mind over matter is the old adage, I believe, but remains true today. I had to resort to shouting and swearing at him, accompanied with an occasional boot up his backside. He found this humiliating and showed resentment and anger towards me. This was the reaction I needed as it had the desired effect of keeping him going. We met again many years later when he was a successful business man and thanked me for getting him through the course and winning his wings and red beret. We became life-long friends.

Another officer who was overweight, idle and more of an habitué used to an easier way of life, failed to show the qualities and determination required; the only solution was to send him back to his unit – RTU. Some years later meeting him at a social function he was overheard to say he had volunteered for Airborne Forces, but declined to continue with the selection course, as a better opportunity was made available to him elsewhere. He was full of bullshit.

Shortly after passing 'P' Company, Captain Philip Bulpin took over as Officer Commanding. This was unusual as Philip was in the same Corps as me and this position was usually reserved for officers of one of the Parachute Regiments. It was a great compliment to him personally, and his appointment was fully justified. He was formidably fit and a great character. We have always kept in touch and, at the risk of boring our wives to death, talked for hours whenever we met, recounting the many shared experiences. This one sticks in my mind: He and his wife, Anne, had invited me to lunch one Sunday. On arrival he was busy changing the wheels on his car. Just finishing off the job, he was interrupted by Anne to say there was no wine in the house and would he go to the Officers Mess to get a bottle. I climbed into the car with him and off we went. Driving along the Farnborough bypass knocking about seventy miles an hour, I noticed a wheel bouncing along besides us as if it wanted to join our company. It hit a stone and soared up into the air determined to get to the wine before us. Amusement changed to alarm when Philip remembered he had not tightened the wheel nuts on his front near side wheel. We were travelling along on three wheels. (do you recall the song 'Three wheels on my wagon?') He avoided using his brake in case the car dropped onto its front axle and then careered into oncoming traffic. With fingers crossed, we continued in neutral, ignoring angry drivers behind us for holding up all the traffic until, much relieved, we came to a halt. I went scampering off to collect the accelerating wheel which still seemed determined to race us to the Mess. As Shakespeare once wrote: 'The wheel's come full circle'.

Philip stayed on in the Army until reaching retirement age, where he spent his last years serving as one of the Army's Court Martial Presidents joining up with another Para to form a formidable twosome. Due to their Para background they became known as "the hanging judges". Many years later when I was running my own travel company, Philip and Anne joined us on one of our holidays to Cyprus, where he kept everyone amused at dinner with his fascinating stories of military Courts martial.

Another moment to pump up the adrenalin awaited me on a drop on Salisbury Plain when taking part in an exercise involving multiple aircraft. I have mentioned the need for *all round observation* once one's parachute had deployed. Checking above to establish the parachute had deployed correctly, then to the left, right and behind, but, this time, forgetting to look below (a major departure from the plan, Fairs). The mistake was realised when I found myself standing on someone else's parachute. Sliding down it and grabbing hold of the occupant, my Second-in-Command as it happened. He shouted to me *"Don't panic Sir"* sounding as though he was Corporal Jones's stand-in, in Dad's Army. Difficult to avoid really, but holding on to him as if my life depended on it, my parachute deflated and his was taking our combined weight down to the Dropping

Zone. The problem was compounded because I could not release my 40kg weapons container strapped to my leg, which should have been released but prevented from doing so because my parachute was all tangled up around me. We landed in a heap on the one parachute. I should have broken my leg due to the unreleased weapons container, but apart from two rather painful bruised heels, all was well. The subsequent five mile walk to our rendezvous was testing. It was my own fault ....must do better.

Having experienced two parachuting incidents best avoided, this would normally amount to more than one's fair share of mishaps. Too optimistic, of course, because, another incident awaited me on an exercise in northern Norway as I was approaching the Dropping Zone (DZ). After several hours in a noisy and uncomfortable RAF transport aircraft, we approached the DZ only to be told weather conditions were unfavourable and the drop was going to be aborted. It was a night drop with good visibility, the temperature was just below zero, but the wind was gusting over fifteen knots, considered to be too strong to meet safety requirements. In the meantime, we had to go through the procedures. Doors were open, we were all hooked up and we took up our positions in the door with the yellow light on, waiting for the red light, which is the signal to jump. With one hand outside the aircraft to keep steady, a strong chilly wind blowing in my face and the Parachute Jumping Instructor (PJI) holding on to me to stop me falling out, the last thing you want at this stage is to be hanging around for too long owing to a large weapons container strapped to your leg. The PJI shouted above the noise of the aircraft that we were about to abort, requiring us to unhook our parachutes and return to our seats. I half turned when suddenly the red light came on and we were bundled out of the aircraft sideways. Once my parachute opened, I could see the rigging lines were all twisted up. This was sorted out and, drifting down on a moonlight night, my parachute made its own decision to head directly, without deviation, for the patches of water glistening below. Getting soaking wet on the first day of the exercise was not a good prospect. Skilfully attempting to avoid landing in water, my efforts were all in vain. I landed in a large area of waist deep water covered in a thin layer of ice. Great. Super. Wonderful. Welcome to Norway. Shivering and feeling more than a little bit unlucky, we headed for the rendezvous. There were always pluses and minuses in any job. This was like any other and we just had to take the rough with the smooth; no point complaining, just get on with it, Fairs. We were already wet. Sodden is another word I could have introduced here, perhaps sopping, soaking or saturated?

My parachuting incidents were not yet complete. We were on a summer camp in North Devon and had the good fortune to be allocated a helicopter for several days to do some parachuting. Jumping out of a helicopter was always popular because one just sat on the sill of the door and, when ready, pushed oneself off. Easy. The problem was, weather conditions that summer day were unsuitable, again, owing to the wind strength which was too high. There was a better Met forecast on the last day, so six of us, all eager as.... as beavers, climbed into the helicopter and prepared to jump. Then the bloody wind got up again with conditions described as marginal. We were given the option of jumping or returning to camp. Not a difficult decision and out we went. I was caught by a gust of wind and drifted well away from the planned Dropping Zone. I was heading for a landing in a holiday camp and just before contact a strong flurry caught my parachute and I landed in an awkward heap. Minor concussion prevented me getting up right away corralled as I was by a group of campers concerned about my welfare. One was a very attractive girl in a bikini, (no. honest), who held my head and helped prevent my parachute dragging me across the grass in the wind. She must have thought all her wishes had come true and this was her warrior from heaven, so I milked it for all it I was worth until a Land Rover turned up to take me back to camp. This was my first introduction to holiday camps. I was reminded of this early contact with campers when I came to run a holiday camp later in my life.

Our much-loved Quartermaster was detailed to attend a course at the Guards Depot. Shortly after arriving at the Officers Mess he made his way to the dining room for dinner and was surrounded by a bunch of young, rather grand, Hooray Henrys' fully engaged in talking about their polo ponies, totally ignoring him, a guest in their Mess. They were contemplating visiting Argentina to buy more steeds. They continued, comparing the quality of the fodder and the cost of saddle soap and similar nonsense. The Mess Sergeant came into the dining room to ask him if everything was alright and was there anything he could do for him.

'Yes, could you go to the stores and bring a large broom and a bucket and sweep up the horse shit underneath the chairs of the Guards officers around me'. Not sure if the Guards officers got the message. Several of us managed a para jump with our Q.M. to celebrate his fiftieth birthday.

We had been training hard for the Parachute Brigade athletics championships but had forgotten we were also entered for the annual Cairngorms Mountains race which involved a four-man team, yomping up the three highest mountains in the Cairngorms, including *Ben Macdui* the second highest mountain in Scotland, *Ben Nevis* and one other, *Braer Riach* if my memory serves me rightly. I was responsible for the Athletics Championships as well as the yomp. The only solution was to race back to the Mess from the athletics and travel to Perth on the overnight train with hardly enough time to grab one's kit. Arriving the next morning, totally knackered from lack of sleep, we made it to the base camp just in time to dump our kit in one of the tents, get to our allotted starting time and hoof our way upwards towards the first mountain. Time allocated to complete the course was twenty-four hours. There must have been over a hundred military teams taking part and our aim was to complete it in under twelve hours. The weather was set fair so we decided to risk it and travel light. Dressed in a shirt, trousers, walking boots and red beret and with no heavy kit to slow us down, we set off in good spirits. There were plenty of streams in the Cairngorms so there was no need to take any water and for food we carried nuts, raisins and chocolate in our pockets, nothing else. Teams set off at five minutes intervals and we were soon passing team after team. Some had overnight camping gear, heavy rucksacks; one group were even seen to be cooking a meal on a primus stove. They had no chance. Despite taking part in the athletics, overnight on an uncomfortable train with very little sleep, we were fit and looked forward to the challenge. Our strategy was to take it slowly climbing up mountains, jogging along the level ground and downhill, often breaking into a run. We made it back in good time before dark and slept, uninterrupted in our sleeping bags for twelve hours. Later we discovered we had clocked the best time and won the trophy. We did not win many trophies at the athletics but the Colonel was delighted when we returned with a cup from the Cairngorms.

I cannot leave this chapter without relating the story of the pig drama. After a Brigade exercise, we were on our way to Land's End on a night drive when we noticed smoke billowing from under the canopy of our trailer. During the exercise we had deployed several trip flares (tripwire, surrounds an area linked to one or more flares). As they were unused and difficult to get hold of, instead of setting them off, as we were supposed to do before leaving the exercise area, we foolishly decided to keep them for future use. Big mistake. They were unstable and we knew right away the movement of the vehicle had set one of them off inside a large metal ammunition box which also included a number of thunder flashes and other pyrotechnics. At great risk to ourselves we undid the canopy and hurled the box over a hedge into a field. Shortly after, there was a colossal explosion as the trip flare ignited the thunder flashes.

How were we to know the field was full of pigs?

Pigs, porkers, boars, sows, hogs and swine generally set off at a porcine gallop, managing to crash through an electric fence, whereupon they disappeared over the horizon as if they were hell bent on catching the last train after a Saturday night out. The farmhouse, on the opposite side of the road, was close in range where the farmer, interrupted his breakfast on hearing the enormous bang. He raced towards us. Judging by his language he was not in the best of moods but, calling us "swine" was unfair and untrue. We came to the rapid conclusion the best action was to be on our way, not the least because he was carrying a shotgun. Off we went like bats out of hell with the rest of the convoy thundering on behind us. Fully expecting to be reported, we were fortunate not to hear anything further, but the farmer had every right to be outraged.

When we reached Land's End, everyone was given time off and to my complete surprise, motor bikes were manoeuvred down ramps from some of our four-ton trucks before heading off to St Ives. Further investigation revealed some vehicles had beds with sheets and blankets, wardrobes, even bedside carpets.

Someone mentioned: 'You told us to use our Airborne Initiative, Sir'. What more was there to say?

CHAPTER 4 (PART ONE)

Down the Nile in a Canoe

"A journey of 1000 miles begins with one step."
Confucius '....or one stroke of the paddle, in our case.'

After four years with Airborne Forces I was seeking a new challenge. It came in the idea of canoeing down the White Nile to its confluence its the Blue Nile near Khartoum. This was sixty years ago when relationships between countries of the Middle East were tense a great deal of the time.

The source of the Nile is generally regarded as Lake Victoria but some believe it starts in the Nyungwe Forest in Rwanda. Whichever is the truth, it is officially the longest river in the world at 4,350 miles. My original idea was to canoe from Lake Victoria through the Sudd swamp on the White Nile to Khartoum. One of the most knowledgeable persons on the Nile was Dr Lawrence Kirwan, Chief Executive Officer of the Royal Geographical Society. To learn more I needed to travel up to London from Aldershot to seek his advice.

To my extreme disappointment, Dr Kirwan strongly advised against my plan due to political uncertainties in the area (nothing has changed and the area has since broken away from the Sudan to become South Sudan, after much fighting and loss of life). Another significant problem was the resurgence of a floating weed called water hyacinth, originally from Brazil, which was clogging up large parts of the river making navigation almost impossible. Coupled with this, the area was infested with large numbers of Nile crocodiles. There was a very real chance we could take a wrong channel which led nowhere leading to our small team disappearing without a trace, Sudan's equivalent to the Bermuda Triangle. Not a pleasant thought. Dr. Kirwan, sensing my disappointment proposed an alternative idea – to start at the confluence of the two Niles near Khartoum and canoe to Wadi Halfa, now on the main Nile river a journey of similar length of one thousand miles with the ultimate challenge of navigating five of the six Great Cataracts along the route.

I had been planning to start our journey in April when the Nile would be at low flood, with the cataracts at their most challenging. We found, with the help and support of the Royal Geographical Society, our plans starting to fall into place.

As everything you do in the Army has to have a clear and simple aim, I thought the following mantra would be appropriate and our aim should be:

"To navigate safely, the five Great Cataracts on the Nile."

I was never quite sure how the word "safely" became incorporated into our premise. There would be no medical facilities, no mobiles (they had not even been invented) no other forms of communication in those days and no escape route such as choppers to get us out in an emergency as much of the area where we were to travel bordered by the Nubian and Sahara deserts was uninhabited. No hospitals, medical centres or a shop selling aspirin for that matter. But, such obstacles made the trip (better word perhaps expedition, as the other implies a Sunday afternoon picnic) even more of a challenge and we could not wait to get cracking.

The time had come to begin to plan the venture. The first task was to select our team. There was no shortage of interest, not surprising in an Airborne unit and I soon settled on Norman a qualified pharmacist in the Royal Army Medical Corps, Jock of the same Corps, James (Jim) of the, then Royal Army Service Corps, and myself, a team of four. We were all serving with 23 Parachute Field Ambulance, part of 16 Parachute Brigade. We were, to a man, all fit and healthy, enthusiastic, with the right temperament to get along well together. Throughout the journey we enjoyed excellent camaraderie and never any disagreements.

As we were serving with a Medical Airborne unit we had to undergo rigorous medical tests. We needed vaccinations against all known diseases in the area and a full dental check-up. The others signed a certificate to confirm this instruction had been carried out. The only one who failed to comply was me! Too busy, planning,

I omitted to have the dental check-up and paid for it on the trip.

The Army has strict rank protocol and the ranks of our team would be a mixture of captain, sergeant, lance corporal and private. Guess who was Captain? As we would be spending several months together in remote areas we needed to adopt a sensible approach to this; it was agreed to use Christian names. No need for "Sir" or "Sarg" which worked well, and gave us no problem, reverting to correct procedures when we later met up with local military or the many other officials who liked to see protocol maintained.

If one has a challenging idea in the Armed Forces, but do not have the required equipment, the Nuffield Trust is an outstanding organization to approach for help. I had learnt how to navigate the system in previous units and provided you prepared a good case, you were likely to succeed. The Army encouraged adventurist and unusual ideas, such as expeditions and activities likely to improve character development, leadership and team building and we were fortunate to have a Commanding Officer who fully supported us. Added to this we did not believe anyone else had navigated the Great Cataracts at low flood before, so this would be a first: not that this influenced us in the decision to make the journey. The accolades came later and quite unexpectedly.

It was during the time when planning was getting under way, I was nominated to attend the Small Arms Weapons Instructors course. In addition to evening coursework, I was also busy planning the expedition, greatly helped by the wife of one of my fellow students. Her typing skills were excellent while, more unusually, she gave me help with one of the projects on the course. The plan was to give a presentation to demonstrate how *'Distraction'* could affect the quality and success of a lesson. In the middle of the presentation, and wearing a skimpy bikini, she walked slowly and provocatively through the lecture room. No one remembered a single thing I had said during this performance but provided me with a good course report.

It was time to train, and train hard. Three shiny, new Tyne folding canoes made in Twickenham, with full equipment, duly arrived, and we were able to start schooling ourselves in earnest. One incident, when canoeing on the Thames, was when we came upon a large, rather elegant riverside house with a garden full of apple trees. Even though it was winter, there were still a few apples on the upper branches. Clearly the owners were not about to harvest them so we helped ourselves. It took me back to scrumping apples and grapes in those halcyon days in Mumbles. I hadn't changed. Just when we were about to leave, the owner appeared, and it was not surprising he seemed somewhat "annoyed". I'm sure he was. We were caught red-handed and apologized. We struck up a conversation and explained we were in the Armed Forces and training for an expedition down the Nile. In a trice the issue was reversed. We were invited into the house and enjoyed his considerable hospitality before setting off again. By this time it was dark and having little enthusiasm for continuing apace, we made it to the pick-up point rather later than expected.

We had been given permission by the Sudanese Embassy in London to take a shotgun with us as the Nile has a plentiful supply of wild duck. Our plan was for *duck à l'orange* possibly once a week, to sustain us on our journey. Oranges might be difficult in the desert ...then, there was the problem of buying Grand Marnier in a Muslim country! So, possibly duck à la...duck? Accompanied by our new shotgun and an ample supply of cartridges, we found ourselves on a Parachute Brigade exercise in the Stanford Training Area, Norfolk, laid up in the middle of a large wood for the weekend with not a great deal to do before the exercise began on the Monday.

We were impressed by the large number of pheasants roaming around so, rather irresponsibly, I thought it would be a good opportunity to test out our new shotgun with a barbecue in mind for the evening. Big mistake! Driving around in a Land Rover and blasting away at anything which moved, we were close to ending up with a decent haul, when an irate gamekeeper appeared, alerted by the shotgun blasts. He came hurtling towards us in a large SUV, shouting and swearing and threatening to call the police. He wanted to look in the back of the Land Rover, but we had different ideas and were not about to give up our barbeque. He then adopted a different approach and sneakily asked to see our shotgun. He said he was going to confiscate it and attempted to drive off with our gun. We were not going to let him do that, so when four paras jumped out of the Land Rover he very sensibly arrived at a different point of view and handed back our weapon. When he was safely some distance away from our group, he shouted out, he was going to report the incident to our Brigade Commander and we would find ourselves in deep shit, well me, anyway. Well-deserved l suppose? I had calculated wrongly, the pheasants belonged to the military because it was, after all a military training area, and not owned by some wealthy landowner. Nonetheless, having accepted responsibility I thought it best to tell the Brigade Commander's P.A. exactly what had happened. Rather than receiving a bollocking I was quietly commended for my Airborne Initiative and he passed on a message to say he was sorry to have missed the barbecue! No further action was taken.

To plan the Nile venture successfully meant we had to pass through a great number of hoops before we could leave. Diplomatic permissions were needed. One reason for caution by the Foreign Office was having to consider what the Egyptian Government would believe to be the reason for four British Airborne servicemen canoeing down the Nile towards the Egyptian border. Hardly an invasion force, but bearing in mind the country's sensitivity about anything to do with the waters of the Nile, altogether very understandable. Egypt has a near total dependence on the waters of the Nile with ninety-five per cent of its population living in the Nile Valley alongside the river bank. Egypt has depended on the Nile since the dawn of civilization five thousand years ago and was granted natural historical rights by the 1929 Anglo-Egyptian Treaty and the 1959 Agreement between Egypt and the Sudan. The Egyptian authorities had refused to abandon these anachronistic treaties causing tensions to continue to exist between Egypt and Sudan. It was further exacerbated when Ethiopia had started to build the Grand Ethiopian Renaissance Dam on the Blue Nile, a hydroelectric project designed to improve livelihoods significantly in the region. The dam was planned to transform the lives of one hundred and ten million Ethiopians, providing many of them with electricity for the first time and allowing the country to industrialize.

As a result, as we proceeded down the Nile, we came across frequent Egyptian outposts monitoring the flow of the river. We stayed well clear. Fortunately, we did receive political agreement to go ahead with the expedition provided it did not include publicity in the national press.

Now for a bit of history. It might help? Khartoum began its existence in 1821 as an outpost for the Egyptian Army after The Sudan was incorporated into Egypt. Due to its position at the confluence of the Blue and White Nile it was quickly established as an outpost for trade and became one of the centres for the slave trade in central Africa. At the time of our visit, Khartoum was a beautiful riverside community, strongly influenced by colonial architecture intermingled with Sudanese and African culture. Its wide tree-lined streets encompassed the many different nationalities and cultures – African, Nubian, Sudanese, Dinka from the south and Europeans – who lived harmoniously together. In 1883, the Mahdi (the Mahdi of Islam or 'The Expected One') proclaimed himself as the Prophesied Redeemer of the Islamic world. His actions threatened all the major cities of the Sudan, including Khartoum where his army had gathered.

General Gordon had been commissioned by William Gladstone, the Liberal Prime Minister, to go to the Sudan to organise the evacuation of the Egyptian garrisons in the Sudan. The Anglo-Egyptian agreement implied that Egypt had been a British protectorate in all but name, but because it had claim to the Sudan, the region came under British protection. Instead of going to the defence of the garrison, the British Government decided to abandon Sudan to self-government. This ensured the existence of a Mahdi state. General Gordon was sent to plan the evacuation but he had other ideas; instead he organised a year-long defence of the city when it was besieged by the Mahdi in 1884. The only way the city could be relieved would require intervention by British Armed Forces. Because of British parliamentary reluctance to provide assistance, it took a year for a British Expeditionary Force to be sent, but Khartoum fell just two days before the arrival of the relief column, by which time General Gordon had been murdered.

Public opinion sought to avenge the death of General Gordon but this was ignored by Parliament for 13 years until an Army under Lord Kitchener was sent to destroy the Mahdist forces.

In 1898 Kitchener restored colonial rule with victory over the Mahdi forces at the Battle of Omdurman, on the Kerreri Battlefield, about eleven kilometres north of Khartoum, thus finally, avenging the death of General Gordon.

General Kitchener had set out to avenge the defeat with eight thousand British troops, a mixed force of seventeen thousand Sudanese and Egyptian troops, and a fleet of gunboats equipped with twelve pounder guns, howitzers and Maxim guns. Against the British forces, the Mahdi's forces Sudanese deployed fifty thousand holy warriors, mostly armed with little more than ancient rifles and spears along with two machine guns; Kitchener's army had fifty-five. During the engagement, the 21st Lancers mounted one of the last cavalry charges in history, but the Battle of Omdurman was essentially won by brutal firepower, including Kitchener's gunboat, the Melik, with its ferocious battery of guns. The Sudanese warriors, with their chain-mail armour and crocodile-skin shields, were no match for the Maxim guns, which could fire five hundred rounds a minute. At least ten thousand Sudanese died supporting the Mahdi and many more were wounded and taken prisoner. Only forty-eight men were killed on the British side.

During this time, Thomas Cook, the oldest and most prestigious travel agent in the world and one of the credits of the British Empire had arranged a huge steamboat flotilla, including the 'Melik', to sail from Cairo for the General Relief Expedition up the Nile to Wadi Halfa, and then onto Khartoum. The Melik was Lord Kitchener's gunboat and was ordered from a Chiswick shipyard by the Admiralty for service with the Egyptian Army in 1896. Construction was rapid, and she was delivered the following year. Following trials in Britain, she was then dismantled into carefully marked sections and shipped to Ismailia in Egypt. The sections were then transported up the Ismailia Canal and then south on the Nile to Wadi Halfa on the Sudanese frontier. There they were loaded onto railway wagons and conveyed on the newly built desert railway across the Nubian Desert to Abu Hamed. In the summer of 1898 they finally reached Abadieh where the gunboat was reassembled to lead a flotilla of heavily armed gunboats in Kitchener's short-lived triumph. At the time of our visit, the Melik had found a new life as the club-house of the Blue Nile Sailing Club and the Commodore and Committee invited us to be Honorary Members of the Club. They offered us storing facilities for our canoes and made us welcome to come along to afternoon teas, enjoy their bar and use some of their boats for a bit of sailing.

•••

As the expedition was officially recognized by the Army, we became eligible to fly out with RAF transport, provided the aircraft did not have to deviate from its route, and subject to space being available. Very soon we were on our way. We took off from

RAF Lyneham on a Britannia flight and had overnight stops in Kano, Nigeria and Nairobi in Kenya before arriving in Aden at one of the hottest times of the year. We were expecting thirty-one degrees in April moving up to around thirty-four degrees in May. This was a good opportunity to start acclimatizing, working on a strict exercising programme and gradually increasing exposure to the sun, starting with a base of twenty minutes a day. The best place for this was "Steamer Point Lido", which was a section of the beach cordoned off by a shark net, but complicated by local military rules which allocated separate parts of the beach according to rank. This meant segregation into areas for officers, NCO's and Junior Ranks. We decided to all be NCOs and stick together. We were not sorry to leave Aden for it was a desolate, forlorn sort of town, with a number of no-go areas. One such, the notorious Crater area was approached by Jock and Jim who attempted to walk around the city rim one day, but inadvertently wandered into a shanty town and were chased off by angry locals.

As members of an airborne medical unit in the Parachute Brigade, there was no shortage of medical advice in preparation for the expedition. One of these was to acclimatise carefully, particularly to avoid sunburn. We were advised to build up a sun tan gradually. That included limiting exposing to the sun to no more than twenty minutes on the first day, then adding five minutes each day thereafter. We were all lazing on the beach in the sweltering heat of Aden on the second day when one of our team fell sleep. Having already exceeded the recommended exposure time, we thought it best to wake him up and get him to put a shirt on. This task fell to Jim, but he immediately regretted it when the person concerned, despite being woken up as tactfully as possible, became aggressive and violent. He might have been having a bad dream but his behaviour was disturbing. Thinking the matter over, I remembered another incident when we passed a group of fishermen canoeing down the Thames. The same person got into a heated argument with fishermen when his paddles got tangled up with their fishing line. Instead of navigating around the fishermen, like the rest of them, he carried on almost relishing the opportunity to annoy the fishermen. I wondered at the time if his temperament was suitable for the expedition, but gave him the benefit of the doubt. It was a mistake. I could not risk the success of the expedition wondering when the next incident would occur and had no choice, sadly, but to send him home on the next available aircraft.

RAF flights to Khartoum were infrequent but we were lucky to thumb a lift on an aircraft travelling to pick up the Sudanese Army's polo team and taking them on to Cyprus for the annual polo match between the British and Sudanese Army teams. The Military Attaché in Khartoum later mentioned to me, this was an important annual event in the calendar and helped to cement good relationships between the UK and Sudan.

The British Military Attaché in Khartoum had planned for us to camp in his garden. On arrival he had second thoughts as he considered it may not reflect well with the Sudanese authorities.

And so we were accommodated in the splendid Colonial-style Sudan Club where, in those days, locals were not allowed to be members. It was very stylish with a cloistered swimming pool, restaurant and lounges. I remember in particular, club rules insisted, if you wanted to attract the attention of a waiter, you had to clap your hands. No shouting or loud voices allowed in the Club. There was a strict dress code at the Club so we all had to wear jackets, collar and ties for dinner in the evening, though the temperature was over one hundred and twenty degrees, that is forty-nine degrees centigrade! One evening, we all duly changed for dinner as usual only to be told by the waiter that April was the start of the official summer time when shirt sleeve order was permitted at dinner. Sense prevailed even here.

Final preparations were going to take us a week before we could set off on our journey. During this time we were taken on several sight-seeing tours, one of which was to the Omdurman battlefield, where we stood where Winston Churchill observed the battle as a young war correspondent. Although it was a triumph, Churchill included in his report, his denunciation of the inhumanity of the neglect of thousands of Dervish casualties, much to the displeasure of Kitchener who was, to say the least, not happy.

Every morning we made our way to the Blue Nile Sailing Club and spent a few hours training before returning to the Sudan Club to swim. We also enjoyed the hospitality of the Military Attaché and his capable wife. They invited us all to tea and were taken to see their pet donkey where their lively young daughter told me, his name was Fart. A dinner party was arranged but, following local custom, all the guests were men. No women, apart from, strangely, the Colonel's wife. There were an impressive number of high ranking Sudanese army officers and the main topic of conversation was the annual polo match against the British Army in Cyprus. After dinner they all stood in a line and peed over the rockery, something of a tradition in the Sudan I was told later. Shame about the pansies.

The Military Attaché wanted to take a ride in one of our canoes, so Jim was duly volunteered to take him out into the Nile. They followed the fast flowing current and canoed down to the confluence of the Blue and White Niles but, when Jim tried to turn the canoe around, the Military Attaché started to lean the wrong way causing the canoe nearly to capsize.

Jim said afterwards that he was visualizing the headlines in the papers. *'Lance Corporal drowns Military Attaché.*

We were impressed by the hospitality shown to us by the Sudanese Army who had passed on information to villages along the river to look out for our canoes and offer every assistance. They had arranged for mail addressed to us via the British Embassy to be delivered to villages along our route. This was a great morale booster, especially for me, as I had a girl friend at home who had promised to write every week.

Sensibly, all the locals in the Sudan wear the traditional abaya (meaning cloth in Arabic) a white robe intended to cover up the whole body save for the head and feet to ensure the wearer remained within the strict Islamic conventions. It also provides protection from the sun. We were often to be seen prancing around in tee shirts and shorts; how unsuitable a form of dress is that for the sweltering heat of Arabia? It was however probably the best form of dress to deal with our daily exposure to the sun, and, once acclimatised, we discarded our tee shirts and developed a good strong ebony brown sun tan. We all wore sun shades and turbans which were essential. Not that sporting a good sun tan was planned, rather what we wore, or did not wear, remained comfortable for our journey. We supplemented this by swimming in the Nile several times a day to cool down. We started the tanning process by using Factor 50 sun blocker but, rightly or wrongly, after a few weeks, did not see any need to continue using it. Due to careful climatization, none of us suffered any skin damage caused by ultraviolet light.

The Sudanese Army provided a most useful map showing our route printed onto a huge piece of linen and sewn together showing navigable channels, dangerous areas to avoid and other useful information. We had our own maps, but I do not know how we would have managed without this. Every morning it would be opened up and positioned on my lap in the canoe. As a result, we always knew where we were.

My letters requesting help to various, carefully chosen companies had also paid off. We were awarded four very fine waterproof and shock proof Smiths watches – one to my certain knowledge still going strong, Basketball boots from Dunlop, Crawford's biscuits and, amazingly for the time, masses of tea bags which were to prove their great value alongside Nescafé, a confirmatory picture of which you will find in the illustrations. Interestingly, one of the watches, apart from telling the time all the way down the Nile and being submerged when we capsized on the great cataracts, has been up the Khyber Pass, down the Rio

Grande and up into the foothills of Kilimanjaro and the highest mountain in Norway, Galdhøppigen at 2,469 metres. Quite a journey since we set out sixty-two years ago.

The time had come to leave the luxury of the Sudan Club. Armed with bags of advice from different people, we set off. We carried our canoes down to the banks of the Blue Nile and were pleasantly surprised to find so many people had come along to wish us bon voyage! Amongst them were representatives from the Sudanese Government, the Armed Forces and the British Embassy including the Military Attaché and his family. It was a hot, still day with the temperature reading one hundred and five degrees. After handshakes and farewells, we were loaded up and all set to get under way.

CHAPTER 4 (PART TWO)

The Nile, April 1961, a Thousand Miles to go

We paddled out into the confluence of the Blue and White Niles which meant we were soon out in the main flow of the Nile itself, with the current bringing momentum to the journey ahead. The 1,000 miles of water ahead would take about two months to cover. Although feeling elated and, yes, excited, after all the delays and worries of the planning stage I also wondered what we were letting ourselves in for, and had I underestimated the dangers by exposing my companions to unknown dangers without any medical backup? As we set off, I recollected a comment from one of the senior Sudanese Army officers.

'David, if you want to go to Wadi Halfa why not go by rail. You can get there in twenty-four hours.'

The first of the Great Cataracts for us was the Sixth at Bagrawiyah one hundred and twenty miles north of Khartoum where the river narrows considerably with one hundred and thirty foot, black rock cliffs, rising up on either side. We first become aware of the cataract by the roar of the water as we entered the narrow gorge of turbulent, treacherous rapids with hundreds of semi-submerged rocks, where just one could smash a canoe into matchwood. We had to use all of our strength to paddle hard so as to be moving faster than the river, otherwise it would have been quite easy to lose control.

Before leaving the UK we were advised to avoid drinking the Nile water and had been provided with several sets of water sterilizing kits which involved pouring Nile water through a mesh to get rid of the sediment. Then to add sterilizing tablets, wait twenty minutes, then add a de-tasting tablet and wait another twenty minutes. I mentioned this to one of the older warriors in the Blue Nile Sailing Club who said that it was nonsense. All you had to do was dip your mug into the Nile, count to thirty for the sediment to settle, then drink half the contents, leaving any remaining grit in the mug.

As we settled into a steady rhythm in calmer waters, pleased to be free of the first of the great cataracts, we turned out attention to the more routine, if still important, activities for each day. We needed to drink about a litre of water every hour to rehydrate our bodies. Advice also was given to avoid the sandy islands as this is where our friends, the Nile crocodile hung out. And they could grow to sixteen feet in length, they were aggressive, and they could swim at about twenty-two miles an hour. Even on land for short distance they could run (at us) at eight or nine miles per hour. We tried to batter our way into the banks, through the reeds but the ground was iron hard even if one could reach it. We had sleeping bags and tents but no camp beds and soon found out that the uninhabited sandy islands in the middle of the river were the best places to sleep. It was too hot for tents and the routine was to stop well before sunset and prepare the main meal of the day before dark. The sand would be baking hot, but we learnt to dig two holes where we were going to sleep, one for the shoulders and the other for the hips so that by the time we were ready to fall into oblivion the sand had cooled and we all slept well until dawn when the flies arrived replacing the need for an alarm clock.

We were told to stay away from stagnant water to avoid bilharzia. This is an infection caused by tiny worms which gather in stagnant water and live parasitically in snails, becoming dangerous to humans if they penetrate the skin. They can have life-threatening consequences, second only in its impact on humans to malaria. We did not come across any stagnant water, fortunately. The Nile travels at a speed of about four knots, much faster in the cataract regions, and this constant movement of water together with the influence of the sun, continually oxygenating the Nile in remote areas, makes it safe to drink. This is not the case in Egypt which is much more populous.

Nothing had prepared us for the region inhabited by the nimitti midge, a tiny black insect that matures a few meters under the water and lives for 24 hours, during which time it can think of nothing better to do than go for your eyes, nose, mouth and ears. A few other places as well. The only protection is to wear an Arab keffiyeh headdress pulled across the face and wait for the sun to set, when they all disappear along with the hordes of recognisably common or garden flies.

Our journey coincided with the Holy month of Ramadan and we were told that our presence could be sensitive to villagers. This turned out not to be true. In every village we received nothing but the kindest of welcome, Islam at its best. As soon as our approach was noticed, the whole village would turn out to greet us. This invariably meant meeting the village Head man, along with his acolytes and being offered a place to rest. If we were passing late in the day, we would be invited to stay in their huts, waiting until dusk when sunset would permit them to give us coffee and food. This was, usually kisra (a thin fermented bread) dipped in goats milk. Towards the end of the journey, when Ramadan also came to an end, culminating in the great Eid festival, roast goat would sometimes be on the menu. It was delicious. On one occasion we were entertained by the local Headman who insisted we stayed for a meal, not realizing it would take four or five hours to kill the goat and then cook it. While we tucked in, our hosts just watched us, though, according to custom, the women were not to be seen. We greatly appreciated the hospitality of these wonderful village people and knew they could ill afford to provide us with food. Mostly however, we continued to sleep on the sandy islands so that we could get off to an early start the next day.

Pulling into a sand bar for the night, one of us would be charged to check out the crocodiles. They could often be found, sunning themselves on the banks but would crash into the water as soon as they were disturbed and remain submerged apart from their eyes and snouts, remaining at a safe distance, while observing us closely, possibly for thickness of thigh or sweetness of arm. We continued to swim in the river several times each day to cool off and, although the crocodiles were always to be seen they tended to stay away from us. Jim was canoeing near the river bank, at which time he disturbed a very mature, sixteen foot long crocodile basking in the sun. It was, of course, a Nile crocodile one of the most aggressive of the twenty-four types of crocodile. The startled reptile made for the water, nearly landing on top of the canoe. Another day, found Norman and Jock canoeing in the middle of the river where they managed to\ run aground on a half-submerged sand bank. Jock got out of the canoe to push the canoe into deeper water. Jim shouted across to him, 'you're brave' and pointed to a rock about fifteen feet away which turned out to be a huge crocodile basking in the sun. Jim said afterwards he'd never seen a Scotsman move so fast.

In one village we were asked to shoot a large crocodile which had eaten the local postmaster for his tea, but unfortunately our shotgun would not have been powerful enough. The incident had occurred a few weeks before our arrival and the crocodile was known to be still in the area. The deceased postmaster had had a girlfriend living on the opposite bank, and having missed the last felucca ferry he decided to swim. He never made it. Crocodiles have no tongues and thus cannot chew, so they drag their prey underwater to decompose, often wedging a body under a submerged log or large rock. The body was never found.

Another bit of advice which I foolishly disregarded, was to avoid contact with nomads. We saw a large group of them on one occasion watering their camels. When approaching them with a friendly gesture, they raced to get rifles from their saddle bags so we thought it would be a good idea not to hang around, leaping into our canoes emulating graceful gazelles straight from the bush, and not looking back as we sped away.

From Bagrawiyah onwards, we passed hundreds of pyramids, fortified castles and temples close to the banks of the Nile making up part of the ancient city of Meroë, which, in its day had rivalled Egypt in its size and power. The area was full of unexplored history, remote and untouched by the modern world, and hardly changed since ancient times, but, quite unlike the antiquities of Egypt. We were privileged to witness a lost world of 2,700 years ago with a treasure trove of history lying in the sand, waiting to be properly excavated by a modern day Howard Carter.

As we approached the next cataract where the Nile met the Atborah river, we had developed a procedure where one of us would go on ahead, beach his canoe and climb to a high point to work out the best route, one which had the least number of rocks. It resulted, one day, in a memorable incident when Jock and Norman had gone on ahead to do the recce, but on our arrival they were nowhere to be seen. Jim and I assumed they had continued down the rapids. We soon realized our mistake when they reappeared, yelling and shouting at us to turn back. We attempted, fruitlessly, to turn our canoes around, but the current was too strong. We managed to get our bows facing down river and paddled like fury down the half mile or so of rapids, hoping not to hit anything. We managed to get to the end safely but the others were not so lucky, hitting a submerged rock, which turned their canoe over. Strong and fit, they were able to hang on until they reached calmer water. Luckily they were not badly hurt; the canoe was quickly repaired and we were underway again. We lost some of our equipment but the main thing was, we were all undamaged. Nowadays life jackets and head gear are essential requirement, but in those early 'sixties' we did not have those attitudes towards health and safety as today. But, the dangers we faced were also, exhilarating in their way and, at our age, we welcomed the challenges.

Between Abu Hamad which sits on an enormous bend in the Nile and Karima we passed through one hundred and sixty-five miles of completely desolate countryside with the Sahara on one side and the Nubian Desert on the other and in the whole of this distance there were cataracts every few miles. Today much of the area is flooded caused by the building of the Merowe High Dam. At this stage of our journey, Abu Hamad was three hundred and forty-five miles north of Khartoum if one had been travelling by train.

Our usual routine would be to get up at first light, brew a cup of tea, eat a few dried dates and biscuits and be on our way. Towards mid-day we preferred to rest from the scorching heat, seeking the shelter of date palms or thorn trees. The evening meal usually consisted of boiled rice, soup provided with the compliments of *Swiss Knorr* supported with vegetables purchased from villages. Duck was on the menu most nights as the

Nile is one of the prolific places in the world for these birds. We attempted to cook one over a fire on our first night, (note my earlier comment on duck à la l'orange) but it turned out to be a disaster, tough as old boots, burnt on the outside and raw on the inside. We soon abandoned the idea and settled on cutting them up into small pieces and dropping them into the soup. It may not seem very appetizing but we were hungry enough to have eaten anything. We developed a good system for duck. I would shoot them, Norman would remove the feathers and Jim would cook them.

Sometimes we met up with local crocodile hunters and invited them to our camp site. After the usual bartering, crocodile meat was on the menu for supper by way of a change. An acquired taste! The official description of crocodile meat states it is mild in flavour, something like chicken but with a fishiness about it with easy, flaking meat. Take your pick. A real treat was when we came across local fishermen with Nile Perch on sale as the main course. This set itself above char-grilled duck and baked crocodile by a long way.

•••

It was after only a few days on the Nile, I developed a raging toothache as only a toothache can be...ache.

It was my own fault for not going for a checkup, as planned, before leaving the UK. The only solution was to have it out, but with little likelihood of finding a dentist on my own, I sought advice from one of the villages. Great news, there was a dentist in a village about ten miles away from the river, so I hired a donkey and guide and set off into the desert, leaving my companions to carry on and arranging to meet further down river the next day. On arrival at the village, I met the dentist in a mud hut – where else? It turned out that his services included not only dentistry but pharmacy and veterinary work – so, a wide range of experience. Surprised at his extensive skills, I asked him if he was qualified. He spoke a little English and said he was only a "small doctor" having completed a four-week course in Khartoum. So that was alright then! Four weeks is almost a month after all. Well, there was a small point about no anaesthetic so it was an experience not to be forgotten. He eventually applied his pliers, possibly borrowed from the garage across the road, around the offending tooth and gave it a yank, made all the more difficult for him as I was grabbing his arm, quite tightly, causing both of us to fall on the floor as the tooth finally emerged, though only partially, as over the next few days I was spitting out remaining bits of tooth. But the pain was gone which was all that mattered. I was pleased to rejoin my companions and carry on down the river.

Jim read out an insertion into his diary which he felt was worth recounting.

"I was canoeing in some turbulent white water when I hit a rock but just managed to stay upright. The impact however had fractured one of the wooden canoe spars. David gave me a tongue lashing saying I should have been more careful and vigilant as it could have been a disastrous end to our expedition. The next day David hit a rock and gave me another telling off for not warning him that the rock was there." Honestly Jim, I was not pulling rank!

There are probably as many pyramids, temples and other antiquities in the Sudan as there are in Egypt. The only difference is that they are largely unexplored or visited by tourists due to their remoteness, although most of them were sited along the banks of the life-giving waters of the Nile. We had seen a scattering of these buildings soon after leaving Khartoum, but came across the largest collection of pyramids in the Sudan near Meröe between the sixth and fifth cataracts where kings and queens from the Meroitic period are buried. They were close to the river so we took time out when stretching our legs to explore.

At Abu Hamad we arrived at the big loop of the Nile mentioned above, and entered the most remote region of our journey. We were greeted by the head of the local police who invited us to visit the Karima Pyramids out in the desert. These astonishing incredibly ancient tombs are extremely remote and therefore little known in those days. Since then, they enjoy the status of a UNESCO World Heritage Site. Built by the rulers of the ancient Kushite Kingdom in an area of the Nile known as Nubia, we were lucky to have the Chief of Police as our guide.

We travelled in a police truck and on the way got bogged down a couple of times in soft sand and had to be dug out. At one of the pyramids, we crawled inside the burial chamber to its centre. Tomb raiders had long since removed anything of interest or value, but it was an interesting if, to me, a claustrophobic experience.

On our return to Karima, and much to the embarrassment of the Police Chief, our truck broke down with a burnt-out coil. A donkey was commandeered from a passing local to allow one of the policemen to go to a village for help. He returned about an hour later having been unable to find a tow rope, so we waited in the shade sipping tea and watched villagers – would you believe - twisting twine to make an instant inch thick tow rope. We arrived back after dark but the last twist to this story (sorry) was a soldier stopping our vehicle and pointing a loaded .303 Lee-Enfield rifle at us. The Police Chief soon sorted that out.

Ramadan was over and the people were celebrating Eid holiday when we arrived at Dongola, capital of the state of Northern Sudan. Previously, it had been the centre for Nubian civilisation. It was market day and the buzz in the air was contagious. My most vivid recollection was the donkey (car) park where hundreds of donkeys were corralled into a space surrounded by an effective stone wall and thorn bushes. Donkeys were so tightly packed in together, they could hardly move, apart that is, for a Jack donkey who had sussed out a Jenny on heat. There followed a performance that was compelling to watch. The Jenny, anxious to avoid the interest from Jack, (well, wouldn't you in the circumstances with everyone watching?) sought sanctuary by climbing on top of her crowded mates before running along their backs for dear life. Jack the Lad was having none of it, the chase concluding with Jack getting his sinful way, which he followed up with a long drawn out bray of satisfaction in response to our applause. I watched the continual movement of donkeys and how the donkey park attendant was able to identify every donkey when the owner came to collect his transport for home.

The only other mode of transport in this whole region was either to take a felucca or dhow; there were hundreds of them in the harbour, well managed by the harbour attendant. With these three methods of travel serving everyone's need in the region. It was quite timeless, as if the world had moved on long ago but forgotten to take Dongola along with it.

I have always liked to be clean-shaven so, after a week or so of an increasingly untidy appearance, I took the opportunity to visit the local barber. Sitting on a rattan chair in the open and watched with interest by a group of locals, I had my first cut throat razor shave experience. I kept a beady eye on the man's razor hand but it did not tremble once, so I was, finally, able to relax.

Dongola was interesting to us Army men as it was the scene of one of General Kitchener's victories in September 1896 over the Mahdist tribes leading to the final Battle of Omdurman exactly two years later. In the town we were lucky enough to be put up at a government rest house so the decision was made to have a bit of R. & R. and catch up with domestic chores before continuing our journey the next day.

We set off again with some dread and trepidation as we approached the Second Cataract, the last and most dangerous on our journey; the first has now been lost, submerged under Lake Nasser. Unknown to us, the authorities had arranged for three guides to show the team the safest route through the worse of the rapids. As we approached, we saw someone on the banks waving frantically at us. It was our guides. Stripped to the waist, one of them, with his turban and shirt tied into a bundle on his head, blew up a goat's bladder for buoyancy and launched himself into the water, signalling for us to follow him. One hand was used to keep hold of the goat's bladder, the other for paddling. Very soon he was caught up in the white turbulent water with us following close behind. Protected by our fitted spray covers we sliced through great breakers of white water surrounded by a savage roaring as the river threatened to destroy us once and for all but, eventually, exhausted but triumphant, we reached calmer water and felt more than grateful to our guide for his invaluable help.

Towards the end of our journey we were surprised to hear what turned out to be a generator pumping water up a cliff. Standing close by was a man in shorts and a tee shirt, the first European we had seen on the trip. We pulled in and were given a warm welcome by this Italian mining engineer and invited to follow him up the cliff to what turned out to be a forgotten gold mine dating from biblical times. We were the first visitors to his mine and although we were anxious to continue our journey, there was no way of avoiding some excellent hospitality, including a tour of the mine and the best meal of our journey. The story, we learned, from out Italian friend, was of him having heard of the existence of the mine in the souk at Khartoum and it was for sale. Taking a gamble and purchasing it on the same day, knowing they only had a limited amount of time before the newly constructed Aswan High

Dam was completed, when the area would be flooded forever. Miners were working around the clock for the elusive gold seam which they were sure was there. We would have liked to learn if they had ever found the gold seam.

Throughout our journey, the weather had been dry and hot except for several occasions when we had to face up to sandstorms, called haboobs. They would begin with darkening skies and high spiraling plumes of sand, which usually gave us time to ground the canoes and seek shelter under whatever cover we could find. One exceptional storm, which we saw approaching, was so strong we decided to carry on until we found a village, but with nothing in sight, we agreed to split up and fend for ourselves, concentrating on keeping our bows into the wind. Although the river flowed in our favour, the strong wind from the north made it almost impossible to make any progress. We soon lost contact with each other, so carried on while trying to keep the sand out of our eyes (if only we had brought goggles). Eventually, I heard a shout from the bank so made my way to an island where a small community of farmers lived in straw huts. Everyone turned out to see this stranger and I settled in for an overnight stopover. One of the locals spoke a little English and said someone had gone to fetch a blind man well over ninety years old, who had been a guide with Kitchener's army. He proudly showed me his medal and spent the whole evening by my side, touching my face from time to time as we were the only European contact he had met since all those years ago. When I awoke in the morning he was sleeping on a *charpai* (traditional woven bed used throughout North Africa) right next to me. In the morning the storm had passed and we all met up again later in the day with different tales to tell about our overnight experiences.

Wadi Halfa at the hottest time of the year and us, arrived together. It was in June with the temperature clocking a hellish 124 degrees F. that's fifty-one degrees Celsius. We had reached our destination and received a friendly welcome from the local people including the District Commissioner and for the first time in two months enjoyed the luxury of a decent bed.

It was as we completed our voyage, an example of one of the strange regulations under which the Army sometimes operates, became evident. Because we were on official duty, we were entitled to Ration Allowance, even though we neither expected nor needed it. Someone had decided we could not receive Ration Allowance unless we also received Local Overseas Allowance, which was more for me, less so for the others, as it is based on rank. As we were not expecting to receive either, this was all a bonus for us and we saw no reason to fuss. There was, not surprisingly, no official rate for the Nile, it was based on the rate for Khartoum, resulting in a comfortable sum of money waiting for us on our return. So what to do with all this money? I suggested we should add the total amount of our individual allowances together and divided the total by four, a not too difficult calculation to make.

The rail journey across the desert from Wadi Halfa back to Khartoum took around twenty four hours. There were four different classes of coach, from absolute basic to the luxury of your own carriage compartment with bed, a bearer and all meals provided. We all agreed to spend some of our money on this bit of indulgence. When I mentioned this to the District Commissioner he said we were guests of the Sudanese Government and there was nothing for us to pay for. We were more than grateful and enjoyed luxurious travel across the desert returning to our starting point.

On arrival, we had the unexpected pleasure of discovering the Sudanese Army had arranged a Reception for us which turned out to be a rather grand affair attended by some of the more senior officers in the Army, together with several diplomats. The British Military Attaché had also arranged a welcome back party for our safe return and, to round it all off another surprise was a Reception given to us by the Blue Nile Sailing Club where we were each awarded a silver engraved ashtray in recognition of our achievement.

After a few more days gearing down to what I would describe as a 'normal' life, we departed for home. The one outstanding memory which will remain with all of us was the tremendous hospitality and friendship shown to us by the Sudanese people.

Our departure went smoothly until we arrived in Cyprus, where we were off-loaded and had to wait for the RAF to find space on another flight back to the UK. After about a week at the RAF transit camp, we were duly informed we couldn't stay indefinitely and had to move out to stay with 2 Para in Limassol. After two weeks of hauling our kit and canoes back and forth to the airport in the hope of getting seats on one of the daily flights, we were beginning to get impatient. We had been away for three months and wanted to get home. There was no email in those days, so I sent a signal to our Commanding Officer in Aldershot asking for his help. He got in touch with Brigade HQ and they set the wheels in motion by contacting RAF Transport Command and very soon space was being arranged for us to come home.

We arrived at Nicosia airport in high spirits but attempting to check-in, a very unhelpful, pompous and unfriendly Movement Control officer said the flight was Category C and unsuitable for passengers. I tried reasoning with him but to no avail. As we were pondering on what options we had, we could see the aircraft sitting close to the fence. At that moment the crew came out and started making their way to the aircraft for departure without us. Using my *'Airborne Initiative'* I climbed up and over the terminal building fence and ran over to the crew to explain our predicament. Luckily, they had been expecting us so we collected our kit and started to load up when the incredibly unhelpful Movement Control Officer ran onto the airfield with an armed guard to arrest us. I had time to explain to the pilot that we were now in for a spot of trouble, but he also used his 'Airborne Initiative' telling him we were classified as "supernumerary air crew" and instructed him to get lost. We were told there would be no meals or proper seats on board as the aircraft was in cargo (Category C) mode and the crew advised us to go back to the terminal building and get something for the journey, but we had no desire to run the risk of another confrontation with the Movement Control Officer. We were also told that the Beverley aircraft we were travelling in had a full payload and if there was a strong headwind they may have to offload us in Malta. Fortunately, this did not happen, so another hurdle was overcome. When we called in for a brief refuelling stop at Marseille, we felt there would be an opportunity to get something to eat. But being a military aircraft we were positioned a long way from the terminal near the perimeter fence. On the other side of the wire we could see lights and hear music from a bar, so we drew lots to see which of us was going to climb over the fence and get some provisions. This task fell to Jock and Norman who came back with armfuls of baguettes, cheese and several bottles of wine. Wine, cheese and baguettes disappeared allowing us to sleep until the next thing we remembered was seeing the lights of London through a window. Shortly after, we landed at RAF Lyneham where our Commanding Officer was waiting to meet us. It was great to be home.

•••

Several years later, I was contacted by Ranulph Fiennes, then an officer in Royal Scots Greys and later to be knighted for his skills as an explorer. He was planning an expedition to parachute over the historical site of Abu Simbul in Egypt, and then to travel up the Nile in individual hovercraft. He wanted to know if he could borrow the map we used on our expedition to guide him through the cataracts, then to be at high flood and more navigable. At first I hesitated, but a couple of meetings later agreed to let him borrow it on condition that I could come on the trip. But due to my next military appointment I was unable to make it. Later I contacted him to try to get him to return the map but received no reply. Many years later and after he had become a famous explorer, he appeared in Waterstones in Kendal to launch his latest book. I introduced myself to him, but he had no recollection of meeting me. I never did get the map back.

But our adventures on the Nile were not yet finished. I was to receive an extremely pleasant surprise. After over fifty years I saw an article, along with a photograph of the team in our canoes on the Nile, in a Royal British Legion magazine written by Jim Dalziel seeking to make contact with his three companions on the Nile expedition. We got in touch with each other and next time I was in London took the train to Essex to meet him. After all those years. I asked him how I would recognize him. He said not to worry about that because it would not be difficult to spot him. He was the only person waiting at the station wearing an airborne red beret!

We had a great time exchanging experiences, and I particularly appreciated the amazing records he had kept, far better than mine, along with a stock of photographs. Also impressive, were his children and grandchildren who had all used his Nile experience for school projects. On our next visit, my wife, Denise, came with me and we were made particularly welcome by both Jim and Joy, his wife. Essex is a part of England we had not visited before and we enjoyed being shown around including the walk to the end of Southend pier, well over a mile long. (1.33 miles long to be precise). We have remained firm friends and keep in touch, sharing various magical memories we experienced on the Nile. Sadly, Jock had passed away and Norman, Jim believed, had emigrated to New Zealand,

It had been a journey of a lifetime. Both Jim and I treasure the time we spent together in true comradeship. The end result to cap it all, was the appointment, I was delighted to accept, for being made a Fellow of the Royal Geographical Society.

CHAPTER 5

Royal Marine Commando

"Better to live one day as a lion than a lifetime as a sheep."

Saying goodbye to my red beret and donning my black *'crap hat beret'* again, I was off to Somerset to join the Junior Leader's Regiment. This consisted of six platoons of junior soldiers aged between fifteen and seventeen in which the men continued with their education while being taught to be future leaders. On arrival, the Colonel said I was to be allocated Ford Platoon where there were difficulties of morale and bullying.

There is a saying: *'There are never any bad soldiers, only bad officers'*.

Not wishing to cast any aspersions on my predecessor, there seemed, nonetheless, to have been a lack of leadership and the Colonel thought my Airborne background could help to sort it out. This was a challenge, but one I looked forward to, and immediately sought permission to take the platoon out of their normal routine to spend a week on Dartmoor. This would allow uninterrupted time to get to know them and help get them back on track.

The day before we were to leave, a weather warning was issued for the area, with heavy snow forecast across Dartmoor. Ignoring this, with everyone on parade and about to board the transport provided for the trip, they found they were in for a surprise. Divided into groups of three, each were given a map and told to get to the camp by nightfall. Questioning the idea, they were told to use their Airborne Initiative, with a prize for the group having the most interesting story to tell that evening. They all managed to get there on time, which was encouraging. The group who won their well-deserved award had thumbed a lift with no less a person than the well-known movie star, Peter Ustinov in a Rolls Royce. Not only were they entertained to lunch in a 5-star hotel but were taken right to the camp. Health and Safety issues would probably prohibit such a sort of thing now, but that's progress?

With Dartmoor covered in six inches of snow, we set off on a ten mile trek, aiming to reach the rendezvous in good time to be collected by 3-ton trucks which would be waiting to take us back to camp. Navigation was difficult due to the snow and poor visibility. I took over as navigator but made the fatal mistake of not believing the compass and, after five miles, discovered we had gone around in a complete circle. Recovering from my embarrassment, sort of, we set off on a compass bearing only to arrive at a farm with a mad farmer, clearly with a hate for the Army, ordering us to get off his land. We could see the road in the distance and the last thing we wanted to do was to go back on to Dartmoor and get lost all over again. I told everyone to ignore him and once we were a safe distance away from him, ran for the road. Just before reaching the rendezvous point, this crazy farmer came roaring up to us in a Land Rover, shouting and swearing and wanting to take me to the local police station. The boys were having none of it and their show of strength warned him off.

Part of my problem concerned three of the lads who had been identified as bullies. My predecessor had segregated them from the others, but far from helping to resolve the issue, they became martyrs to a cause, demanding the rest of the group clean their kit and get things from the NAAFI for them. The remaining group dared not report this behaviour for fear of being beaten up. It was time to see how tough they really were. Walking across the moor in the snow we arrived at a river in spate. The plan was for each of the boys to jump from a bridge about twenty feet above the water into the freezing, turbulent frothiness below. It was more than a little daunting, but perfectly safe as each would be hauled out by the rope tied securely around their waists. Stripping down to swimming costumes, I asked for a volunteer to go first. It was one of the bullies who jumped off without fear, shouting 'Geronimo' on the way down. Others followed until the other two bullies were seen lurking behind the others, hoping not to be seen. I accompanied the next bully, holding his hand, and after some hesitation we jumped together, much to his self-esteem. The ones who found it the most difficult benefited most as it increased their confidence. There remained the last, who not surprisingly, was the third bully, who absolutely could not be persuaded to jump. Most people consider humiliation to be degrading and unnecessary, but in those days, freed of 'do-gooders' interference, it was acceptable, especially if the end result was successful. What was the purpose of all this and what was the result? The third bully was later discharged from the Army, the second one settled down and did well while the first one had excellent leadership abilities which had gone unrecognised. The next term he was promoted to the rank of Junior Sergeant.

All military and sporting activities outside the education programme were competitive. These included drill, live firing, map orienteering, cross country running, athletics and an assault course for choice. At the end of each term, one could be declared champion platoon. From being last over the previous twelve months, we managed to win and in recognition of our success were offered the chance of assisting at the Annual Game Fair. This involved setting traps for shooting competitions, arena control and helping with the fishing competition. There were plenty of restaurants and cafés on the site of the Stately Home, our venue, so it was agreed with the organisers, vouchers would be handed out for the boys to exchange these for three meals. In retrospect, it was not such a good idea as it turned out, because after three days, although given enough for three meals a day for a week, they mostly had none left. They discovered that vouchers could be exchanged for cigarettes.

That had to remain their problem.

Returning to camp coincided with preparations for our Annual Inspection. Anxious to do well, the lads had been putting in extra effort to clean their barrack rooms. The evening before the inspection, I wandered down after dinner to see how they were getting on. There was no one in sight which caused some concern. They were in the woods next to the barrack block in their sleeping bags where they were to spend the night so as not to undo all the good work they had put in to preparing the barracks. It was a warm summer's night; the inspection went well.

•••

It was itchy feet syndrome again. I was missing Airborne Forces. The Special Air Service (SAS) selection course in Hereford felt right for me and tempting. Being mid-winter, it was not the best time of year to be clambering over the mountains of South Wales. but it was good to be back with elite forces again and I completed the first week without difficulty. The next test was an overnight individual map and compass trek over the Brecon Beacons. There was no moon and the ground was covered with a heavy frost. Trying to avoid clumps of frozen mounds of grass, I went over on my ankle which gradually started to swell. Continuing, I arrived at what I believed was the rendezvous point. Approached by an SAS Sergeant, his remarks did not exactly fill me with confidence: '*Where the bloody hell have you been. As an officer you should be setting a better example, so get the hell out of my sight.... and it's pathetic to use your ankle as an excuse*'. I asked the way and he pointed out a long track leading into the distance. After a few paces he called me back and said '*Well done Sir, you are the second to arrive. Go around the corner and you will find a truck and some hot tea*'. The psychology behind this was to see if you lacked determination and prone to giving up easily. My comments at the time were kept to myself. Just as well. Returning to camp, I saw the Medical Officer who, after a cursory glance recommended returning to my unit and going on the next course.

I was twenty-seven and should have been preparing for the rather daunting promotion of Captain to Major examination. Looking after the lads was a full-time occupation, much like, I imagine, a house master would be at a public school, but with a military flavour. In addition, I ran a canoe club (surprise, surprise) which involved being away most weekends; together, there was little time for studying.

The promotion examination involved taking six subjects and achieving a 40% pass in each subject. If you did not pass all subjects, the ones you did pass were credited to you and permission would be given to retake the following year. It was not uncommon to do that, whereas the Staff College entrance examination included nine subjects with the requirement to pass all subjects in one year with over fifty-percent in each paper. I thought a reasonable plan was to take three subjects in the promotion examination and sit the remaining exams the next year when life would perhaps be a little less demanding. Big mistake. I took the three subjects explaining to the invigilating officer what my plan was and he did not see it as a problem. When the results came out, I had failed. Checking on the marks I had achieved, they were all well over the required level. Following this up as an official complaint, it escalated all the way to the Ministry of Defence, who decreed that had I submitted blank papers for the other subjects, I would have received credit for the ones I had passed. As it was, I had failed all subjects. It made no sense at all, and I felt much aggrieved for a long time.

The summer holidays arrived and three of us were off to Spain, driving overland, and looking forward to some time in the Mediterranean sunshine. Only one of the cars stood a reasonable chance of managing the long journey but, unfortunately it was a two-seater sports car. At the last minute I was detailed to stay behind as duty officer and was unable to travel with them. This solved the seating problem for the journey south, while giving me time to do some revising for the promotion examination next year. A few days later, with rucksack packed, the railway allowed me to meet up with my friends. First though, arriving in Paris, my holiday began to look up when I found my sleeping couchette was to be shared with three charming French girls. I was delighted to help them out with their cheese and wine to sustain us on the journey. The trouble began in Barcelona. Although I had a rail ticket, I had omitted to book a seat and was not allowed on the platform. Getting on that train was essential because I was being met on arrival and had no idea where the others were staying and had no desire to spend ten nights sleeping on the beach. Time to use my *Airborne Initiative.* I left the station and found my way to a marshalling yard some distance away from the railway station. Climbing over the high fence and, careful not to be seen, I made my way along the sidings and rail lines to the platform where my train was about to depart. Waiting until the last minute, and leaving it until there was no time to be kicked off, I nonchalantly climbed aboard and walked down several carriages until finding a vacant seat. Collaborating with some of the passengers around me, I made my way to the lavatory and remained hidden inside until the ticket collector had passed by. I'm sure there was a film which copied my escapade.

Our time in Spain disappeared all too quickly and we were due to face the daunting problem of how to fit three of us into a two-seater sports car. Apart from the driver, we took it in turns to sit crouched in a most uncomfortable position between the driver and passenger seat. Fortunately, the weather was good as it would have been impossible with the hood down. It had not occurred to us to bring goggles, shades of haboobs on the Nile. Stopping at a small country hotel in rural France, two of us checked-in while the other lurked around the corner. We could not afford two rooms so by the spin of a coin I was destined to spend an uncomfortable night on the floor. Next morning the hotel owner asked if we knew anything about the smell of cooking in one of the rooms the night before. Quelle horreur! With facial expressions of total innocence, we commiserated with him as to how anybody could do such a thing. Quietly, we packed the primus stove in the boot of the car. *'Nous ne pouvons tout simplement pas y croire!'*

While applying myself to these future leaders, a name fell into a box at the Ministry of Defence. Some faceless controller of destinies pulled it out and reviewed the history on the card.' FAIRS! That mad buggar, on that bloody big river. For God's sake.' It was he who allowed destiny to take a hand in my future at this point. Just as I was about to head off back to Hereford, the MOD thought if I was stupid enough to volunteer for Airborne Forces and the SAS, I could be a good candidate for a posting with the Royal Marines. Instead of replacing my black crap hat with the sand-coloured beret of the SAS, it was to be a green one. Sand or green berets depended on passing the selection course, which was by no means a foregone conclusion. My over-loaded MG sports car left Taunton with me squeezed in tightly where we headed for the Royal Marines Commando School at Lympstone, to attend the six-week Commando Course. The Royal Marines do not accept anyone into Commando Forces unless they pass this course to qualify to wear their green beret. I was, by this time, twenty-nine years old and at the peak of my fitness. I was well prepared to meet the challenge despite most of the others being much younger than me.

One of the more colourful officers on the course was a Captain in the American Special Forces. I had never met anyone so fit and determined and we became good friends. He persuaded me to join him in attempting to break the record for one of the tests, which was a ten-mile road walk and run involving ploughing through mud, swimming underwater through a large pipe and ending with firing your rifle with marks taken off or added for accuracy. There is no point getting to your destination unless you were still physically fit and ready to fight, as was later demonstrated to good effect at Goose Green in the battle for the Falklands. I kept up with my American friend for half the distance, while he went on to break the record; I was content just to have completed it in time. Keen to show him some of England with a Stately Home to begin with, where we stopped for afternoon tea. The titled son of the aristocratic owner was serving us and my friend gave me a sideways look when I was asked : '*Who is going to be mummy?*' This one proved quite difficult to explain to an American Special Forces officer. In the end, I held my hand up tentatively before grabbing the tea pot firmly. He understood.

I cannot think of a better example of describing how diligent the Armed Forces are when it comes to getting things done on time. We were on a night, map-reading yomp on Dartmoor and had to arrive at the rendezvous point by a certain time, with no room for error. The reward was the smell of fried bacon and fresh coffee for breakfast. A group of four young Marines arrived just one minute late. They were denied breakfast and given the option of being back-squadded, (that is, put back behind the next group to leave) or driven back to the start point to complete the six-hour yomp again. Are these not the same thing? To give them credit, they voted to do it again without complaint and arrived back totally shattered. But they did it. Army time is always five minutes early and if you follow this rule, you are unlikely ever to be late for anything.

Then there is slit trenching. 'Do you need to know about slit trenching?'

We were on a defence exercise when we had to dig a four-man slit trench and, once complete, to spend 48 hours without leaving it for any reason. It was constructed as a 'W' and it was important to get the angles right so as to get in and out easily. We failed to do that. The two middle parts of the trench were firing positions while the outer trenches were covered as protection and for sleeping when off guard. There would be two on and two off at any one time. After much bending and wriggling, I managed to get in to my sleeping bag when it was my turn to sleep for a couple of hours. I woke up suddenly, totally disorientated and feeling very much as if I was in a coffin. In total darkness and having forgotten which was the way out, I was beginning to feel claustrophobic again, but managed, finally, to get out after much panic stations and roping around.

Sharing a trench with three other potential commando colleagues is an interesting experience. One would quickly get to know those with a bad temper, those whose feet smelled in a wet trench or someone who snored so loudly that a would-be enemy would be able to locate our position from several hundred yards away. After a couple of days on stodgy compo rations, you would even learn of one another's bowel movements and when to stay up wind. On completion of this testing, nay, challenging experience, we were purposely directed out through the campsite of the directing staff. We had only recently had a cold tinned breakfast, while they were tucking into sausage, eggs and bacon. Later, I questioned this performance and was told they had completed their commando training, and when you pass, you too can look forward to this sort of privilege as well. I can see the logic and incentive of this idea, but had totally different ideas at the time.

The last test was a thirty mile yomp across Dartmoor, which had to be completed within eight hours with rifle and full kit weighing around forty kilos. The first half was across moorland with the second half along country lanes. At the half way mark having completed the toughest part, most of us were well behind time, and had to speed up by running most of the way along these lanes, spurred on by the Royal Marine Instructors. I made it in time, but only just, and collapsed in a heap, like most of the others with lots of blisters. The following day we were all sufficiently recovered to attend the award ceremony and receive our green berets. Proud, very proud moment. It meant I was off to Singapore to join the Headquarters Staff of 3 Commando Brigade, this time without the luxury of overnight stops.

Arrival in Singapore coincided with the news, Brigade HQ had shipped out to Kuching in Sarawak due to the stepping up of border incursions by Communist Terrorists and elements of the Indonesian Armed Forces who were seeking to take over Borneo before Malaysian independence. The war in Borneo was a funny old war. Frankly, it wasn't even a war as we might understand it, though it did involve the deployment of some 10,000 British forces at its peak. Britain never declared war but supported the Malayan and Brunei governments under our Treaty obligations.

This was a small, enclosed, secretive war, forgotten or just unknown by many, in a part of the world where white faces were few. We did lose men, we had wounded also but, on reflection, they were within acceptable limits – if ever there can be acceptable limits these days – and it turned out to be a brilliant, jungle-fought campaign. Raiding parties had been initially confined to Indonesian incursions where retaliatory raids were permitted but with limited penetration, and in total secret. Operations were all carried out in remote and difficult jungle terrain with a heavy responsibility resting on the shoulders of local commanders right down to Company and Platoon level. Success depended primarily on the initiative and resourcefulness of the man on the spot.

My stay in Singapore was thus short lived as I was flying on to Kuching where we were to remain for six months on active service. Brigade HQ was supporting a Commando, a Gurkha Rifles Battalion, Malaysian Scouts, SBS and SAS, all strung out along the border. There were no roads to speak of and replenishment was either by river or air drop. My job was to make sure units on the border were resupplied with ammunition, food and any other requirements. This was mostly conducted by parachute. One request, not on my usual schedule of supplies, was a request from the Gurkha Regiment to drop live goats for Dashera, one of their festivals. As one does! Scratching my head for a solution, I approached the Chinese owner of the local supermarket who had previously said nothing would be too much trouble as he was anxious to help. That put him on the spot. 'Live Sir? You did say live Sir?' But he produced the goats. They were loaded into panniers and dropped in unfavourable winds, of course, naturally missing the Dropping Zone and landing squarely on the attap roofs of the longhouses of an Iban village, much to the amusement of the villagers who found the whole performance hugely funny. The laughter came from the fact the goats had, finally, broken out of their panniers and, being peckish, had begun to eat the roofs with obvious relish. When the Airdrop Completion Report came in over the radio, it said '*goats dropped on the roofs of an Iban village and headman requests compensation because goats have eaten attap roof of longhouses*'.

Longhouses are one-story wooden buildings raised above the ground on stilts with palm-frond (attap) roofs. They are the homes of the local Iban tribes, famed for their reputation as head-hunters. Their balconies were adorned with shrunken human heads, revered trophies of the tribes past battles. Many years later when I took a group on a Langdale Walking Holidays to Sarawak, we visited a longhouse but could not see any shrunken human heads. Seeking information from our guide, he introduced me to the headman and was taken up a very rickety ladder to the attic and shown a huge basket. It was full of human heads, though no longer on public display to avoid upsetting the tourists.

•••

When Royal Marines officers are first commissioned, they are placed under the watchful eye of a platoon sergeant, particularly when on active service and are required to follow his directions until gaining enough experience to command their own troop. There was a sad situation with one such officer who was on duty in one of the border posts and wanted to relieve himself. Rather than trudge all the way back to the field latrines, he took a short cut and went into the jungle on a dark night and on return was asked for the password by the sentry. I should explain here that passwords work like this: If the password is, for example, *dark night,* the procedure is for the sentry to whisper *dark* and the approaching person whispers the reply - *night.* The sentry then whispers the well-known phrase: *'advance and be recognised'*. It was pitch black and everyone was alert for a possible attack. The officer had forgotten the password and was shot dead by the sentry, which, although was the correct procedure was more than unfortunate.

Leaving Sarawak on completion of two tours of active service, we were all looking forward to a more normal form of life in Singapore. We embarked on the Commando Carrier and, sailing into Singapore Harbour with all hands and embarked Commando lining the deck, we were greeting by the sweet sound of a Royal Marines band, and the jetty thronged with family and friends. It was a very emotional day.

Serving with the Royal Marines was going to be one of my most valued experiences. They are part of the

Royal Navy and everything was in naval terminology – the room you slept in was a cabin and having an evening away from camp was known as a run ashore. I asked the Special Boat Service officer, whose cabin was next to mine in the Officers Mess, what were the circumstances for his award of his Military Cross while in Sarawak. Modestly, he said it was completely unjustified, because he had no choice in the action taken. He was leading a patrol across a series of paddy fields when coming under fire from a CT patrol base which was only fifty metres in front of him. Turning around to seek cover was more than twice the distance than to move forward and would prevent them from returning fire. Making a quick appreciation, and firing from the hip, they advanced at speed and managed to overwhelm the base. It was the only thing to do. What he omitted to say is the Communist base was destroyed along with its occupants. On the next emergency tour to Sarawak, he was awarded a bar to his MC for gallantry. Again, and typical of the SBS, he said it was completely underserved. Once perhaps. Twice, that is bravery.

From time to time, we were allocated an aircraft for parachute training. On one occasion we were flown to a disused airfield on the east coast of Malaysia where the drill was to disembark, get fitted out with parachutes and carry out the drop. The aircraft would land and the procedure repeated. Having left Singapore well before dawn, we were well and truly knackered when the time came to fly back. Sleeping soundly, I was awakened by a new event for the aircraft which was quite alarming. Sitting right next to where the door should normally be, we were flying over the South China Sea at what seemed to be an altitude of twenty feet. No exaggeration because, as we flew over a group of fishing boats, we could see the crews diving onto the decks and flattening themselves into small balls of humanity. It appeared as if their last hour had come. Careful not to fall out of the aircraft, and making my way along to the cockpit I asked the pilot what was going on, as many of his passengers were scared to death. We really did not want to crash into the sea. He mentioned something about some low flying experience he needed to improve upon, and he had left the doors open because it was so hot. I returned to my seat (not a seat, but a nylon harness) and remained now, wide awake and fully alert for the rest of the flight. On other occasions, if we were lucky, we had taken part in parachuting into the sea. Today, we could almost do this without using a parachute!

Brigade HQ Officers Mess was a requisitioned tea planters house, situated next to the golf club. We were quite comfortable there with six of us to a room on camp beds. Brigade HQ was an attap hut built by a local construction firm. We attended the Brigade Commander's nightly briefing, attended by political officers, Brigade staff and others as required. One particularly interesting briefing involved concern that the Communists were carrying out nightly raids across the border. Because we were not allowed to retaliate by crossing the border for political reasons, there was concern the enemy could return safely to their camp without fear of being attacked. The Brigade Commander got hold of a map and said: *'Border, what border?'* The demarcation-line was ill-defined and orders were given in secret to destroy the camp.

•••

Three of us would go water skiing in Singapore harbour, ostensibly test driving SBS boats for border raids, and on one occasion we nearly got into more trouble. One of us had taken control of the boat, the other was keeping a sharp look-out from the bow for floating logs, while the third took a turn at water skiing. The "sharp" lookout had clearly failed this time for we hit a submerged log at speed causing the two in the boat to be dumped into the water. The 'two' of course included me. The steering lever locked and the boat started to career around in circles at top speed.

Surfacing, I found the empty boat racing directly for me, and to avoid the very real possibility of being cut up by the approaching propeller, I dived, emerging only to find the same thing happening again, until the boat, in ever increasing circles ran out of petrol. It was a close call and a great relief to my two companions as they had great futures ahead of them. One was Paddy Ashdown, later to become Lord Ashdown, Leader of the Liberal Democrats and High Representative for Bosnia and Herzegovina. The other was Geoffrey Tantum who left Oxford with a First Class Honours degree in Classical Arabic and spent the best part of his life in the Middle East. He was awarded the Order of the British Empire (OBE,) Companion of the Order of St. Michael and St George (CMG) and knighted for services to his country. The third member of the party, yours truly, received the Grand Order of the Boot (GOB). Geoffrey and I remain firm friends to this day. See his Foreword.

Some of my best recollections in the Officer's Mess in Singapore were the Sunday movie nights with a curry while persuading the Royal Marines band to entertain us and our guests on the patio when HMS Bulwark the 22,000 tonne Centaur Class light fleet aircraft carrier was in harbour. All the Royal Marine officers who formed the staff of Commando Brigade Headquarters were exceptional, outstanding colleagues to work with, particularly on active service in Sarawak. In addition, there were four Army officers, myself included, and two Royal Naval officers, an Aviator and David, a Medical Officer. David was something of a rare character and believed Royal Marines were indestructible and would rarely need medical attention. He believed, anyone claiming to be ill or damaged in some way was likely to be malingering. When we were in Sarawak, a marine reported sick as he could not sleep and thought he would be able to sleep better if he could return to his family in Singapore. David agreed, this was indeed a serious matter and something had to be done. He made out a note addressed to the Quartermaster, not the pharmacist, which struck the marine as odd. But he did as he was told. The note said this marine is unable to sleep and should return his bed along with bedding to the stores as it would be more useful to someone else.

It was my turn one morning when I woke feeling particularly rough and attended his surgery one minute after closing time. I met David coming out of the surgery on his way to breakfast in the officers' mess and told him my troubles. He, kindly, asked if I was dying. 'If not, come back tomorrow.' Nothing was going to keep him away from his fried eggs.

Life was not always relaxing in Singapore. We left the city on a major amphibious and jungle training exercise in the Philippines, along with contingents of warships and amphibious forces from the United States, Australia and New Zealand. We set sail from Singapore and after a naval exercise, landed by helicopter into a jungle clearing to start the next phase of the training exercise. I was based with the American Marines which provided the base camp for the manoeuvres. This was a new experience with all the comforts of home including, showers, lavish tented accommodation, great meals, even ice cream. I was allocated a vehicle and radio operator and wearing a white arm band, acted as an umpire, adjudicating between the two protagonists, with the Australian SAS as *the enemy*. I had been alerted to a planned attack on one of the gun positions and was on hand to judge the guns had been compromised. Telling the Battery Commander, a Major, that his guns were umpired out of action for several hours, he pulled rank on me and told me to 'fuck off'. Not to be outdone, I was about to report this on the radio, when he had the good sense to reappraise the situation and reluctantly decided to comply. Two weeks passed quickly enough, until the exercise ended allowing us to be picked up by helicopter and returned to the ship. Had we seen anything of the Philippines? Yes, but only the jungle. Oh, and more jungle as well.

Several more amphibious exercises followed. One of the most pleasing aspects of life on board the carriers was the quality of life. The Royal Navy looked after us very well and arriving on the flight deck after days or weeks in the jungle, we looked forward to being reunited with our kit and sitting down to dinner the same evening, all washed and cleaned up and feeling smart in our red sea rig for dinner, followed by the luxury of one's own cabin and nice clean sheets on the bed. One of the rituals prevalent at the time was the daily issue of rum to all embarked personnel, apart from officers. What a performance. Each deck would submit the numbers entitled to this daily ration, and these were gathered together to calculate the quantity of rum required. Supervised by the duty officer, he proceeded to the store where the rum was kept and the correct quantity was poured into a huge copper cauldron in the stern of the ship, while representatives from each deck lined up to receive their allocation. I observed this procedure several times as duty officer and was astonished to discover that, despite painstaking care being taken to decant the correct amount of rum, there was always a large quantity left over. What did they do with it? There was a small ceremony, followed by the leftovers being tipped overboard for Davy Jones, who must have been smashed out of his mind following the ship.

Back at our base one Friday afternoon, we were placed on standby in the wake of a reported amphibious landing by a contingent of the Indonesian Armed

Forces. Contingency procedures were followed, a Commando Company earmarked to standby while I had to arrange for the release of additional ammunition from a local depot. I made contact with a Major at Singapore Base HQ, whose responsibility it was to authorise the release of ammunition, but he had gone home for the weekend. Contacting him at home and trying to explain this was an emergency, he told me to put the application in writing and send it to him first thing Monday morning. It was difficult to find the right words to describe this idiotic response. But there was a bit of history here because I did not get on with this particular Major, for reasons that eluded me at the time. He was always extremely awkward to deal with at the best of times. Everything was Top Secret and he had not been kept in the loop, so I bypassed him, which did not improve my relationship with him. Everything was eventually sorted but first thing Monday morning, fully recognising the need not to allow personalities to get in the way of operations. I thought it best to go and see this character to establish what the problem was. At Brigade Headquarters we maintained an easy relationship with everyone on first name terms, regardless of rank, apart from the Brigade Commander. It was how the Royal Marines operated. In the Army it was different. As a Captain, I would normally be expected to address a Major as

Sir, but having enjoyed the way the Royal Marines and Airborne Forces operated, such formalities were overlooked. There was no need to hide behind one's rank and it was always better to display good leadership attitudes to gain respect, rather than relying solely on one's position in life. This Major did not see things our way, and I suspected, he did not like me, a Captain, addressing him, a Major, by his first name. I arrived at his office, gave him a smart salute, called him Sir and we were best friends for ever!

Recollecting the disgraceful rules and the class-conscious British attitude of the times, where I was shamefully prevented from inviting Chinese guests to the Officers Mess in Hong Kong, I was again saddened to learn two of my fellow Army officers faced a similar problem in Singapore. They wanted to invite their Indian lady friends to their Officer's Mess for the annual ball but faced the same barrier as Hong Kong. I raised this at the next Mess Committee meeting and my friends were immediately offered honorary membership of our Mess. The ladies were welcomed on their first visit to the Brigade Officers Mess by the Brigade Commander. They were later both happily married to these delightful Indian ladies.

CHAPTER 6

Staff College to Command of a Squadron

"No man is a leader until he is ratified in the minds and hearts of his men." The Infantry Journal

I had been extremely proud of wearing my green beret. It demonstrated, clearly, I had reached a stage in my career through physical hard work as well as applying my brain successfully, while working closely with colleagues at all levels. It had taken me on active service, twice to Sarawak, two years running and, despite the light-hearted times when we parachuted goats into the jungle, there had been unremitting pressures upon us from constant Indonesian infiltration forces. There was never a time to ease up from our watchfulness. Deep, dark, very hot jungle was a difficult place for the average Englishman, to feel comfortable, let alone fighting and working in it, even if we had been trained to operate in all environments.

But, I had come to a point in my career where I had to make some serious decisions about my future. I had, behind me, the Para. Brigade, my exploits on the Nile, the Royal Marines and I was still only thirty-two years of age. It left one big gap. Promotion.

I had been advised by the Brigade Commander, I should push ahead in applying myself to pass the Staff College entrance examination, a step necessary for the higher ranks, having now dealt with the thorny issue when I had not submitted blank papers which had failed me last time. For some reason, he felt I should move on and up but it did require me to go back to school to swot in a fairly serious way for the next nine months if I was to have any chance of passing the exam.

Amongst many other advantages, the Army was able to allow me the time to do this though there was a catch. It did not enable me to skive off my other duties. My boss provided the support mechanism whereby I did not have to start my Army tasks until ten in the morning. It thus involved me rising each day at four in the morning and working on my books until I had to get back to my Army duties at ten when breakfast was but a distant dream. The work, though, quickly became obsessive as I realised, if I was successful now, it might mean a Regiment of my own later on. That would be the next feather in my cap. It was to be my new target, a new focus.

This was going to be my world for a year or so. There would be no thoughts of flying in supplies to the Gurkhas; it was going to be replaced with books, pens and pads, aware always, I had to be ready each day for my life in the Army and there was always the chance of an emergency arising somewhere in the world which might require the services of the Commando Brigade, which would take precedence over everything else.

Worse, in its way, was the long wait for the result of all this effort. First. Had I passed? Second. Had I been allocated a space if I had passed, and to which college? Most applicants would end up at the Staff College, Camberley. Me? Yes, I did pass and my place was rather special and unique. I was going to be the British Exchange Officer at Kingston, Ontario in Canada; moon, delighted and over came instantly to mind

So, what is a Staff College all about? It is there to prepare military students (me) for higher command. If you wanted to get on in the Army it was considered a necessary step for the higher ranks. Kingston, Ontario is the home of the Canadian Armed Forces Command and Staff College. (sorry, a bit of a mouthful) where it sat on the edge of the waterfront where the St. Lawrence river runs into Lake Ontario. Kingston is similar to Sandhurst in the U.K.

Not wishing to give the impression of blowing my own trumpet, I was proud to be selected as the British Army's exchange student to attend this famous military college. I found myself the British Representative on the course, a reflection, I think, of previous service to be chosen to represent one's country. To me this was an honour.

Life meant being split into syndicates of twelve, mixing infantry, armour, engineering, the whole shooting match (sorry, again) with a top-class American instructor with significant decoration on his chest to wonder just what he had done in the past. Daily, we would include discussions of our own experiences and I contributed here about my time in Sarawak though I do not believe I mentioned the episode with the goats eating the roof of the headman's house. There would always be tactical problems to solve and I was told it would always be better to offer a wrong solution than none at all. Have you ever seen the amount of military books published? We had to read many of them before offering our own solutions on the success or failure of a particular battle or campaign.

In 1966, now fifty-seven years ago, half a century of living and ageing has changed everything; life was quite unlike the old days of the Commonwealth. Canada was going to be a world away from how we know it today. Then, Ontario was parochial, insular in many ways, genteel and peaceful. Canadians were and are decent people, fanatical about sport and they liked to enjoy themselves. These were two elements snatched out of my precious time there, which could intrude into my serious learning stuff, perhaps too often at times.

The advantages the Army provided, extended to the manner in which my wife and I were transported to Canada. Not a troop ship, not a lumbering RAF Transport but a Cunard liner no less...ah, first-class cabin of course, I almost forgot to mention. And all the way to Montreal. The ship craned my shiny new car aboard into the hold as lightly as a feather, before we set off for five days of utmost luxury, all care of the British tax payer.

Seeing Quebec for the first time from the starboard rail, I remarked to a Canadian local returning home from a holiday in the old country, that I couldn't see any coon skin hats. It was my first attempt at humour in the new country. Canadians do not, or, did not fifty years ago, understand British humour and my fellow traveller assured me at great length, that the pioneering days had long gone – yes, quite – and no-one wore them anymore! 'Well Sir. Thank you for getting me up-to-date. I never would have known that. That is very kind of you.' Strange how wrong I could be.

It had been recommended, I should "acclimatise" myself to the Canadian way of life and Canada itself, before commencing upon the concentrated Staff College course now reduced from two years to one but having no reduction in content. Suggestions on how to do this, came thick and fast with one, in particular, which attracted us. This was to take off for some wilderness camping in Montana and Wyoming, an area of forest and lakes covering seven and a half thousand square kilometres. It had, we were told, everything from bogs to beavers, Moose to Mosquitoes, Wolves to woodpeckers…and loons, the bird with the curious call. We were captivated by signs to such places as Whiskey Rapids and Ox Tongue river and we couldn't wait to load up our rented canoe which took me back five years to my happy days on the Nile.

We set a course, paddling for about two hours until we found a suitable landing place and an ideal camping ground. Again, I was reminded of the huge contrast between trying to find a camping spot on an over-heated sand bank, shoo-ing crocodiles back into the river against the ease of selecting one of many sites on the edge of the lake backed by forest rather than impenetrable reeds. I suppose, the one clear link between the two trips was, although we had no crocodiles to be wary of, we did have bears which, we imagined, would put up just as good a fight as *Crocodylus niloticus*.

We had been provided with some very reasonable advice on what to do at night. On closer examination I realised, all that stood between me, my wife and a bear were three ounces per square metre of raw but flimsy canvas (pre-polyester days) as it felt to me – although I have to admit at being no expert in such things as bear claw size, diameter of mouth and how much of a punch the average brown bear could pack. After doing my research I learned these brown bears could grow heavier than a grizzly due to the amount of fish they ate and weigh in at 1,320 kilograms, 2,900 pounds, with a height reaching 2.8 metres, that's a tall nine feet. And, of course, they can run faster than humans, swim quicker than Mark Spitz and climb a tree to outpace Lenny the lumberjack! It was thus essential we built up the fire every night and keep all of our provisions we had bought for a week, inside our tent. As well as bears, there were raccoons, real scavengers to think about. In all, we received excellent advice from many people who knew what they were talking about. Regrettably we ignored it all, or, to be more kindly, we forgot.

In the middle of the night, we awoke to hear what sounded like a wrestling match. The scuffles continued until I poked my nose through the tent flap, its zip eased down by three inches, but enough to see a). the fire was out completely and b). the last raccoon running off with the remainder of our food store. Our next job, having missed crispy bacon, fried eggs, fried bread, bagels and jello was a two hour canoe paddle back to our departure point: 'Back so soon David?' to reload with another week of provisions.

Horse riding here was a natural. I had been taught to ride in Hong Kong when I was a Lieutenant but not taken it up since. Here in the Big Horn mountains which topped out at thirteen thousand feet, it was suggested I also could get back onto a horse with a bit of trail riding and a pommel on my saddle which would look good in the occasional photo. The scenery was stunning, the air clean as though it had been filtered by a giant, the track had inviting hidden bends. This was going to be a doddle – to the uninitiated it means a pushover. I climbed up on the horse, or is it onto the horse? Curiously, the animal had not passed on to me its only desire was to get back to the ranch as soon as it was able. Oats, straw and rest probably came to his mind, all at the same time. There is always one horse in these stories which is just… blinking difficult. While the animal was playing silly-buggars, I wanted to get my full money back with a jolly good 'giddy-up, a technical term known to thousands of young pony riders. Do you recall the day when a pal of mine wanted to get his full money's worth when hiring a rowing boat on a pond even though it was pouring with rain. The decision was made to cut my losses on that particular wet day. Today was not the same. It was dry and hot. I kicked lightly somewhere in the region of his belly but the horse merely grunted, leaned forward as though it was going to move, then subsided into its original position, eyes focussed towards the ranch. I tried again, harder feeling its ribs under my toes. More grunts but this time, no movement forward. Turning round to my riding partner to ask her what to do, I relaxed my grip on the reins and lo! The horse began to walk, before breaking into a trot…straight towards the dude ranch (a dude ranch is a ranch geared towards tourism). Saying 'woah' made no difference, nor did 'Christ!' when the stupid stallion took off into what is known as a gallop. Here was a slight change in tempo. Its ears laid back, my legs flew astern in the roar of the wind, hooves pounding on the uneven ground and me screaming in considerable alarm at the idea of leaving the saddle to connect soon after with this potholed dirt track at high speed. But, we did arrive. The horse was steaming like a laundrette, me wondering if I could find a spare pair of underpants in the dude ranch without having to ask embarrassing questions. I handed back my Stetson hat knowing I looked daft in it, and realising that a green beret looked far better on me than anything else. But I was safe to fight another war.

The loons laughed, the wolves wailed but we suffered nothing more than swollen ear tips from gnats and midges. The trip did bring to us peace, tranquillity even, as we, regretfully, turned back to allow me to learn how to be a senior officer in the British Army.

Staff College meant cramming just as I had done for the entrance exam. I had one year to learn just how to lead, how to command, directing me, hopefully to commanding a Regiment of my own.

I mentioned briefly, the inordinate amount of time spent by Canadians on sport which, combined with the course demands was often hard on our wives. The College, generously invited our wives to accompany us on some of the excellent tours arranged for guest students, including Western Canada. Other activities included ice skating on frozen lakes, downhill and cross-country skiing. We even went on a winter sleigh ride into a snow-bound forest to see how maple syrup is farmed. This was hospitality beyond the call of duty.

As the months moved quickly through my diary I began to understand what life was all about. I knew now, I had been right to relinquish my hold on the Royal Marines, to learn, instead, what makes a first-class officer, elements which would remain with me when I set out to form my own travel company.

On my last day I was asked to attend at the Deputy Commandant' office. He sounded me out in confidence to see if I would like to transfer to the Canadian Army. I had to be flattered by such an offer, and I was extremely tempted, for I had grown to love this huge, beautiful and generous country and its wonderful people and the offer was more than tempting but the proposal came tight up alongside my promotion to Major which meant I would be taking off for Germany, back in Europe with all its political issues to balance. A challenge in other words. I turned down the officer's attractive pitch to live and work in his country and, instead, watched as my car was re-hoisted back on board our liner. In our cabin, was a huge bouquet of flowers along with a message. *'Canada will miss you.'* Perhaps somewhat unbecoming of a former para and commando, something had crept annoyingly int both of my eyes. but I have to admit I did find something had crept, annoyingly, into both eyes.

•••

You, the reader, will have picked up by now that we, in the Army, enjoyed a considerable amount of comfort and a high standard of living – when in peacetime. It must never be forgotten, our *raison d'être* was to defend our nation and its way of life.

We were in the midst of planning a joyful Christmas when an urgent message came through from the Colonel. The fact we had little contact with him made the call that more important. Christmas was cancelled, making it sound like Alan Rickman in the *Sheriff of Nottingham,* when he declared '…and call off Christmas.'

Christmas had indeed, been cancelled without our knowledge, as the Ministry of Defence had decided, in its wisdom, to reinforce Northern Ireland with an additional transport squadron. Just a few days later, found me seeing to the loading of our vehicles to be shipped to Belfast from Marchwood Military Port. Marchwood would have another revival in 1982 when it became into its own again, loading the thousands of tons of equipment onto ships bound for the Falklands Islands eight years later.

The Sergeant Major and I formed an advance party, flying out ahead of our transport in poor weather which compounded the gloom of our non-Christmas which, naturally had originally included a whole range of parties and celebrations.

But, we had our duty to perform. End of story.

The removal of the greatest festivity of the year from our families caused concern at a higher level for our morale, but this issue never raised its head above the parapet as we settled in quickly, driving our armoured cars around the streets of Belfast and Londonderry. We had discovered on our arrival, our role was to convert to armoured personnel carriers in aid of infantry battalions. We had to draw up a rapid plan to train our drivers into these APCs' meaning our four ton trucks which we had shipped over were redundant and now were parked up on the barracks square in Lisburn. It did, though, ensure the APCs' provided greater protection to the infantry.

Arriving almost unplanned, we managed to find accommodation for the men but not for us officers. The

Officer's Mess was full, requiring us, initially to sleep on the unyielding floor of the Garrison gymnasium though, soon, we came up with a cunning plan. A regulation, obscure, I admit, permitted us in such circumstances, to rent local accommodation. We duly found a terraced house which had no heating, just as the weather turned into January wet and cold. Cunning plan number two enabled one of our officer's to scrounge some paraffin heaters, one of which was only a quarter full. My driver, good as gold, went off to purchase fuel unaware my source of warmth had to be charged with paraffin and not petrol. Surprise, surprise, the bloody thing caught fire with a whoosh but it did not end there, as the flames greedily consumed *all* of my bedding and a*ll* of my clothes. I stress the word *all.* Two of us hurled the red hot, useless heater (mine) out of the bedroom window where it continued to make the few weeds in the garden believe spring was on the way, as the flames warmed our neighbours front plots.

Each day, usually two vehicles in each armoured patrol holding eight to ten men would drive around to give a presence, getting out from time to time in suspected problem areas. Compare this, the normally dismal streets, brightly illuminated with Catholic and Protestant Christmas lights, yet there was always the possibility of instant death even as the greatest peace festival of the year was being celebrated. It was almost 'normal,' as if nothing had ever happened in this troubled country. Living as we did in a Protestant area we found the locals helpful and supportive in every way. They appreciated what we were trying to do in an almost impossible political situation.

Meanwhile our patrols had to go out for several hours each time, including night patrols, though never the same route for obvious reasons. I was not on patrol as all officers were out all day for Christmas attempting to visit every soldier and, where possible, celebrating the Christmas meal which, traditionally, we served to our men. Later that day, seven of us officers managed to cobble together some delicious bacon sandwiches to observe Christmas in our terrace house.

Christmas also brought another "delight" this time right to our back door. A blocked drain. So what, you ask? With the weather as it was, the back yard, paved over, began to fill until it was several inches deep. It could no longer be ignored and, guess who volunteered to sort it out? The only way to do this was two-fold. One, strip down to underpants. Yes, the Army provided for these, and two: lie flat on the ice-cold paving's now four inches of water covering them, and pull out, by hand, the offending articles. It was well-blocked, probably building up over years of neglect and included empty cans, bits of bottles and, politely, unmentionables, the latter of which had managed to wrap themselves around all the rest of the junk. With a gurgle and a gargle the water eventually rushed past my frozen body leaving the paving stones cleaner than they had been for years. I showered and brandied (is there such a verb 'to brandy'?) and returned to my normal self.

There was to be a nice ending to our six-month tour which made up for our cancelled Christmas. Terence O'Neill, Prime Minister of Northern Ireland recognised our Squadron's contribution to the security situation with an award; the spin-off came with an invitation for my wife and I to attend a garden party at Buckingham Palace. Nice sandwiches.

•••

I began to realise, during this part of my life, as I was moving around the world, that more and more countries were becoming crystallised in my mind. In the last few years there had been Canada which led to Cyprus, on to the Orkneys, changing down a gear for the British Virgin Islands and up the road to Bermuda and back to Germany.

I had no idea at the time how much information I was storing away which was going to be so useful to me in later life. My mind was loading up useful detail along with the rubbish but cruise ports, distances of airports to cities, cities themselves, hotel locations, places of interest and walks of course, it was all arriving like buses in London. The beauty of the idea of walking holidays was that one person or a full tour group could walk anywhere in the world. Outwardly, I was not ready to take the leap, indeed I probably had not even taken it on board as a viable alternative in my later life for more powerful voices were directing me up and forward as I needed to prove to myself I could command a Regiment. Having achieved this maybe, just maybe, I could think of other things to do.

•••

I mentioned Cyprus in my list of countries visited. From condoms wrapped round empty tomato soup cans in the wet and cold of Northern Ireland I was asked by the Brigade Major if I was interested in taking the Squadron to Cyprus for training. Interest? I should coco. Blue skies, warm clear air, sand on the beach was all a hell of a contrast. So I said: 'Yes please Sir.' This was, despite the knowledge General Grivas-Digenis had returned to Cyprus to found EOKA-B to oppose Archbishop Makarios. In many ways the comparisons between Cyprus and Northern Ireland were close. These jumped up despots never learn, do they?

Arriving in August, we moved to tropical routine, another clever Army rule which meant we worked from seven in the morning until one o'clock at which time we took the rest of the day off for recreational activities. Lunch under a sun brolly in other words; brushing sand from one's toes? We had arrived in paradise, an enormous contrast with the slate grey of Northern Ireland.

The infantry battalion, scheduled to go instead of us, had been reassigned to Northern Ireland at short notice. This good news was further improved with a request from the Brigade Major to include a detachment of the Brigade helicopter squadron to make up the assigned air lift. We were to be established at the Sovereign Base of *Dhekelia,* so swimming was a natural. Meanwhile, the Helicopter Detachment Commander was on the look-out for pilot training opportunities. I, very helpfully, suggested the *Troodos* Mountains topping out at six and a half thousand feet, would be a good destination where there was excellent hiking, and a relaxing break above the sweltering heat of the coast.

One of the training exercises was to be map reading carried out in small groups. Deciding to go to the rendezvous point to meet everyone on arrival, I found the journey took longer than anticipated. I made a short stop to rest under an olive tree to keep out of the sun. Falling soundly asleep, I was awoken, rather rudely, by strange noises, more mellow than trumpets or cornets and clearly, more difficult to control in the higher registers. I should have recognized them. Like a series of flugelhorns it was a flock of several hundred mouflons, the local sheep, often wild, with all of them taking it in turns to fart, almost in tune at times, as they 'marched' past me in 'threes'. I did not take the salute.

Back at base we were tasked with organizing a logistics field demonstration for the Staff College in Camberley. We had previous experience of this and found most students showed little interest in logistics, so we calculated something different was required. With several hundred, rather bored looking, future staff officers, gathered around waiting for me to introduce the programme, I announced my notes had been left back at the Squadron and a motorcyclist had been sent back to get them. After fifteen minutes or so there were rumblings about incompetence and patience was being stretched to the limit. Eventually, the motorcyclist, a very large Army rugby player, roared up dressed as a gorilla and presented me with my notes, which was a piece of paper the size of a postage stamp. One of the officers was heard to make disparaging comments when, to the amusement of the other officers, he was picked up by the gorilla corporal and dumped in the woods, an action which was greeted by loud applause, probably because the particular officer was, by a stroke of good luck identified as a pain in the ass. Later, I met several of the officers who witnessed this performance. They remembered the gorilla incident but nothing about the logistic demonstration which I had spent so much time in preparing.

Having been elected President of the Brigade Officers Mess for twelve months, I enjoyed arranging social events, the entertainment and dinner nights for Brigade HQ including my own Squadron. During this time came more pointers of the direction I would one day take with me into the leisure industry. Using the Brigade Commander's name, I approached the Commanding Officer of the Green Jackets, which formed part of the Brigade, and obtained agreement to include their Band and Bugles as the cabaret for our summer ball. On another occasion the Band, Pipes and Drums of The Royal Irish Rangers featured as entertainment for a ladies' dinner night. I was to meet up with The Royal Irish Rangers again when running Holiday Club Pontins at Camber Sands who provided the best cabaret evening of my time at the Club. Little by little, I was gaining expertise in what the public would go for and the necessary knowledge I would need to achieve it.

Away from candelabra and cut glass, I took part in an exercise on Salisbury Plain where it was decided, an 'emergency crash out' would be practiced. (Emergency crash out – that is to say, training for an imminent simulated attack.) There was no such attack of course, but an exercise in the procedures whereby you just get the hell out of the area and practice making way to the alternative location. There is always an alternative location, and navigating your way there at best speed is the test. Not something we did very often as you have to return later to clear up everything – fill in trenches, take down camouflage netting and pack it all up, loading up kitchen equipment and cookers, that sort of thing. When you leave a military training area, everything down to the last blade of grass has to be restored to its original state.

The Squadron was tactically positioned in a wood. Our vehicles were covered by camouflage net. When the signal was given, everyone had to make their way at speed to an alternative position. At seven on a summer morning we moved, and, after much confusion, everyone finally got into action. We had not anticipated driving at speed through a sleepy local village on a day, unfortunately coinciding with the annual meet before their Hunt. Horses kicked sideways in panic upsetting the otherwise calm demeanour of the riders in their fine pink coats who now became more than a little disturbed at their sherry staining their immaculate breeches. Well, in fact, bloody furious, as only those riders in pink coats can be. Following up in the rear, my Land Rover was stopped by a very red faced, and angry hunt master. It didn't help much he was a retired Brigadier (aren't they all?) and was after my blood. Trying to be as polite and tactful as possible, had no effect, and he was certainly going to report me personally to the Brigade Commander with the aim of either sending me to the Tower or, at the very least, terminating my career. My Brigade Commander had already supported me and got me out of a number of scrapes, but I could not but wonder if this incident would be a bridge too far, quite an apt cliché I feel. On the contrary, how can an Army exist without realistic training? 'Sit down and have a coffee, David'.

Life moved on again and it became time to take up a new staff appointment. As this was to be in Salisbury it meant I did not have to 'up sticks' and could stay in our newly bought house in the area. On my departure from the Squadron, the officers had clubbed together to present me with a solid silver 'Shiny Seven' made by Garrard's of Hatton Garden. This was a solid silver figure of a Chinese 7 representing Shiny Seven, the Squadron's nickname. Very nice.

Finally home for the weekend, someone contacted me. "Congratulations David". "What for?" was my reply. "On the announcement of your promotion to Lieutenant Colonel".

I spent the weekend wondering if this was correct until, on Monday morning, sure enough, I received the official confirmation. Very soon after this, a posting order came through on my desk. It stated: to be the Commanding Officer of 4 Divisional Transport Regiment in Duisburg, Germany, an all ranks regiment of six hundred men. Commanding one's own Regiment is widely regarded as the very best appointment in the Army, and I was delighted. What a privilege and a significant step in my military career.

CHAPTER 7

Command of a Regiment

"A good leader is a person who takes a little more share of the blame." Arnold Glasgow

Germany again, but this time to Duisburg. No sooner had we settled in than we received a visit from the Area Commander who had called to express his extreme concern about ill- discipline in the Regiment and, in particular, the deteriorating relationship between the City of Duisburg and the Regiment which had fallen through the floor. This was at a time when the British Army's continued presence in Germany was being questioned. Politics was raising its head again on the matter.

A few days before our arrival coincided with the opening of a new railway station opposite the Barracks and, as life was, often in those days, a bunch of soldiers from my Regiment, returning after a drunken night out, decided to break as many windows as possible; six hundred and counting. To add to the problem, the next night another bunch from the Regiment smashed around twenty or thirty grave stones outside the local undertakers causing several thousand Deutschmarks worth of damage. The local newspapers were, rightly, full of anger, and the reputation of the Regiment severely damaged. The Area Commander had every right to be concerned especially with the on-going negotiations in Parliament. Having just arrived, no blame was attributed to me, of course, but it was made very clear, my career was on the line if things were not sorted out: *'Pretty damn quickly'*.

This was not quite the welcome I was hoping for having pumped myself up for my first Regimental command. To cap it all, there was a fight at a local hostelry involving soldiers from the Regiment and local Turkish guest workers. More headlines in the papers.

I was lucky to have Steve Knowles as my Regimental Sergeant Major and, together we drew up a plan. As a Lieutenant Colonel of a Regiment. I had powers of command which included awarding up to twenty-eight days detention, normally in the cells of our own guardroom, or with another regiment if ours were full. We decided to make every offence, no matter how minor, which involved damage to our reputation with the local population, a serious offence, with an automatic punishment of twenty-eight days detention and no argument. The Army calls it a *Prevalent Offence.*

Our guardhouse, the only one in the camp, had sufficient cells for eight. It filled quickly and we soon had to seek overspill lock-up accommodation from other regiments. Being locked up is not a pleasant experience but, we could see it was not going to be a sufficient deterrent. I asked the RSM, if he knew of a suitable person to be in charge of the guardroom and prisoners; we needed, urgently someone who was feared and respected.

A Corporal was identified and we asked him if he would like to be promoted to Sergeant with the caveat that, under his control, everyone sentenced to twenty-eight days would never, ever, wish to go back inside. The corporal visibly rose several inches and accepted the offer without hesitation.

Promotion from Corporal to Sergeant in the Army is significant, and on Saturday he was dined-in at the Sergeants Mess. It was midnight and his wife was tired, but, before leaving he called in at the guardrooms one after the other, to check the prisoners were comfortably settled, if quite cramped, for the night. He then ordered all the inmates up and out of their beds, getting them to stand by their beds while he carried out a more than thorough kit check. He went further. It was the custom for prisoners to be marched to the cookhouse where they took their meals. No longer. Yes, they were marched to the cookhouse, there to collect their meals but made immediately to about-turn and were marched back to eat in their cells; no longer in the cookhouse. Each had been given two mess tins, and they were permitted two selections from tea, main course and dessert. Everyone opted for tea and main course. Guardroom staff then marched the defaulters back to their cells at the double, making them run on the spot every few yards. Our aim was to ensure every drop of tea slopped over onto the main course by the time they got to their cosy, cramped cells. Result, one course of tea studded delicately with fried tomatoes. The holiday camp regime in our guardroom came to a rapid demise.

Daily exercise for prisoners included marching drill on the main square every day with full kit, but not at a time when families were arriving by bus to go to the NAAFI located close to the guardroom to do their shopping. This was to avoid humiliation of their partners. We did not miss the opportunity. This was soon changed and their drill took place exactly at the same time as the arrival of families. Humiliation as a form of punishment is questionable, certainly in these more puritanical days, but we were in a very serious situation with a hostile town on our doorstep, and the bad behaviour had to be stamped out at any cost.

On release from their twenty-eight days detention, the RSM and I would interview each soldier in turn and, without exception, all agreed they were not going to get locked up again. It was a tough time for us all but the problem was sorted.

These days with all the talk about human rights and other nanny state regulations, many would say this unorthodox corrective punishment was doubtful. But it worked and discipline was greatly improved. Besides, why should the town have to put up with louts running up and down their streets throwing up every few yards?

The Regiment was particularly fortunate having Steve Knowles as my RSM and I made it a priority to get him commissioned. The Ministry of Defence said *'You do realise that if he is commissioned, he will immediately have to be transferred to another unit'*. Another strange regulation, I disagreed with, but eventually was able to convince them to drop the idea and I could turn my attention to other more important matters.

We had a great Officers Mess, ideal for entertaining, and our dinner parties moved up a scale to become popular social events. In previous units I had served, it was the usual custom to have male only regimental dinner nights and I could never understand the sense of men dining together and leaving wives and girlfriends remaining at home. It was a time when our Squadrons were moving back and forth to Northern Ireland, at least once a year, so wives saw precious little of their husbands anyway; it made no sense excluding them from dinner nights as well. During my three years in command of the Regiment, we never once had a dinner night where it excluded the ladies. As a further, positive point it was always noticeable, officers behaved much better when there were ladies around. Not exactly rocket science to understand this.

Regimental dinner nights are something of a tradition in the Army and most regiments would hold at least one a month. All officers had to attend. For the ladies it was optional. We would all wear mess kit and music would usually be provided by one of the regiments in the area. It was the custom that the sound volume of the music would be such that you could talk comfortably to the person sitting next to you. These events were hugely enjoyable, including the tradition of the loyal toast to the Queen. The President of the Mess sitting at the head of the table would tap his glass and ask Mr. Vice, usually a junior officer, to pass the port around the table. The cut-glass stopper would be removed with considerable reverence and the decanter passed around the table in its time-worn direction to the left. When all glasses were filled, the President would say 'Mr. Vice. The Queen'. Mr. Vice would then say 'Ladies and gentlemen, the Queen'. If you were a field officer, meaning the rank of Major of above, it was acceptable to add: 'God bless her'. This procedure would be carried out with everyone standing. After toasting the Queen, the Colonel's wife would rise from the table and invite the other ladies to join her in the Ante Room while the men would linger awhile, but not too long, to see off the port and tell a few jokes.

Anyone reading this and without any knowledge of the Armed Forces might well think such a performance was old-fashioned and out of touch with the real world, but in the best tradition of the Services, it does work, securing the loyalty and patriotism of the Regiment. In the Royal Navy the tradition is different, the loyal toast is taken sitting down, in recognition of days when warships did not have sufficient head room to stand up in the wardroom.

There was always a shortage of available ladies to accompany some of the junior officers, so we contacted the local military school and invited expatriate lady teachers as guests, offering them accommodation and chaperoning by our junior officers. A year later this resulted in being invited to the wedding of one couple and to give the bride away. The Daily Mail got hold of the story and published an article headed *'Colonel Cupid'* but no-one dared take the mickey out of my new label.

General Sir Frank King was serving in a senior NATO appointment in Germany at the time and, being an ex-Para, I invited him and his wife to one of our dinner nights. Sitting next to him, he asked me, as one Para. to another, if I had any problems he could help with. I did and regretted it the next day. The previous day I had need to call a UK telephone number trying to locate one of our NCOs who might have got himself into a bit of trouble. But British Army of the Rhine regulations did not allow telephone calls to the UK unless approved, in my case, by Divisional Headquarters. Following procedures, I sought permission from the Duty Officer, a Captain in the Royal Army Education Corps, who was unaware of the regulation, and told me to call back the following morning. I thought this to be stupid beyond words and mentioned this to the General. He was astonished. First thing the following morning the shit hit the fan. The General had sent a signal, no emails in those days, to all units ordering that such a ridiculous regulation was to cease forthwith and commanding officers were to be given more support in commanding their regiments. Rather than thanking me for drawing attention to the problem, staff at Divisional Headquarters thought I was being disloyal and why had I not asked them to sort it out first. The French say 'tant pis!' I say 'b....cks.'

We had become good friends with the *Oberbergmeister* (Mayor of a large town) and his wife and they become regular guests to our dinner nights in the Officers Mess. This led in a roundabout way to our being introduced to the Director of the Duisburg Zoo. The Director was an influential zoologist and the development of this friendship led to several of us being invited to the zoo for dinner parties and, on a couple of occasions, swimming with dolphins when the zoo was closed. We were particularly honoured one night when all the officers were invited to a barbeque in the aquarium, with black buck on the menu and beer provided by the local brewery. I met the curator of the City's museum and, remembering the historical artefacts borrowed from the Tower of London when serving with 7 Squadron, I asked him, tongue in cheek, if he had any artifacts, we could borrow for display in the Officers Mess. Like all museums, most of their collections are hidden from view, there being no room to display the complete stock. He was delighted to invite several members of our Mess to select whatever we liked on loan, provided we insured it. The Officers' Mess was transformed. Not like a museum; more like a stately home and much admired by Mess members and visitors. One would hope, by now, for the reader to understand we were developing excellent relations with our German neighbours, which apart from cementing good Anglo-German relations, made our tour in Germany all the more enjoyable. It did mean a tight control on one's waistline was required.

It is worth explaining at this stage, the role of the Regiment. There were three Squadrons, each consisting of around hundred and fifty to two hundred men and transportation providing logistic support for the three Brigades in the Division, along with an HQ Squadron, a Royal Mechanical Engineers Workshop who provide the mechanical serviceability of a fleet of vehicles, altogether some six hundred personnel of all ranks. As we were at a distance from Divisional HQ, we also had our own NAAFI, Padre, Guard Room, Church, Medical Officer and Medical Centre. It formed a completely self-contained outfit bringing pride to our independence.

Our task was to provide logistic support for 4th Armoured Division based in Herford, known for its music and theatre, some four hours away on the autobahn, which involved a considerable amount of driving back and forth to attend meetings. I was fortunate to have an excellent Driver on the establishment, but following my Para, days, never used him as a Batman; he remained only a Driver. We were caught speeding one day by the over-efficient German Police. My loyal Driver sought to protect me when we were both ordered to get out of the vehicle to be searched. When they drew their weapons, we considered it prudent to follow their instructions.

One of the most important events we had to undertake during my tour of duty with the Regiment, was to take part in a field trial to re-evaluate the logistic resupply system in the Divisional area. The system of resupply to forward units was the provision of ammunition, fuel and rations which had to be moved from our rear bases to forward bases. It required a huge amount of unloading and reloading of vehicles.

This was a particular problem with ammunition, can be heavy stuff, so a plan was devised for ammunition to remain loaded on vehicles and taken direct to gun positions. Removing the detail, it was a good plan, well considered and those involved with the trial believed it would work. The truth brought to light was that most staff officers did not have a clue or the slightest interest in logistics, preferring to focus their attention on the tactics of infantry, artillery and armoured units. It gave me more flexibility on how to proceed. The report took a huge amount of my time before being sent to Divisional staff for its stamp of approval. They either did not understand it, or were not interested, or both, which meant it went off to the MOD without alteration. One of the net effects of delivering direct to front line units was to reduce the number of logistic units. This conflicted with the same department and a worried senior staff officer in my Corps pointed out, it would result in the loss of a number of units and officer positions. They asked me to modify it. Although there was no implied threat, my career prospects could, nevertheless, have been in jeopardy. I agreed to make the changes with reluctance. Years later the system was implemented and everyone started to take logistics more seriously.

One of the more enjoyable diversions was our link with a wine grower in the Moselle Valley. Yes, I know, another jolly, you say, but what could I do? I was under orders. I inherited an arrangement between the Regiment and the owner whereby volunteers from the Regiment would help harvest the grapes. There was always a shortage of labour – nothing changes. As we moved into October, we would expect a call from the Estate owner of the vineyard to say the grapes were ready for picking. Once the grapes were ripe, they had to be harvested quickly before the frost came. It was all on a volunteer basis and the soldiers involved would be on official leave and get paid by the owner for their effort, an arrangement approved by the Army as it was considered to be good for public relations. It also demonstrated goodwill towards our host country. We were invited to visit the vineyard and chat to the fifty or so soldiers who had volunteered and quickly began to understand the attraction to them of grape picking. It was quite evidently not the grape picking itself, which was very hard work, but the village harvest dances and festivals attended by all the local fräuleins with some serious wine tasting to boot.

Visiting one of my Squadron Commanders on a field exercise, coincided with a major incident which required his immediate attention. Calmly, he started to sort it out when one of his junior officers inappropriately started querying the menu for dinner the following night. John took a long look sympathetic look, sighed deeply as in the fashion of a basset hound wanting its dinner, and without in any way humiliating him replied: *'When you are up to your elbows in alligators it is not a good time to start thinking about menus'*. A wise and considerate response, I thought.

I was asked by the Area Commander to assess the abilities of a Captain who had received poor, annual, confidential reports. With my Para. background, the request was for me to toughen him up and advise whether he was a suitable person to remain in the Army. The captain turned up looking scruffy, unfit, overweight and unimpressive. I formed my opinion in five minutes. But to be fair to him, I asked this Squadron Commander to take him under his wing for a couple of weeks to give me his own opinion. After a couple of days, he approached me to say the officer was useless and not fit to command a dustbin. I reported back to the Area Commander and, as a result, he was sent back to his unit. What was the outcome? He was posted to a less challenging, cushy rear unit, where he was allowed to soldier on. What a disgrace to the Army. My Squadron Commander meanwhile, also stayed in the Army and became head of the Corps as a Major-General.

After three years, I received a posting order to the Joint Warfare Establishment near Salisbury and we looked forward to returning to the UK and, in particular, our own house in a Hampshire village. It was not far from my new place of work making our return so much easier to settle back in Britain.

It proved to be a good idea to get back because our tenant, an artist would you believe, had stopped paying any rent for the previous six months. Tackling the tenant on the non-payment of rent his reply was: *'You are paid by the tax payer but, for me, I am a painter, and have to wait until my clients pay me and I have not been paid lately.'*

Our once immaculate garden was neglected and instead of the well-groomed lawn, there was a huge studio right in the middle of our garden. After a few weeks I sold the studio in an effort to recoup some of my losses. The artist had the cheek to turn up with a truck to dismantle the studio and take it away, only to realise it was not there anymore. I had neither patience nor any sympathy for him and told him to get lost.

But there was more to come before leaving Duisburg for the last time. It was to come in the form of a big surprise. The Oberbergmeister's office rang to say the City of Duisburg had voted to honour the Regiment with the Freedom of the City before my departure ten days later. Time was short, but the Corps band and drums based in Aldershot dropped all their engagements and arrived in good time for the Regiment to march through the city and enjoy the hospitality of the City's Rathaus.

In the greatest traditions of the Army, I was towed out of the Barracks on my last day of command by all the Senior NCOs, supervised by my masterful ex-RSM, now a Captain. It had been a good three years and for the Regiment to receive the Freedom of the City showed that the relationship with the city had been restored.

CHAPTER 8

Leaving the Army, Leaving Life

"It is the courage to continue that counts." Winston Churchill

Little did I know at the time, but this was to be my last posting before leaving the Army. Life needed to be enjoyed because a bumpy ride was coming up. 'Crikey' to coin an old phrase. Nightmare was to be more apt than 'bumpy'. For weeks after I left the Army, I stared into a dreadful abyss having to use all of my Army resolve to maintain my head above water. But, I go too fast.

My new unit, the Joint Warfare Establishment consisted of a small team of senior officers representing all branches of the Armed Forces and a United States Exchange Officer together with specialist instructors in Joint Warfare; hence the title. My specialty was Logistics, and our role was to teach all aspects of warfare to senior British, NATO and Commonwealth officers.

One of the standard presentations inherited from my predecessor, included a supporting 35 mm slide which showed a picture of a wizened old man in a bone dome helmet with the caption: *"I couldn't get a cockstand about logistics'.* That sort of attitude reflected the opinion of many of the so called *'teeth arm'* officers of the time (Armoured Corps, Infantry, Artillery), as they had little time for something as boring as Logistics, far removed from the excitement of action their reason for joining up.

During my first presentation, a senior German officer asked me: '*Vat ist dis cockstand?*' I was obliged to tell him there were many uses of the word 'cock' in the English language, including 'Cockney', 'cockshy', 'cockeyed' and the useful 'cocking' as in cocking one's rifle or pistol. '*Ach, so,*' came the reply which also gives my readers a bit more flavour of my surroundings at the time. Feeling that to add 'cockleshell heroes' might be too close a reminder of one of our more successful sorties against the enemy in the last big war I did not add to the list in case I inflamed old memories.

It was noticeable that my presentations were usually slotted in immediately after lunch, which was the best time, or so the delegates thought cleverly to go to sleep during the talks, usually for those who had imbibed in an extra gin and tonic during the lunch break. I ditched the slide show, but a few years later, during the Falklands Campaign, these same 'teeth arm' officers found they had a few urgent lessons to learn about the importance of logistics; much has changed since as a result of that campaign.

Joint Warfare was a motivating place to work. It was headed up by a Commandant, Major- General who insisted every presentation had to be thoroughly rehearsed in advance, at least once. Just as well we stood behind a lectern in the gloom because at my first presentation, my knees began to knock together and continued knocking. And I had worn the red and green berets. We were not allowed to read from notes, but the secret was to write out a list of headings and glance surreptitiously at these from time to time. From kn…knocking knee nervousness at first, by the time of my final presentation to an audience of several hundred senior officers at NATO HQ in Brussels, I found I had become full of confidence, not even needing a list to refresh my memory. I was reminded of these presentations when, later in life, I had to face down a howling mob of over a thousand, outraged holiday guests, keeping them from tearing me apart by balancing their rage against my confidence in dealing with the issue by talking. With training and experience, everything is possible.

The Commandant, a Royal Marine Major General, had a preference for presentations to be punctuated with suitable jokes; these also had to be rehearsed thus removing – often – the punch from the punchline. Giving a presentation at the Army School of Transport, I could see several United States Army officers in the audience. Thinking on the hoof, I remembered a joke that could be appropriate, even if it had not been rehearsed. Never mind said I, full of this new found confidence, until reaching the punch line I found it had disappeared into the far reaches of my temporal lobe. Nonetheless, you will be pleased to learn I managed to keep my composure and the reward was a bigger laugh than the joke should have merited. Lesson learnt? Probably not. Here is the joke, well-rehearsed this time, and my profound apologies if it does not appeal to your sense of humour.

'An American visiting one of England's well-known stately homes, met the daughter of the wealthy landowner and, after spending the evening together, he declared she was the most beautiful girl he had ever met and wanted to marry her. She considered the idea and asserted that the man she would marry would be required to have, amongst other things, a castle in Scotland, be a millionaire and, because she enjoyed sex, a male attachment (putting it politely) that was minimum of at least half a foot in length. The American considered this and they agreed to meet at The Ritz for dinner the following night.

'Well' she said, 'How did you get on today?' 'I had the most interesting day. I charted an aircraft, looked at all six castles currently up for sale in Scotland and put a deposit on one that I know absolutely, you will love. Regarding the second point, my father owns several oil wells in Texas and money is not going to be a problem'. 'What about the last requirement' she said'. The American replied 'I just had time to visit a leading surgeon dealing with this sort of thing in Harley Street who assured me we can get it cut it down to whatever size you like'. Hmm!

Two of the Squadron Commanders in my Regiment were students at the National Defence College. I well recall a time at the Canadian Staff College when brownie points were awarded to students who asked suitable questions directed towards guest lecturers. Believing it to be the case, we cooked up a plan. for each of them to ask a question, appropriate to the subject and to which I knew the answer. *'I would like to compliment you on the quality of that question etcetera'*. I replied. I observed Directing Staff sitting towards the back of the lecture hall making favourable notes. If one asked a stupid question it could always backfire, of course. At the Staff College, one student asked a two-part question which included an opinionated answer. The guest speaker glared at him and after a pregnant pause, said nothing looking around the audience, ignoring the question completely and saying: *'Next question please'*. He was also one of those bullshitters always proposing a last question just when it was time for lunch, an important meal for us, so was quite rightly rather unpopular and ignored if he overrode the time to finish.

One of our most popular destinations was the National Defence College of Malaysia in Kuala Lumpur. Led by the Commandant, we set a week's study for the students based on a notional enemy called Redland, an amphibious invasion somewhere on the Malaysian east coast. We flew out via Hong Kong where we stayed for several nights. Arriving at Kai Tak Airport, I was expecting to be met by Tom, one of my Troop Commanders from 7 Squadron days but he hadn't turned up. Conveniently, there was an announcement over the airport's public address system for: *'Mister Lieutenant Colonel David to go to the Service Desk'.*

That would be me. Surely?

Greeted by a very smart Gurkha Sergeant, he drove me up into the New Territories to enjoy their hospitality. Our Commandant was a personal friend of the Deputy Chief of the Hong Kong Police Force, having been students together. Come the evening, we were entertained to a magnificent banquet at one of the best restaurants in Hong Kong, as guests of the Deputy Police Chief. No payment appeared to be made at anytime but I cannot believe the Police Chief would have forgotten to pay! Surely? Maybe he went back later?

Moving forward to our destination, and courtesy of Cathay Pacific, we arrived at Kuala Lumpur and were in for another a surprise. As soon as the aircraft had come to a stop and the doors had opened, all passengers were instructed to remain in their seats while our small group disembarked. We were met by the Commandant of the National Defence College together with the British Military Attaché where we boarded the staff cars positioned as close to the bottom of the aircraft steps as was possible, without damaging the shiny paint on the wings. The usual Customs formalities were ignored, if they ever existed and we were whisked away with a Police escort, sirens blaring. We were all impressed by the style. That's my sort of style. Our luggage was waiting in our hotel rooms on arrival and, with hardly time for a shower, we were off to a reception given by the British Military Attaché, followed by dinner at one of the best restaurants in KL.

The next day we felt we really had to get down to business. A Royal Malaysian Air Force VIP aircraft had been placed at our disposal to allow us to carry out a reconnaissance of the east coast area allowing us to search for suitable amphibious landing beaches and possible sites for amphibious landings. I was familiar with the region from my 3 Commando Brigade days, which made life a little easier. Plans were completed and the following days were filled, instructing officers from the Malaysian Armed Forces on military contingency operations.

Towards the end of my tour, the Commandant asked me to research a subject that had logistic implications. Its title was: "The use of Civilian Transport in the Event of War" a dull title with fascinating implications. Hovercraft were beginning to come into their own at this time. The Army had an established hovercraft unit. As the Commanding Officer was a colleague, time was spent evaluating Hovercraft performance while, coincidentally, we swanned around the English Channel learning all about the capabilities of different types of these flexible craft. They were remarkable vehicles and it was an interesting experience, but regrettably, to me, they were not found any significant role in the Armed Forces. Interestingly, I discovered that some cruise ships, in a time of war, would be hunkered down in South America, along with the aircraft fleet of Scandinavian Airways System. Some of the components were neutral like Sweden itself, and they did not want to jeopardize their neutral status.

There came further planning for a possible war in the future. I learnt about further planning for conflict and was intrigued to discover the American Government had a policy of fitting a proportion of newly built commercial aircraft with reinforced floors and larger doors so that, in the event of war, they could be requisitioned to carry armour and other heavy equipment. The US government paid for the additional costs of construction and the extra fuel required to fly the heavier aircraft. In Britain, our cross-channel ferries would also be requisitioned by the Government of the day, for troop and vehicle movements. European canals would all be mandated for the war effort for which compensation would be paid to the owners. Railway rolling stock would be deployed and would also be subject to requisition. There were many more examples but these give a intriguing insight to how some Governments viewed contingency planning during peacetime.

Back to my presentation, it was backed up with a mass of photographs, including one spectacular video shown to close the meeting, of aircraft carriers launching multiple fighter ground attack aircraft accompanied by Rod Stewart singing: 'Sailing'. It was an immediate success, and the Commandant invited MOD staff offers to see the presentation. The next thing I knew was having to present it at NATO Headquarters in Brussels.

•••

I mentioned earlier that, well before it was time to leave for my next posting, I had been giving serious consideration to leaving the Army. There were all sorts of reasons, each one conflicting with another, making it extremely difficult for me to come to the right conclusion. It was an unsolvable dilemma, so adopting a well-practiced staff college doctrine, I started to prepare a Military Appreciation, listing the advantages and disadvantages to see if a clear road could be found, any one of which could alter my whole way of life.

The advantages appeared to outweigh the disadvantages in a ratio of 7:4.

Advantages of leaving the Army:

- *Young enough to start a new career, hopefully in the leisure industry*
- *No need to send my children to boarding school*
- *Settled in our home in a lovely Hampshire village*
- *Stay connected to the many friends we had made in the village*
- *The challenge of seeking civilian employment*
- *No need to rent our house again (and risk another bad tenant)*
- *No longer running the risk of a posting to the MOD in London, which I would have loathed*

Disadvantages of leaving the Army:

- *Missing out on further promotion*
- *Missing out on becoming a Military Attaché (a military expert attached to a Diplomatic mission or an Embassy) which I had been recommended for*
- *Missing out on the camaraderie of Service life*
- *No longer able to wear a uniform, which I was always proud to do*

From this I came to a life-changing career decision.

'Ready fore the first trek.'

600 steps Great Skellig 2007.

'On the way up to the beehives. Little Skellig out to sea.'

Lava flow island of Fernandina.
Galapagos. 2005. 'About 2,200degrees F. First to get there.'

Antarctica 2013.

America's Cup yacht. 2008. *n.b. 'Author's carefully nonchalant style with hands in pockets.'*

Galapagos. 2006. *'Wet landing in one of the zodiacs'.*

Cabin Trunk *Capt.D.T. Fairs*

Rajasthan

– PART THREE –

RETURN TO CIVVY STREET

'For those of you who have done well. Well done!
For those of you who didn't do quite so well.
Bloody well done anyway!'

It may be a little simplistic, but if the Advantages outnumber the Disadvantages, then, surely, I should follow its result through to the winding up? But I had not considered personal happiness in the equation not realising this would become a major issue over the next few years; I missed the Service life enormously and continued to do so. Unbeknown to me at the time, my Royal Marines Commandant had recommended me to Commando Forces as the next Colonel Adjutant Quartermaster of Commando Forces, in the rank of full Colonel. It was not long after this recommendation, the Argentinian junta began to look dangerous, to say the least, for the Falklands Islands. Commando Forces struggled to find a Colonel from my Corps who was Commando trained, I might well have been a shoe-in for the position. Following British success in the Falklands, the person who did eventually fill the vacancy later became the Commandant-General of my Corps. To balance this equation, I might have got shot and killed at Goose Green or Mount Longdon but, to coin a phrase, I would have gone like a shot if asked.

Mixed with all this was my future? I was beginning to see it much more clearly as ideas coalesced. There was excitement at times; I wanted to get ahead, to put plans, half-formed perhaps, but plans nonetheless, wrapped around the travel industry. It just seemed right to want to walk around the world accompanied by fee-paying guests behind me. But, how to do it all?

There was a bloody big cross-roads ahead of me. Something the size of Spaghetti Junction in Birmingham. It was filled with queuing traffic, some with indicators out, some unsure of where they wanted to end up, one or two drivers were leaning out of their windows trying to give me advice but none of them appeared to know any more than me. Everyone had been doing one job since they left school. Some were wanting to stay on in the safety of their past lives; others, more adventurous, were studying maps of roads stretching into the far distance. For me the decision was how far did I want to go, and, did I want to join them or strike out on my own? So many decisions, each one becoming muddled with my daily Army duties which had to come first. Slacking was not in my lexicon of thought.

I thus found myself in an extraordinary position, one I had never been in before. If I looked back, even a few months, I could still feel the warmth, the pull of the camaraderie of the Army, my life for twenty-five years. Security, a knowledge of my place in society and a firm future in place. If I looked forward as I now was obliged to do, it was hard to find any of these elements. Putting aside the first two, I had to have, above all, a job, but one I would need to love as much as the Army, even if it might be quite different from my past life. One thing was fixed in my firmament. It had to have connections with the travel industry.

I knew also there was need to be involved in a type of work which would allow me to develop it constantly. I liked to polish, to see a better model emerge from my energies. There was always, in my book, room to develop, expand and advance my tasks. Duisburg as one example, had been a personal triumph as I worked alongside the local residents to rebuild their confidence in me. I began to sum it all up in my mind. Experienced in world-wide travel, an ability to get along with peoples of differing origins, a growing knowledge of the hospitality industry, particularly in ensuring these same people were entertained in a manner which they could expect. I knew how to lead, my logistics training could be one of my greatest assets. All I needed now was to gain experience of working in civvy street, quite an alien place for someone such as an ex-soldier. Dealing with civilians was going to be quite different to Army personnel. There were not going to be tiers of rank protocol handing down orders, no pyramid of officers, just me sitting above a flat line of travellers.

To a man recently having left the Army, I found the world quite odd in many ways, muddled and disorganised. No-one jumped to orders, leading to significant delays in executing plans. There was going to be a lot to learn, a lot of control on my part, but, at the end of the day, I could see, for the first time a way forward, a bridgehead, so to speak. I just had to grasp the idea and carry it directly to the other side of the wide river.

I now found myself on my own with no hope of returning to the Army, with no job to make me feel useful, needed, active and responsible. Although I tried to push the needles of fear to the far boundaries of my mind, the same repeating "what-ifs" intruded daily.

'What if I couldn't find a job I wanted?'

'What if I had to take a job which I didn't like, perhaps not even connected with the travel industry?'

'What if I found myself trapped between the two worlds of my old life and my planned future?'

And only I had got myself into this mess. I couldn't blame anyone else.

I do not go for modern clichés such as: 'Being in a very dark place,' which half the children of the world seem to be using as an excuse for not turning up to school. To an ex-Army man it was not an idea we took to our beds. It was for us to get the world out of these 'dark places'. Not for me to create it in the first place.

And yet, I knew I was sinking, like being in a quaking bog on Dartmoor where the more one struggled the more one sank. Keeping still slowed the whole thing down but, of course, it also meant it prevented one from going anywhere.

A dark place can be loneliness. It can be a very emotional journey where one's emotions are thrown about without reason. Many sufferers might well fall back on depression in the family. But, if one has never suffered before from depression nor known of anyone in the family with this difficult to control illness, where does one go to receive help?

Should a proud bearer of the Red and Green berets really have to seek help when one, just one management job offer in the Hospitality Industry could change the lights from locked red to green go. While these thoughts swirled around in my head, like several nightmares each trying for dominance, I had to get up each morning and pretend to be busy cleaning the tops of drawing pins with Brasso and making sure all the curtains were pulled back to the same distance.

Looking for further time fillers, during my long days there were some aspects of our village life which were missing. It included the need for a village green. As there was a piece of land right in the centre of the village, eminently suitable, a few of us started putting our heads together with the aim of making our homes a better place to live in, and this required a village green. But, there was a snag. (There is always at least one snag in these stories.) The parcel of land was part of the Vicarage where the Vicar of the local church lived. It was neglected and uncared for, so our initial thought was to approach the Parish Council. We turned up at the next meeting in the rather dilapidated village hall with the aim of seeking their support. Steeped in bureaucracy, we were put in our place when told we had to give notice of items to be added to the Agenda in advance of the monthly meetings. Following this advice, we then discovered the next meeting was cancelled and the following one would not take place due to summer holidays. From the discipline of the Army to the quantum leap of Council disinterest and disorder was, simply, quite breath-taking.

When we did manage to get our suggestion added to the agenda, we were firmly advised it was a matter over which they had no jurisdiction. Putting it another way, the right phrase was: *'They could not give a monkey's.'*

Not to be outdone, we convened a meeting in the village hall, which was attended by most of the residents. It was hugely encouraging so it was decided to form a Village Association. For my sins, the appointed Chairmanship landed on my shoulders and supported by three other residents we agreed to establish a village Association..

The first step of the Village Hall saga was to approach the Vicar. He immediately declined even to consider the idea, as he had an arrangement for a local resident to keep her horse there. We paid a visit to the horse owner who, when we explained what we were trying to do, readily agreed to move her horse, if we could find alternative grazing. We knew a few local farmers and managed to secure the promise of one of them to accommodate the horse. Returning eagerly to the Vicar with the news, he brought up more objections and declined to discuss it further. This, note, is the Vicar of a small village church one of the pillars of community life? We were shown a closed door just like his mind. What to do now? We approached the Church Commissioners in Winchester explaining our project. They put up all sorts of barriers and clearly were not interested in helping, (more closed minds at a higher level), even though we were prepared to raise the funds and, provided the price was reasonable, willing to organize a number of events to raise the funds. These included an auction, a village fête, a horticultural show, events in the village hall, a raffle, naturally and, I'm sure we had a 'Bat the Rat' to round off the ideas. We kept up the pressure, but they again declined. It was time to use my airborne initiative. It had remained there, dormant perhaps, but ready to be activated despite having left the Army. This took the form of approaching Southern Television who thought it would make a great story. We thought it only courteous to let the Church Commissioners know our plan and that the story was to go live the following Friday. On the Thursday, the day before the TV programme was to be scheduled, we received a letter from their solicitors saying they would agree to sell it to us but at an unreasonably high price and provided completion would be within seven days. This was a deliberate attempt to make it difficult for us to complete in that short space of time and, more importantly, raise the money. It put the whole village in a spot, but we were not prepared to allow them to get away with it and four of us agreed to take out a bank loan acting as personal guarantors at the same time, which in effect risked us losing our houses if we failed to repay the money. Risky for us but it was a challenge, and we gave ourselves two years to raise the funds. We succeeded in one year. Our enthusiasm was infectious and fully supported by the village. A very unpleasant event took place at this time involving the same church. Having believed, all my life, the church was there to help the worshippers, this story took the biscuit. My neighbour was about to get married. He had been married before, but not his partner, who very much wanted to get married in the local church. As best man, I accompanied them to meet the Vicar who raised all sorts of objections to a marriage ceremony in his church, as the groom had been married before. A compromise was reached, where the ceremony would take place involving the singing of a few hymns and little else, with the marriage ceremony having to take taking place in the Town Hall. Extraordinary behaviour from one of the supposed pillars of society. I wonder what Lambeth Palace would have made of it? On the day, the bride's train was delayed. I collected her from the railway station and by the time we arrived at the church, they were singing the last hymn. Finishing in silence, the Vicar disappeared into the vestry. To him the service was over. He had managed with no help to put a bride in tears on the most important day of her life. Angered by this, I made my way into the vestry, seeking an explanation. He said the service was agreed for a certain time so how was he to know when the bride did not arrive? Explaining in words of one syllable I 'advised' him of how he had lost his own way in life – a very sad man. It reflects, I believe, why attendance at church is so low these days.

The village also became involved, this time with a local building contractor. Having completed a new housing development in the village, he blocked off a lane bordering on land they owned, next to a electricity sub-station. This effectively stopped children using the route to go to school. There were no pavements between the village and the school, the road very narrow and it was causing a safety problem. We held a meeting with the Directors of the building company who offered to remove the wire fencing on payment of a large fee. Outraged, we tried to think of a solution. After several weeks of fruitless negotiations, it was time for some airborne initiative again. (This is becoming repetitive I know). Arriving home one dark night after a party, two of us, armed with heavy duty Army wire cutters, cut the barrier and dumped everything in a ditch half a mile away. It was a job well done, and, for some reason remained unnoticed by the building company. The safe route for children to get to school remains open to this day.

After several months seeking suitable employment in the area, the realization came upon me I had hugely overestimated the potential for suitable opportunities in the leisure industry and had no choice but to cast my net further afield. Leaving the Army, to me, had been all about settling down in our village and working in the leisure industry nearby. What a mistake I made. Something would have to give for I had no idea how to come to terms with civilian life.

The opportunity came when least expecting it while reading *The Daily Telegraph* on the London Underground. It leapt out in front of me – *We seek an experienced Overseas Manager for the Mediterranean area. Must have two European languages, etc.* Impatiently and impulsively, I jumped off the train at the next stop and rang the Company requesting an application form. After a brief conversation with the Personnel Manager (now Human Resources) he did not hold out much hope as I lacked industry experience and languages. However, he did recognize some parallels with my time, planning overseas exercises for the

Army, and agreed to send an application form which I rapidly returned, accompanied by my CV. I felt the interview went well, then heard nothing for a month. Out of the blue, a second interview request arrived. It turned out their first choice had changed his mind, the second had poor references and the third choice had undisclosed problems. I wonder what that was all about? When offered the job, I admitted not having the language qualifications specified, but they said it was not important as everyone spoke English and contracts were all in English anyway. At last the future looked brighter.

The only problem was their Head Office was in Welwyn Garden City, several hours away from our Hampshire village, and I would have to live in the Area. Fortunately, the Company owned a house used by managers arriving back from overseas visits and I was permitted to stay there until I could find my own accommodation. My four weeks induction training started with a visit to Malta to coincide with the Directors tour of the Eastern Mediterranean in a private jet, (how else does one do the job?) to recce new destinations for the following year's brochure. In Malta, we were tasked with setting up a meeting between our Directors and the Minister of Tourism. Over dinner, and meeting the Managing Director for the first time, he outlined an idea he had which involved a two-centre holiday, taking in Gibraltar and Tangiers. He needed someone to get over there right away. The task, to find the hotels, sign contracts with local agents and agree pricing for the brochure, shortly to be published. The Operations Director, my boss, said there was no one available. The MD said: 'What about David?' He replied: 'He has only just joined us'. That seemed to be exactly the right reply for action. Decision made, it appeared, for the next day I was on a plane heading for Gibraltar and onward to Tangier. I now had a job, my darkness was lifting quickly, my back was straightening, my independence was returning. I took to the work like a duck to water. Further induction training was considered unnecessary and I congratulated myself having begun my new career in the leisure industry.

•••

However, all was not well domestically. My family were reluctant to move to the area, and irregular commuting became a strain. Small issues became large problems. Expecting to be home at the weekend, we had planned a dinner party for the Saturday. I had flown from Gatwick to Ibiza to plan the Balearic Island programme and was expected to fly back on the Friday morning.

Sitting in my seat waiting to depart, I was asked to leave the aircraft as it was over loaded. Stranded for a couple of days, I eventually hitched a flight back to the UK, but not to Gatwick, where my car was, but Luton. This happened a few times and became an absolute pain in the arse. It was a bit like the old song: *'Oh!, Mister Porter, what should I do? They are taking me off to Birmingham and I wanted to go to Crewe.'*

This contributed to putting additional strain on my marriage. Misguidedly, I had believed, by returning home to the village, it would make things better. After a year in work, giving me real enjoyment again, and travelling to many Mediterranean countries, I found myself talking to the Managing Director at my farewell party. Seeking the reason for my departure and suspecting it was for domestic reasons, he said if things did not work out at home, he would re-employ me right away and there was a good chance of being made a Director. That did not make it any better, in fact, it was extremely frustrating, knowing I could hold a job down at high level in the industry I had chosen for the second part of my working life. With great sadness, desperation in some ways, my thoughts began again to revert back to my happy Army days and occupied my thoughts for a considerable part of each day. I packed up and headed home to our Hampshire village where things had sadly become quite distressing. This was one area of life I was not trained how to handle.

Being out of work was not an option. I had tasted the alternative and responded to an advertisement for the position of: *regional manager for a leading leisure company*. I had no idea what the product was, but thought it worthwhile attending an interview. It was not far from our Hampshire village, it paid well and attached the all important company car to the contract. As the interview unfolded, it turned out the product was to supply fruit machines and juke boxes to pubs and hotels, not work I had ever thought about, but it fitted the bill for the time being and allowed me to resume my home life. My offices, in an old brewery, were co-located with the Head Office. My position was Regional Manager with a staff of around seventy and, as it happens, was more interesting than I had imagined. Quickly getting to grips with the work, the realization dawned, all that mattered was to achieve or surpass the budget's objectives. Co-operating with the breweries and publicans was all important, because any underperformance was quickly punished with the withdrawal of equipment. Dealing with some of the pub managers was particularly difficult, sometimes humiliating, but a good rapport developed with the breweries, often managed by ex-serviceman.

Taking an overview of my position after twelve months, there were issues clearly unresolved. Some things were just plain wrong. Engineers had poor radio equipment, causing difficulties in contacting them in the evenings and weekends; vehicles were unsuitable and had no lifting mechanism to load and unload heavy equipment and budget objectives which triggered bonuses for staff, were set unrealistically high. Making my recommendations to Head Office all were either ignored or refused. Then, a disagreement arose with the Personnel Director who said the Managing Director had complained that some of my own staff did not recognize him, causing him some degree of offence. One of my responsibilities was to run Visitor Reception with staff provided from my department; I posted a picture of the MD and described his role and the importance of his position, much as we used to do in the Army when expecting VIP visitors, so everybody knew who was visiting. Sensitivities became scorched when the Personnel Director went potty, tearing down the picture and upset my receptionists. I was not prepared to put up with this, so I tackled him and his ludicrous attitude, which he simply chose to ignore. As my recommendations were to improve the business and as the Personnel Director was an asshole, I decided to resign. The MD called me into the office, seeking to know why I was resigning, so I told him everything. This was just before going home on Friday evening and he asked me to list all my concerns in writing and to come and see him first thing Monday.

Came the day we went through them one by one and he agreed all my recommendations, even calling in the Personnel Director to give him a bollocking in front of me for the way he behaved, having used his name in vain. Everything was sorted and there was no longer a reason to leave. Profit margins went up, and this was followed by two more years of steady growth. But after three years, just like the Army system, it was time to move on. The MD again called me into his office and offered me the position of Personnel Director if I was prepared to stay. It was tempting, but I was now free; I had learnt how to work in civvy street, I knew I could make it work. Pastures new were beckoning.

CHAPTER 9

Holiday Club Pontins

'Not much different from basic training'

I felt the past three years had been valuable in making the painful decision to leave the Army which had been my whole life, and get my feet under a Civvy Street desk. I must have applied for over a hundred jobs without success, mostly without even the courtesy of a reply. I decided it was time to use my *"airborne Initiative,"* creaky, but still available with a touch of 3 in 1 oil, and began to revise my CV allowing it, this time to spin a bit, just a bit you understand, but now giving each line a gloss with each version tailored to the specific job application being applied for. I would often exaggerate, no, sorry, embroider or embellish are better words, my background experience and, with tongue in cheek, included some colourful anecdotes in an attempt to generate attention. It worked. After so many disappointments, in the course of one week I received three interview offers.

The first was a commercial manager's position with a well-known brewery. I was invited to meet the Chairman at his office in Norwich, not an unattractive place to work, and with a reasonable salary, a company car and a number of perks including a monthly allocation of beer. What more could one ask for. The Chairman had been the Commanding Officer of a local TA County Regiment and it was not long before we were engrossed in Army matters. Realising how much time had been taken up with this discussion, he suddenly looked at his watch, got up and thanked me for coming along to the interview, saying he had arranged to meet his wife for lunch and would get in back in touch. I intervened as I shook hands with him asking about the interview result because we had not discussed anything much relating to the job. He apologised and said: "When can you start".

Needless to say, I was delighted, but still thought it sensible to go along to a second interview, just by way of comparison. This other position was for a General Manager of Pontins Holiday Club at Camber Sands, East Sussex. It was close to Dungeness. The interview went well advising me I would be the first General Manager they had appointed without previous experience in the industry, so they would be taking a risk with me. Nice? I might have retorted 'likewise' but the job interested me, for it was a challenge and one I believed, even then, I could get on top of.

The job offer arrived in the post. The salary was not as good as the brewery, but accommodation would be provided in the form of a bungalow on the site. It needed an army type recce to Camber Sands to see what had been omitted from the offer which might have a bearing on taking the job. It was not what l had expected, but, then, l did not know what to assume because l had never been to a holiday camp in my life.. They don't like to be called 'holiday camps' by the way, but that is how most people describe them.

I took the job, putting aside the brewery offer.

Arriving at a huge prison-like building, painted rather gaudily in blue and yellow, and six hundred and seventy-eight basic – I mean, basic - two storey self catering chalets, they were not unlike an Army camp, in fact, I should say very like a basic training camp. Both entrances had barriers and managed by security guards who had yet to be instructed in the niceties of being polite to guests. The whole 'camp' (Stalag?) was surrounded by a lethal looking fence topped with barbed wire, leading me to ask myself whether this was to keep out unwanted trespassers or to keep the guests in? I discovered later it was both. There was sufficient accommodation for 3,000 guests and at peak times was completely full, so it was a significant operation.

The rise of British holiday camps became popular for people looking for an affordable holiday at the end of the Second World War. It was a brilliant concept. Billy Butlin started it all off, closely shadowed by Fred Pontin. In the early days, campers were awakened by a loudspeaker summoning them to breakfast and to take part in humiliating competitions, before being ordered back to their chalets to be shut in for the night, much like the popular TV series Hi-de-Hi. Bed and Breakfast businesses and seaside guest houses could not compete and the British public considered holiday camps to be great. Cheap package holidays to the Mediterranean eventually arrived leading to the beginning of the end for holiday camps, apart from the few which they managed to adapt. Camber Sands was one of them.

One of the reasons motivating me to leave the Army in mid-career, was to start a second career in the leisure industry, but my visit to Camber Sands convinced me it was not the right vehicle for me, so I replied to my letter of appointment thanking them for the offer, but declining to accept. Shortly after, I received a call from the Chairman who said he was disappointed I had turned down the position but he wanted me to know, he had it in mind to appoint me as a Director in due course, but wanted me to understand the importance of gaining experience of the whole operation. I quite understood. There were no promises but it did put a different perspective on it. It might, at very least, be fun, and it was more related to the leisure industry than a brewery which was my other offer. After some consideration I started to take a different point of view finally accepting the position.

Moving to Camber Sands coincided with my continuing marriage difficulties, so, with the offer of accommodation, it provided me with an escape route and the adoption of a new family. It turned out there was a great bunch of people forming my staff, ready to back me up at all times, professional, yet fun, most of whom were seasonal staff accommodated on the site.

One attractive feature of the resort was its complete orientation towards the family; the only problems which arose was when single people booked in. They had little regard for other guests, drank too much, and generally were selfish and inconsiderate to everyone. My first task ensured the acceptance of bookings from families, banning all single people. Despite misgivings from Head Office about the commercial sense of this decision, and mutterings about exceeding my responsibility, this proved to be a success. This left only the problem of local single men sneaking over the fence wire presumably to get to the bars, and the ladies. Of course, these points might be the other way round?

My car was packed to the gunnels, when I duly arrived at the main gate, a few days before opening the Camp for Easter. I received a rather cheerless welcome from the security guard on the gate. It did not matter he did not know who I was as I explained to him the importance of greeting all arrivals with a friendly welcome. The title "security guard," may have had something to do with it so, once settled in, I changed the name to "security and hospitality staff". When serving on the staff of the 1st British Corps in Germany, the Corps Commander was very particular about greeting visitors correctly on arrival because he believed first impressions were all important and there were many from NATO, Government and other organisations of a sufficiently high rank who expected to be treated with respect. This had particularly applied to security checks on arrival and the customary drink in the Officers Mess before lunch. The barman had to be carefully vetted. Also, when I commanded my regiment in Germany, the Regimental Sergeant Major always tried to find out what a visitor liked to drink before arrival by contacting his staff officer, so that when offered the customary welcome drink, we collected a lot of brownie points when the barman asked our visitor if he: *'wanted the usual sir'*.

Back at Camber Sands, the word soon spread, and security staff thereafter, displayed an improved level of politeness and offered a warm welcome to guests and visitors.

My arrival coincided with the Camp's opening for Easter and there was a great buzz like a hive of bees in the air seeking nectar where ever they could find it. On check-in day, I made a point of observing, as well as greeting guests, and was surprised to discover how many maintenance jobs had to be sorted out, such as toilets not working, lighting and heating problems, locks sticking, the list appeared endless and each one would mean a guest with an issue. The previous day I had met the permanent staff including an electrician, plumber and carpenter and wondered why they were not available to sort out the growing list of maintenance problems. I was told, they worked a five day week which excluded weekends and bank holidays, so two additional handymen were employed to do their work on these days. During the season most bookings were Saturday to Saturday with the result our maintenance team were never on duty on the days when they were most needed. It did not make sense and it required resolving quickly.

The only solution was to amend their contracts of employment by saying, in future they would be "working five days a week spread over seven" which meant they became eligible to work weekends when required, with a wage increase in compensation. It went down like a lead balloon. I had not made any allowance for the Union reaction. Something missing in the Army thank goodness. The Union representatives arrived in the form of a ton of bricks. Various leaders visited to show their huge salaries were being deployed usefully, demanding to see the staff involved. I told them they could meet with them after normal working hours, which also did not go down well. My Army background gave me no experience of how to deal with such a stupid situation as this, but after much discussion and negotiation, it was all resolved. Nowadays I am sure my actions would have upset one or more shop stewards but these were the sensible days when sanity did prevail from time to time.

•••

When our guests had returned home after Easter, I took a trip into Rye. It was a Saturday and here I came across other old fashioned and out of date habits. This was civvy street in the raw to me. It was lunch time so I called in to what appeared to be a decent café for lunch. I was 'greeted' with a frosty reception and told it was the staff's lunch time. The café was closed to customers at peak dining time despite the sign on the door stating the shop was open. I sought out the Tourist Information Kiosk. It was closed because, as I discovered later, staff only worked Mondays to Friday. I rang the Director of Tourism at Hastings for a chat and asked him why the Tourist Information Kiosk in Rye could not be open at weekends, a time when the town was maxed out with tourists. A few days later he came to visit and to find out how I had managed to get around the problem with our tradesmen and the Unions. A week or so later I invited him to bring his leisure department staff over to see how we operated. They were offered the usual hospitality and after thanks all round, the visit ended around 1:00pm. I noticed several of them were still in the bar at 4:00pm and they confided in me that if visits extended to 4:00pm they were not required to go back to the office.

It was becoming clear to me, that my twenty-five years in the Army had taught me to live in one particular way. This 'way' was poles apart from the world I had now chosen to live in. Over the years I had diverged further and further from the manner in which Britain wanted to work…or, in this case, not want to work. On re-examination I realised I had not diverged, it was working Britain which had changed, in those days controlled by the Unions who, in turn, controlled Downing Street. Attitudes of staff to customer were a very long way from what I saw was acceptable. Politeness costs nothing, saying: 'yes, of course,' brings immediate relief to the enquirer.

We had a small permanent staff and a seasonal staff establishment in excess of two hundred. Surprisingly, it was not difficult to recruit staff for the season, and most stayed until the closing week with many returning again the following year. When looking back now, in some respects, with the sole exception of the Unions attitudes, our work retained some resemblance to the Army. I used to hold weekly management meetings attended by Heads of Departments. Minutes were taken by my very efficient Secretary. Tasks were set with clear instructions on what had to be achieved. There the similarity with the Army ended. I had been trying not to be too "military" in my approach and more inclined to "request" staff to do certain tasks, rather than issuing "instructions, "orders" or "dispatches". A sort of soft approach? It simply did not work. Engaging high gear, I reverted to the military way of doing things by setting the task, getting the person to agree to it, and, naturally a deadline for completion. There was the proviso that, if it could not be achieved in the time agreed, the employee would report back with good reasons for failure. In such a way, there could be no misunderstanding. The following week those who had completed whatever tasks were agreed on time would receive praise; those who had failed would have shown up their weaknesses and seen to be letting the side down. Today, any H.R. Department would throw a fit applying all sorts of protocols and procedures to my thinking but, my way worked, and those who changed for the better were, in my opinion, better fitted out for life in the future. The system succeeded, the team was beginning to mould into a fine shape.

I was disappointed with the way some of the staff looked after their accommodation, particularly amongst the men. Many of the younger, seasonal staff had probably not been away from home before, and were not used to doing things for themselves, much like Army recruits on arrival in the barracks. In the Army, accommodation was regularly inspected with the familiar bawl from the Sergeant Major of: 'stand by your beds'. Everything had to be immaculate so it soon became second nature to the recruit. The seemingly ridiculous habit of boxing blankets and sheets served the purpose of recruits having to shake them before boxing off, which was a cunning way of getting air to their bedding every day. Such an idea, while attractive in its way was a bridge too far at Pontins, particularly 'standing by your beds'. But what did work, was to tell staff in advance, some of the chalets were going to be visited each week by the manager. If they wanted to be in attendance, this would be welcomed. As an incentive, there would be a weekly prize for the best chalet, with results published on the staff notice board for all to see. The girls always won.

Trouble arose one day when a staff chalet was found to have been trashed. A local lad had had an affair with one of our young female kitchen porters. As so often at that age, she became fed up with him, fell in love with someone else, a member of staff, and attempted to ditch the local lad. He took exception and this triggered a reaction of hitting out blindly. One night he drove to the back of the camp, and not only trashed her chalet but injured her quite badly. He was nearly caught, but legged it back over the fence and scarpered before he could get to his car. The Entertainment Manager reported the incident to me so we could decide on a plan of action. I told him to use his airborne initiative. (repeats like this can get boring but I need to make the point). The next morning the Head Gardener came into my office distraught. His prized rockery had disappeared.

'Overnight Sir! Not a bloody thing. Not a rock, not a stone, not a bleedin' pebble.'

The intruder from the night before, had made the mistake of leaving his car behind having made his escape over the fence. As a result, the Entertainments Team removed every single stone from the prize rockery and threw them, one by one, with as much force as they could muster, into the car, smashing every window to pieces and ruining the interior of the car. Justice was not only done but seen to be done.

While a complete cleaning programme was put into effect after Easter, there were several arson attempts to set fire to some of the chalet blocks. It was more than a worry. Attempts to burn them down had been made by turning on an electric hob and placing a pile of bedding on the red-hot rings. On each occasion, the cleaning staff managed to raise the alarm before the fire got out of control and the speedy responses by the local fire services saved the day. To counter our arsonist, the power was turned off at the mains but further attempts were made demanding we try to catch the culprit. By checking staff rotas, we discovered that the son of one of the chalet cleaners, someone of a dodgy character, happened to be working on each of the days when the arson attempts were made. It led to the conclusion it was too much of a coincidence. When interviewed, he seemed very nervous, further raising our suspicions. Nothing could be proved, but keeping a close eye on him, we chanced our luck by dismissing him for poor attendance when he was late for work twice. There were no more attempts to set fire to the chalets. Arsonist 0. Camber Sands 1.

Apart from the Christmas and Easter holidays, the camp was only open for the summer months. One of my tasks was to find other organisations to use our facilities in the shoulder months outside of the summer's bucket and spade brigade. The only organisation already booked in was a well-known religious group who had traditionally reserved the camp for several weeks immediately after Easter. One strong point Pontins retained, was being renown for its cleanliness, so when this group sent a strong advance party of cleaners and started to clean everything from top to bottom, leaving our staff with nothing to do, I found it more than mildly offensive. Their message was clear; our standards were not good enough for them. I then looked into the rate they were paying and was surprised to find how little this was. It made it all the more reason to identify other organisations to take their place. The group even stuck large pieces of brown paper over the windows of our shop, amusement arcade, sports hall and the bar, as if to say they did not want to contaminate their congregation with such things. To add insult to injury, on the day they departed I was presented with a brown envelope full of ten pound notes which I refused to accept until my Assistant Manager, put me in the picture. There was a pecking order of renumeration for all the Heads of Departments and if I refused to accept their money, it could jeopardise what they received as the organisation could take it as a sign of contempt. We had a few good nights out at their expense.

The group wanted to book again for next year, but by putting up the price by several hundred percentage points to encourage them to go elsewhere, they resorted to complain to Head Office. But I stuck to my guns, and we never saw them again and managed eventually to fill the gaps with some interesting organisations, who were prepared to pay commercial rates.

The first seasonal staff to arrive for the summer season were the Bluecoats (Butlins call theirs, Redcoats) and it was fun watching them rehearse their shows which were professional and very enjoyable, entertaining. We attended auditions to select two groups of musicians we needed to engage for the season; a showband for the ballroom and a group for the night club, known as the Rye Bar.

The few permanent staff lived locally, including a superb team of maids who looked after the chalet cleaning, administrative staff, two assistant managers, head chef, head gardener and tradesmen. Shortly after my arrival I had a difficult run in with the chef who was not happy with his salary and had threatened to leave unless given a respectable increase. Not wanting to lose him nor to increase his salary, thus distorting the remuneration paid to the other staff, I mentioned this to the Regional Director who had known him for a number of years. On his next visit he agreed to interview the chef in my presence. He said: 'I believe you have been offered a job on the oil rigs so wanted to wish you all the best. Please let David know when you will you be leaving so we can give your successor a starting date'. I liked his style and we never heard any more about a pay rise.

A good working relationship with the Entertainments Manager and his staff began to develop. They were all exceptionally professional at their jobs and always popular with the guests. One member of staff was a professional football player who worked with one of the sports organisers. He was at a loose end for the summer and looking for a change. Towards the end of the season he took off for the States where he found a job as a personal fitness instructor at an exclusive club in Florida. He kept sending us messages about his latest adventures and the last I heard from him he had been employed by a wealthy widow as her personal trainer with not only a good salary but a house and a sleek sports car. The phrase: "falling on your feet" seems to come to mind.

Our Head of Security had taken his job in retirement after serving forty years as an Inspector with the Hong Kong Prison Service. He was normally quite a reserved person, that is, until he had a few drinks when he would open up on his past life. One of his stories was when he was called into the Governor's office to be asked if he would like to accept the job of Hong Kong's official executioner. Capital punishment was still extant in those days in the Colony. He felt it quite useful to mention he had had no experience of hanging a turkey, let alone a human being, but, how do you practice for such a job? He mentioned to the Governor he had had no experience of being a hangman, but, after some interesting discussions as to how he might become an expert, he was persuaded by the salary increase to accept the job offered.

His book could be a best seller.

I arrived at a time when new regulations were being introduced into Britain for the operation of swimming pools. It was arranged, I would attend a short course run by the Royal Life Saving Institution. As a result I became the acknowledged "expert" on swimming pool safety for the Pontins Group, resulting in being tasked with running courses for all the lifeguards in all our holiday centres, some twenty-four altogether. Amongst other things learnt, was the need for a greater number of lifeguards than were currently employed. This was to allow for frequent changes, such as the maximum time a lifeguard could remain alert, being now judged to be twenty minutes.

Whilst on the subject of lifeguards, I received a disturbing telephone call from a News of the World reporter one Saturday. He was in Rye to write a story about one of our members of staff and wanted to interview me to find out why we had employed a lifeguard who had been certified as HIV positive. I assured him this was absolutely not our policy. They gave me his name and we agreed to meet that afternoon as the newspaper was going to publish the story the following day regardless of whether or not I agreed to meet him. If he was HIV positive, the information should have been recorded on his employment application and a quick check revealed that it was not. Our Head of Security contacted the local police station on the old boy net where the lifeguard lived. Not only were they aware that he was HIV positive, but he also had a police record. The lifeguard was interviewed and dismissed on the spot for Gross Misconduct. When the reporter duly arrived to write his story, I was able to say he was no longer employed by us, thus diluting the story. Although a watered-down version was published the next day, we managed to avert what could have been a major PR damage reparation.

During the summer season, the programme included various sporting competitions and new regulations were coming onto my desk all the time. One such Government requirement required all sports staff to hold the new Sports Organisers Certificate. Fortunately, I had some contacts at the Army Physical Training Corps School in Aldershot, so managed to enlist support in arranging for one of the instructors to volunteer to run a course for us, not only for my resort but all the other Pontins resorts. An arrangement was made whereby one of his Senior Instructors would run the course in exchange for his family to enjoy a complimentary holiday at our centre. On the first day a rather motley collection of Bluecoats showed up, including several girls who were late, dishevelled and half-awake after a late night. They were in for a surprise. Apart from a dressing down they had to endure the humiliation of fifty press-ups in front of the class. The instructor said anyone who was late again would be kicked off the course. He also mentioned that Army time was always five minutes early. No one was late again.

Surprisingly, no qualifications were required for the weekly donkey derby.

The one competition I disliked most of all was the talent competition. Each week, monotonously, at least one guest would sing: 'I did it my way.' I never want to hear that bloody song again.

If faced with a tricky staff problem, it was always best to deal with it face on, rather than kicking the can down the road. We had a new trainee Administration Manager who unfortunately, had a body odour problem. The girls in the office asked if I could do something about it, but I thought it was a matter for the Admin. manager to deal with so I hauled him into the office and told him to sort it out. He found it too delicate a matter to deal with so, handing it back to me, I got the lad in the office and told him straight out that his level of hygiene was unacceptable and not fair on the others in the office. He was mortified but clearly unaware of the problem. But that did not solve the issue as the odour persisted because, although his personal hygiene improved, he omitted to have his clothes dry cleaned. After a visit to the cleaners, everyone was happy.

Young trainee managers learning the ropes would always need watching carefully. Some spent time skulking around, disinclined to engage with the guests. One of them never cleaned his shoes and was a bit of a scruff bag. I told him to sort himself out by cleaning his shoes every day and to smarten himself up, also, to mingle with the guests. He was a very likeable person and responded well to advice. Every time we met he would say: *'still mingling.'*

Every year, to remind me of my lost life, I liked to go to the Military Tattoo in London or attend the Beating of Retreat on Horseguards and thought it would be good to invite my Assistant Manager and a couple of others members of staff who had not experienced the thrill of these events. I discovered the Tattoo was sold out during a visit by the Guinness representative who, sensing my disappointment, mentioned, he might be able to get some tickets. He contacted his office and not only did he get us four tickets, but an invitation to attend a pre-tattoo Royal Reception. On arrival, the Master of Ceremonies asked each of us for our names and in a loud voice introduced us to the other guests and members of the Royal Family. One of our member's of staff had a broad Lancashire accent so when introducing him the Master of Ceremonies thought he was a Brigadier. Thereafter, and forever, he became known as the Brigadier.

As the end of a season moved closer, it became something of a tradition for me to invite Heads of Departments, girls in the office, and some of the band, to a barbeque. Careful not to upset neighbours, I made a point of inviting them as well, thus ensuring, noise arising from the revelry and music did not offend sensitive ears. At one particularly successful party where I happened to know the Commanding Officer of The Royal Irish Rangers, based in Dover. I asked him if the Pipes and Drums could put on a performance in the ballroom during an event we were hosting – the British Majorettes National Championships. The Pipe Major had heard about the staff party and offered to come along later with some of his pipers and drummers to provide some entertainment for us, which turned out to be a storming success. In those days the Army was always keen to ensure it was *'keeping the Army in the public eye,'* and he offered to speak to the Director of Music, so the visit would be on a voluntary basis. The whole band, pipes and drums wanted to come along and the deal was, they could bring their families and enjoy complimentary accommodation. As one family put it: *'Wow!'* To cap it all, on the Sunday morning the band, pipes and drums led a parade of two thousand majorettes around the camp, something, almost certainly Pontins had never experienced before.

I did find it surprising when Head Office staff turned up for a visit without any pre- announcement, as if they were trying to catch us out. In the Army, visits were always planned in advance and everyone knew who the visitors were. One of the auditors, who was ex- Services, confided in me, that not many years before, one of the managers somehow got away with letting out a whole chalet block for himself, with revenue going into his personal bank account. This may have been the reason for the unannounced visits.

As General Manager, the working day extended from early morning to midnight when the show bands and Rye Bar closed, so it was not possible to be present all the time making oneself available to staff and guests. This suited me well because most afternoons in the summer I would head off to the Rye Tennis Club. Through the Club, I met a number of members who had their own tennis courts in the local area, usually local residents with oast houses, vineyards and smart homes who liked to gather together in the afternoons for a couple of hours of tennis. As most of the men were at work, I was something of a 'spare man', obliged, well…delighted, to be invited to these events which were followed by tea, scones, strawberry jam and cream in that order, in their gardens. Better to be strengthening relations with the locals than waiting around for Head Office staff, too impolite to let one know they were visiting. Most of these staff would ask to see the General Manager. When mentioning I was not around when they visited, my reply when I did talk to them, was to say I had been given no advance knowledge of their visit and suggested, the next time they should let me know in advance. The habit was, however, well engrained and I never did make much headway with it. Sir Fred Pontin was a good example. He lived in the area and liked to visit but would never let me know in advance. He was popular with the guests and enjoyed getting up on the stage at lunch times to say a few words. When he wished everyone a Happy New Year at Easter you could see there was a slight problem arising in the future.

Most of our guests came from the south of England, particularly the East End of London, and during the summer season, these families turned up, determined to have a good time, not only enjoying a packed programme of entertainment, sporting events and children's events but to wallow on Camber Sands' wonderful beach right on our doorstep.

We received very few complaints but to explain the vagaries of this other world balanced by the capriciousness of our guests at times, the idea of how to handle such an operation can differ from day to day.

A lady had brought her granddaughter for a holiday and complained there were fleas in her chalet. Moving on to the defensive, I suggested they could be ticks from sheep grazing the land around us. She disputed this and asked if she could prove it. 'Absolutely, madam.' I agreed with some alacrity though not expecting her to lift up her skirt, pull down her knickers to reveal unmistakably, hundreds of flea bites on her bottom. I did not see it as a bribe when I offered her another chalet, with a full refund, and all meals included as complimentary. The lady was a retired head teacher and called to say thank you at the end of the week. There were no repercussions and I had to assume the bites had retired from her bottom.

Two more ladies complained about the quality of their dinner and insisted on seeing the General Manager. By the time I arrived in the restaurant they had cleared their plates, so it could not have been that bad. But I refunded them the cost of the meal along with a voucher for another meal, having learnt that the best solution was always to be generous. I do believe some guests saw me coming! Or more than some.

One rather more disturbing incident occurred during Darts Week. There was a group of darts players with their wives and supporters occupying a large table in the Rye Bar, including one rather aggressive man who was generously buying rounds of drinks for his group. The bar staff delivered an order including tomato juice for his wife. Unfortunately, the glass had just come out of the dish washer and the bottom of the glass fell off spilling tomato juice over her dress. The end of this affair was never going to finish satisfactorily because her husband went mad, well, not made, per se, but extremely angry, and insisted on seeing the General Manager right away. Fortunately, or unfortunately, I was in the bar at the time and received considerable abuse and no amount of apologising was going to resolve the problem. I suggested we met in my office first thing next morning to resolve the issue. I arranged for my security officer to be present as a witness. Still defiant, he said the dress was very expensive and the only solution was to pay compensation as it was ruined. I suggested we should get it dry cleaned. This infuriated him further, repeating it was a very expensive dress, but trying to draw a line under it, I said that was our final offer, to which he stormed out of the office accompanied by a vocabulary of several unmentionable swear words, last heard of on the Parade Ground. Pondering his aggressive behaviour, he shortly returned with the dress and threw it on the floor instructing us to get it dry cleaned. After a quick look at the Marks and Spencer label, it was taken to the dry cleaners and collected in good time for the lady to wear that evening. In the Army we were taught if you met an obstacle, it is best to go around it. Ignoring him and presenting his wife and mother with bouquets of flowers was the right thing to do. They were delighted. Wife and mother called in at the office to say thank you, commenting that her husband was inclined to get rather excited, but was not a bad person. Later that evening it seemed like his wife had persuaded him to come over and apologise but when I saw him approach out of the corner of my eye, I pretended not to notice him and left. The following night the same thing happened and he offered me a drink. Even though they say the customer is always right, I was not inclined to forgive his behaviour, so declined. The next night was the last night, so the same performance happened again. This time I had a drink with him and as he went back to his table he said: 'you're alright mate'. The following year he greeted me like a long lost friend.

Security problems would quite often arise, caused by intruders climbing over the barbed wire fence during the peak summer period on Fridays and Saturdays and making a nuisance of themselves. A troublesome man stumbled into the Rye Bar to watch the cabaret one night ending up by standing right in front of a family group. When asked to move he told them to *'f**k off'* and just stayed, attached to additional expletives. I was aware that one of the professional wrestlers in one of our shows had fallen for one of our Bluecoats and had formed the habit of staying on for the weekend in her chalet after the wrestling performance on

Friday afternoons. I suggested to him, he could be given permission to stay and provide him with meals, if he could help out with security. He took the work seriously. Next time the intruder came in, the wrestler calmly lifted him up by the seat of his pants and his hair and took him outside. I asked him what happened to the difficult gentleman. He replied: *'You don't want to know, David, but I put him in the picture.'* After a few other similar incidents, we had no more intruders, apart from one totally unpleasant individual who goaded us by saying *'...you can throw me out as often as you like, but I will be back again.'* Late one Saturday night his boots were taken off him and driven miles away to Eastbourne, where he was deposited, without his socks. We never saw him again either. Unorthodox, unlawful – maybe - but effective.

One exception to the rule of not accepting singles, was a Soul Music Weekend, a non-family event and only attended by single people. Before accepting the booking, I spoke to the organisers expressing my concern. I was re-assured by the security company employed by the organisers to manage the event that there would be zero tolerance. The manager was also ex- Army and knew what he was doing. His team constantly patrolled the area and kept in touch by portable radio. He and I were in the bar when a report came in about someone causing a problem. Without a second thought, he was removed from the camp. Word of mouth was the best form of communication. The word got around; there were no more problems.

Out of season special events were beginning to take off and one in particular was memorable because I received my first, real death threat. Every chalet had been booked for the appearance of the *Chas and Dave Weekend*. The roadies arrived late and not enough time had been allowed for setting-up and to complete sound checks with the result that one of the performances ended suddenly, due to power failure. The system had become overloaded and would take time to repair. Fumbling around in the dark looking for candles, I noticed Chas and Dave climbing into their car unaware of the problem they had left with us. I pleaded with them to stay, but they apologised continuing on their way, dropping us in the proverbial. They had no intention of staying. Angry guests started gathering in the reception area asking when the concert was going to resume. Time went on and guests were getting more and more agitated and aggressive. A real mob began to form, slow to start, like Watt Tyler's Peasant Revolt in 1381. It meant we had to pull down the reception security barrier to prevent guests climbing over the counter to threaten us. One singled me out with a death threat, which rather accelerated the idea of doing something. After a discussion with the Entertainments Manager, he announced that the General Manager would address everyone in the Rye Bar, by now packed to the rafters with well over a thousand unhappy guests. (n.b. for unhappy, better to read, *on the warpath*).

I hadn't a bloody clue what to say, but made my way to the Rye Bar flanked by security staff as if I was the Prison Governor interviewing Charles Bronson, where I was confronted by a lady screeching down the microphone getting everyone frothing and foaming at the mouth. After some unpleasantness, I managed to get the microphone off her. A silence hung like Damocles sword over the sweaty mob as everyone pondered on what I was going to say. I told the truth and said we had tried our best to persuade Chas and Dave to wait while the electrics was sorted out, but they had left. Guests had paid for three nights and while Chas and Dave were the main attraction, there were other cabarets and entertainment for everyone to enjoy. If they decided to leave the following morning, they would get a full refund. If they decided to stay, they would all receive a 50% refund. This solution was thought up on the hoof without regard to any financial consequences, but the result was immediate, and a cheer went up; everyone was happy. The man who had threatened to kill me now wanted to be my best friend, but it was a wish which was not going to be granted. There are limits even for an ex-Army officer, and I kept him in the cold.

Having always been a fan of country music, it was exciting to host a Country Music and Western Festival. The camp was at maximum capacity; shortly after the first guests had checked in, I received a deputation from the "Unionists" assemblage who wanted permission to fly their flag at our main entrance. There seemed to be no problem with that until the "Confederacy" deputation turned up also wanting to fly their flag at the main entrance. They were offered the flagpole at the exit gate, but that was not good enough, complaining preferential treatment had been given to the Unionists. A "pow-wow," it seemed the appropriate word, was convened and after some discussion the matter was resolved by allowing both teams to fly their flags at the entrance and exit gates.

A tall, dignified man seen strolling around the camp was the Sheriff, fully equipped with two six shooters and the obligatory black hat; he played a most solemn and sombre part for the whole week. On the second day of the Festival, he approached me and after taking a cautious look around to make sure nobody could hear, rather like a cliché, second-hand car salesman, he sought permission to ambush the noddy train which trundled around the camp packed full of children every hour or so. He wanted to capture the female Bluecoat who travelled for security purposes in the rear seat. She was made up to be a Unionist and the Confederates sought to hold her for ransom. (Are you still with me on this?). The Bluecoats were warned what was going to happen and all was agreed - "as long as rape was not involved", affirmed the Bluecoat with a twinkle in her eye. She was duly captured and tied up, thoroughly enjoying the experience.

The next day the Sheriff again approached me to say they wanted to stage a hanging. I mentioned we had been a bit short on hangings lately, so the same girl was selected and enjoyed all the attention she received during her mock trial. She did not bat an eyelid at the noose. At the end of each evening there came the flag ceremony in the ballroom, with participants of both the Unionists and Confederates blessing their respective flags accompanied by stirring music. It was, in my simplistic view, very realistic and quite emotional with participants openly weeping as the finale was celebrated. The guest of honour at our festival was a well-known country singer from Nashville, Tennessee. His singing brought the house down. It was a great pleasure for me to invite him and his wife to stay in my bungalow overnight, but I never took up his offer to stay with them in Nashville.

At the end of my first summer season, the camp closed down. I had forgotten the gates would be locked overnight, so arriving back from a night out in Rye, I discovered, to my annoyance, I also was locked out. The high fencing which surrounded the whole camp with its string of barbed wire along the top, was clearly designed to keep people out. However, using my *airborne initiative,* I attempted to climb over and although I succeeded in getting in, thus avoiding a night in the car, I managed to tear my trousers and cut my leg, requiring stitches. So, two things here. 1. Quite an effective barrier and 2. I was not very good at climbing over a barbed wire fence, which, once I might have done in very different circumstances.

It was at this time my marriage dived again, this time permanently. This gave me the opportunity to get out of the bungalow where I would be locked in at the end of the season removing the need for escape committees! Driving around, I came across a property which would suit me in the nearby village of Peasmarsh. It meant becoming integrated with a new community of great neighbours, including Paul McCartney. Meeting Paul outside the school and the village shop on several occasions, I was impressed by his friendliness and ability to remain at the same level as all the locals.

I joined the Hastings and District Conservative Association and was pleased to be invited to a social event in the village, to meet our local MP. Introduced to him with: 'Have you met David before? He runs the Pontins place at Camber Sands, you know.' He replied: 'Jolly good,' and promptly moved on to talk to somebody else more likely to vote for him at the next election. Later in the evening, someone else introduced me to the same man with: 'Have you met Colonel Fairs?' Apart from not remembering we had already been introduced, he said rather gushingly: 'Colonel how jolly nice to meet you and how are you settling into our community, blah-blah'.

I omitted to renew my membership the following year on the basis my vote could have put him into the House of Commons and then where would be?

Invitations continued to flow in. I was encouraged to join the annual village fête committee run by the church and, as I had some experience of these things, felt my contribution could be of value. The first meeting was in the Vicarage, but one (dear) lady objected because she had never seen me at any of the church services. The Vicar overruled her and for the next five years some of the staff at Pontins contributed greatly to the success of the fêtes, relishing becoming involved by supporting the local community.

As mentioned above, I was fortunate to have very good neighbours in Peasmarsh. This included (another) dear old lady who lived next door in a small, wooden house. We would chat over the fence like two washer women. Whenever we were having a party, she would always be invited; her reply was always the same: 'It is wonderful to see you young people enjoying yourselves.'. One day she was not there anymore and there was someone in her garden burning her carpets. I asked him what he was doing. It was her son who gave me a pretty dusty reply with instructions to mind my own business. Making enquiries, I discovered she had been admitted to hospital. Visiting her, I asked why her son was burning her carpets and discovered he had decided she would be better off in a retirement home, and he was busy emptying her house. Seeking to find out why she wanted to leave, it was soon clear she loved her house and did not want to leave, but her grabbing son wanted to get his hands on her house. Looking into it further, it seemed her main anxiety was keeping the garden in good shape. Not a problem, I told her, and the next day some the gardeners at Pontins volunteered to join me in sorting out the garden for her return from hospital. We arranged a welcome party for her and she was delighted with her rejuvenated garden. The son was told to get lost in plain language, and for the next couple of years, one of our gardener's volunteered to spent an evening a week in his own time looking after the garden for her. It was a great pleasure to see them taking tea together in her garden and chatting about her plants.

•••

Ownership of Pontins changed hands twice during my time there as a manager, and we became part of Scottish and Newcastle plc, which also owned Langdale Leisure Limited, a luxury resort in the English Lake District. After the take-over I was privileged if very uncertain to be asked to move north to run it, the resort that is, not the brewery! Not for a moment did I regret going to Camber Sands; it was just one big family. I greatly enjoyed my six years there, but I was being asked to move my career forward another notch and I had to take it up. The Lake District was calling, a big unknown to me, and a challenge as well.

CHAPTER 10

My Breakthrough, The Langdale Estate

"Let nature be your teacher." William Wordsworth

The Lakes lie at latitude 53 degrees 27 minutes north with the UNESCO World Heritage site occupying 2,362 square kilometres of pure, unadulterated Cumbria. Some of you, many of you perhaps, will have visited the area at some time as the park receives 15.8 million visitors each year despite eighty inches of rain falling on the sodden shoulders of these walkers. Daniel Defoe described the region after he had visited it as '*… the wildest, most barren and frightful of any that I have passed over in England or even in Wales.*' So, he seemed to have got this one wrong but, when I went to work there, all I could think of was my house in East Sussex with a six-hour drive from door to door. This I made every two or three weeks, planning the best times to travel to avoid the madness of the motorways at the weekends.

All this is a lead-in to the idea of a breakthrough, confusing in itself, for I found it difficult and trying in coming to terms with The Langdale Estate which I did not know and had no affinity for, like sharing a leaky boat with Daniel Defoe.

Pontins directors, in their wisdom, decided I should take over the management of the up-market (very) timeshare resort and hotel in the Lake District. The reason for this decision to move me was unclear at the time. I believed it to be my ability to manage, profitably, any operation in hospitality. The owners of the one hundred timeshare units, were, privately, appalled that 'someone from one of those *"Hi-de-Hi camps" is going to run Langdale.'* And a lot more in a similar vein, I could have added.

Pulling out the books on my arrival, and sitting down with the accountant, revealed the real reason for my appointment. The whole place – timeshare, hotel, spa, Wainwright's pub and an exclusive country house – were losing money at an unacceptable rate. My job was, quite simply, to turn it around to allow the whole shooting match to be sold. This would involve me as well; being dumped later, that is. It just did not fit into the brewery's plans which was self-evident from the manner in which they had by-passed deploying any investment for years. I would be useful – for a time - but, on success, disposable material.

There was anger, rage, intense annoyance at the manner in which I had become a soft target, and an Army officer at that! I should have seen it coming. But, I had worn, not only a red beret but a green one; at that first meeting I resolved to use all of my skills learned over twenty-five years in the Army to bring the Estate to a level of excellence the owners had yet to experience.

As I had driven up the M6 for the first time, turning off for Kendal, I took in the absolute beauty of my new world. The fells dropped away; stone walls, hundreds of years old, proudly stamped out farmers' boundaries. As I drew nearer, I saw a woodland wrapping itself around the Estate like a green, warm blanket and beyond, like a moat to its castle, ran a brook. Here I was to live, though for months, I had to take any empty room available, making me a wandering hermit, a recluse with no roots, forever hankering after my cosy and settled life in the south. I need to point out here, however, not all my boats had been burnt. My house in Peasmarsh still existed, with my daughter Elly keeping it safe and secure. It could still prove to be a safe haven if a storm blew up out of the blue.

There will be readers mystified at the manner in which I had accepted a post at a timeshare. The concept of timesharing had gone through a very mixed reaction over the years from those who '...liked it very much' to, '...I don't like it all'. Costly management fees, continually rising each year, based on feebly, thought out excuses by the directors regarding costs of running such an establishment did not help its image. And, here I was, my car loaded up with my possessions, eyeing up the tired entrance signs and already having experienced the surliness of the staff at the Estate's pub. The fifty acre site was not only beaten and worn out, but exhausted of ideas. There was a singular lack of training which had been replaced with arrogance – the Estate knows best…always.

The first urgent action was to bring all of the staff together which was achieved following my introduction to them by one of the Pontins directors. The fact they were told I had come directly from Camber Sands caused several smirks behind discarded menus in some quarters. It only reinforced my desire to get cracking as soon as the director had departed for his comfortable office.

Freed of any directorial direction, I began to relate to the staff, my incognito visit to Wainwright's Inn where, despite being in time for supper I was informed: *'We've stopped cooking now.'* There had been no apology. I told the many staff, now much more silent and cautious, that such attitudes were going to stop, 'today' if they wanted to keep their job. Play the game, learn to become a professional, make the guest the most important person in the world, was to be their daily mantra from now on. More silence, but I noticed some were nodding their heads in agreement, others perhaps even of approval.

It became essential that I walk round the Estate every day to enable me to get to know the layout, the weaknesses, the owners and my guests. Out in the open, away from my depressing hotel bedroom which had to be "home" for me, I found agreeable company, and often a welcome cup of coffee at many a lodge where views were expressed which proved useful. I learned quickly, that if any issue was disturbing or upsetting an owner, it was best to tackle it head-on the same day. It showed my willingness to co-operate while keeping the 'Action' file at a non-stressful level. The owners were able to see immediate improvements were on their way. Nevertheless, while wishing to please the owners, the priority, every time, came back to costs which were disproportionately high against revenue. Of these, as always, were salaries which had become wildly out of control. Where ever I looked there were too many of everything. Too many managers (that old chestnut), too many Heads of Department with the sales staff on laughably high commissions. As for consultants, enough to say there were too many chiefs and not enough Indians.

My plans to deal with this main issue began in a small way. Then, like Topsy, they grew, verily. Purdy's Restaurant in the hotel had a resident pianist and guests were able to enjoy a tinkle on the keys as they ate. I asked him to play a tune for me, receiving a mumble about the Musicians Union which required him to take a break…at that very minute. Fair enough?

When he returned he had forgotten my request – I'm being kind – and, soon after, closed the piano up for the night, much earlier than his contract stated. Next morning, looking at his Terms of Agreement, even I could work out he was very overpaid for the little time he spent entertaining the guests. His own good time was, shortly, to come to an abrupt end; I had a cunning idea.

I drew up a business plan based on purchasing a piano which could play itself, using CDs. I balanced the cost against the man's continuing employment. The scales came down firmly on my side, a "no-brainer" is the term, with pay-back within twelve months. The pianist became my first redundancy. The advantages kept coming, for the piano was able to play throughout the day, with no Musicians Union involvement, and could continue as long as diners were eating in the restaurant.

A nice touch, I think arose when a small child remarked one day: 'No-one is playing the piano mummy.' Indeed so. We were surrounded on all sides by sheep so I came up with the idea of having a Herdwick sheep, the animal which dominates the Fells, made of cloth and stuffing, which went ahead, although there was a slight delay as the first model turned out like an ass, or rather for decorum's sake, a donkey. Success with the second, meant it could be sent to its new home sitting on the piano stool pretending to play the ivories. The end of this story is that 'Larry' remained at the keyboard for many years until some bastard stole him one dark night. Unknowingly to the thief, Larry had been chipped. The thief must have heard of this device so ensuring Larry's safe return to the entrance gates of the Estate one day. He was much loved, to the extent I placed him on the payroll despite my need to get the costs down!

When costs do get out of control in any company, the rot spreads like gangrene to every cost centre. One small area had been the piano…now I focussed on a much larger leak, a veritable open sluice gate. Sales.

Whenever the sales office made a timeshare sale, a bell would be rung in the office, a bottle of champagne would be opened and one of them would rush into my office seeking to be congratulated. They were paid reasonable salaries and earned high commission for each sale. I was aware most sales had been generated by existing owners looking for an additional week, so the sale had nothing to do with their sales skills. Investigating it further, and taking into account commissions paid, the profit margins were quite limited. Taking a huge risk, the positions of Sales Manager, Assistant Sales Manager and Salesman were made redundant. The office staff proved themselves quite capable of taking telephone sales enquiries and greeting prospective customers visiting the office. Future sales resulted in the doubling of profit and accomplishing a reduction in the wage bill, ensured we were starting to get our costs down.

The wealthier one is, the more inclined you are to seek discounts. From time to time a secretary to one of the directors of the brewery, or Pontins, would give me a call to ask for complimentary accommodation for some important person or other. My standard reply was, I had been sent to Langdale to turn the business around, converting their loss into a profit, and it would be inappropriate to reduce prices. That would always set the cat amongst the pigeons, resulting in a call from the director himself explaining how important it was to look after so-and-so. Reluctantly I would offer a reduction of just five percent. Not much of a concession but they were then happy to have succeeded in negotiating a discount. The only sensible reductions I did give were to the parents of staff wanting to stay in the hotel in the interest of good staff morale.

From my arrival, I introduced weekly management meetings attended by all Heads of Departments. It was not only useful for allocating work, but keeping everyone informed of the daily changes and issues arising. Minutes were taken and the following week we went over what action had been taken. Not much! It was a talking shop, with all sorts of excuses emerging why this and that could not be done. How unlike the Army where it would have been unthinkable for action not to be taken. The gulf remained; the professionalism of the Army was always going to win in such circumstances.

Here it was different and that had to be sorted out right away. This was Pontins all over again. It was a malaise rife in the country at the time. Do as little as one could get away with. My thoughts at the time were that any meeting had become a total waste of time and I might as well go out selling bananas in the local market rather than listen to excuse after excuse. It was infuriating. I was trying my best not to follow the Army way of doing things, rather to seek the co-operation of everyone by asking them, politely, to accept their personal responsibility and execute their allocated workload. It simply did not work. So, I reverted to the tried and tested Army style, again, instructing everyone given a task, to agree to take ownership of it and get it done, and by an agreed time. If, for any reason it could not be done, to report back well before the weekly meeting with a damn good reason why not. The currency of what appeared to be laziness, an abrogation of any responsibility began to have a sea change.

Over the next twelve months we sold all the off-site accommodation and built more staff accommodation on the Estate, which turned out to be the best decision to have been taken. There was an attractive, Lakeland cottage called Brackens tucked away on the edge of the Estate, occupied by several Heads of Departments. I was reluctant to check this out at first, to avoid offending the occupants, who I thought, as Heads of Departments would be more responsible. I could not have been more wrong. Looking through a window from the outside on one of my regular walks, it was disturbing to see the garden in such a mess. I warned the occupants of my intention of taking a look inside and invited them to be in attendance if they so wished. Behold yet again, communal areas absolutely out of control, with nobody taking responsibility for looking after them and each blaming another. The cooker, refrigerator and freezer were in such a bad condition they had to be scrapped. Every time they had a barbeque, the ashes were tipped on the lawn with rubbish littering the site. This presented me with a solution to my accommodation problem. In agreement with the Pontins director I was directly responsible to, I cleaned the cottage from top to bottom, re-kitted it out, moved my own possessions in where they now had a good chance of remaining in place and sat down with a contented sigh. Home. I realised I was beginning to think less and less of my house in the south.

In a further effort to control costs, I discovered there was no purchase order system and Heads of

Departments could buy whatever they liked. To start the ball rolling, and giving the Financial Controller time to establish a system, Heads were instructed to obtain advanced approval for all purchases during the interim period; not an unreasonable arrangement bearing in mind our dire financial situation. At lunch time, one Friday, I discovered an invoice for a large amount that had not been cleared in advance. I tried to contact the man responsible but was told he had gone off for the weekend and would not be back until midday on Monday. Not only was he going to miss the weekly management meeting that afternoon, but had not sought permission for the time off. Feeling more than irritated, I had to wait until Monday afternoon before he was gracious enough to put in an appearance, and spare the time to come and see me. He advised me that as a Head of a Department he did not consider it necessary to extend the courtesy of seeking permission for extra time off. Neither did he consider it necessary to seek permission to purchase a cover for the back of the new company pick-up truck, costing several thousand pounds. We parted company by the end of the week when his position was made redundant and his perfectly capable assistant took over.

I was invited to attend a Sales and Marketing meeting attended by several consultants employed at great expense to give us the benefit of their long experience in the industry. After half an hour or so I realised I had no idea what they were talking about, so made my excuses. Learning we were all headed for Oxenholme Station to go on the same train to London that afternoon I took a lift in the duty vehicle while they took taxis. Meeting up on the platform, one of them suggested we could travel together. The only problem was to find they were travelling First Class, while I had booked a standard class ticket. Naturally. To save any unease, I paid extra to accompany them. Having been looking forward to two or three hours relaxing with a book, instead, I had to listen to an unending session of sales and marketing speak, also known as blather, all of which I found utterly boring, and worse, incomprehensible. None of it related to my day to day activities. Back at Langdale a few days later, and checking what it was costing us to enjoy the pleasure of their consultancy advice, I discovered, not only were they being paid pretty high retainers, but displayed no restraint in selecting the most expensive items off the menu at dinner, and enjoyed several bottles of our most expensive wines. Another saving was achieved by making their positions redundant. Amazingly, no-one missed them at all and another cost saving had been achieved. Not that I enjoyed getting rid of people for the sake of it, but if I failed to get the business under control it would be my head that would have been on the block.

Recalling the priority the Army placed on its presentation to the public, with impressive large shiny signs and flags at the camp entrances, large new slate signs and several flag poles were ordered and erected at the entrance to the Estate, replacing the rather old and tatty ones. One flag pole was for the union flag, the other for the English flag and the third would be in honour of any foreign guests staying on the Estate, mainly Americans, staying in the hotel. This coincided (collided?) with the Langdale Society, a self-appointed group of unelected local whingers and whiners whose main aim appeared to be to put a stop to anything new or innovative happening in the Langdale Valley. They began with me, making a great fuss about our flags and said they represented unwanted commercialism and if they were not removed, they would complain to the local authorities. I had done my homework and learnt that planning permission was not required for displaying national flags, only commercial flags. I told them to take a sharp turn to the right and fall out. That did it. They did complain to the local authority only to discover, pretty quickly, they were mistaken – plain wrong in other words.

All this fuss led the "Society" to invite me to one of their meetings where one of them mentioned they had a love/hate relationship with the Estate – they loved us because of the money we gave them, but hated us because we were there. They offered no apologies for being intolerant, so it became the last time I had any anything to do with them.

In sharp contrast to this flaccid group, I developed a good working relationship with the elected members of the Owners' Committee. It was the custom to meet regularly, and their responsibility was to represent the over four thousand lodge owners; mine, to carry out their instructions. We did not always see eye to eye and had some heated debates. I had to remind them it was their job to tell me, as head of the operating team, what they wanted to achieve, while it was my duty to carry it out. No matter how many differences of opinions raised their furrowed heads at our meetings, we always made light of them afterwards and enjoyed some enjoyable dinners, getting together after each meeting. We were a good team and I wondered if the other owners realised just how lucky they were to have such capable and professional representatives looking after their interests. These committee members became board members later when Langdale Leisure Ltd was purchased on behalf of the owners and so the relationship continued when they became directors.

•••

One of the lodge owners, Tricia, had mentioned calling in for coffee on her next visit. Never slow to come forward, I called to find her lodge full with family and friends, including her sister, Denise, who she had not previously mentioned. A puzzle to solve when I called in, it took very little time before there was only one other person in the room, as we shared kayaking experiences and a whole raft (sorry) of other experiences we had in common. I was totally captivated and could not wait to see her again but it left this impossible situation of gaining enough courage to ask her out. And me, the man who jumped out of a plane eighty times!

Just before Christmas and acting completely out of character, I asked Tricia to ask Denise if she would like to go out for dinner with me. Coward is the word here. Tricia was not sure, and thought it best to leave it until the New Year. Patience is not one of my virtues, but as much out of curiosity as anything, I suspect, she agreed to meet me when, finally, my invitation was received.

But, disaster loomed. It was going to prevent me seeing Denise, and after all the planning which had been going on in my head. Sitting back in an armchair with friends, chatting away while at the same time eating nuts and drinking wine, a nut became lodged in my windpipe, preventing me from breathing. Managing to get the occasional gulp of air and feeling quite alarmed, I was taken to hospital where the nut was removed. Due to scarring of my throat, I lost the ability to speak. I was advised my voice would gradually return over a couple of weeks. In the meantime, and determined not to miss our date, we met at an Italian restaurant in Lancaster, where I had to communicate, like Beethoven with his Conversation Books with his friends, across the table to Denise as best I could. I assumed the evening would put her off for life having to listen to my croaky voice (not exactly sounding like Richard Burton) instead, resorting to passing Denise written notes. I had to assume this would be the last time we would meet. No-one wants to go out with a frog sounding like a toad on heat.

Strange, we have been happily married ever since.

Long before smoking was banned in most public buildings, I introduced a no-smoking policy in the lodges and the hotel. This generally went down well, except for the staff. I announced at one of the management meetings that the same rules must apply to staff and they could only light up outside. One smoker at the meeting asked how they were going to manage if it was raining, when they could catch pneumonia. 'Better than dying of lung cancer,' I replied.

Front of House is the focal point of any leisure resort or hotel and it is critically important that its appearance and quality of staff were both second to none. Initial impressions when guests arrived were all important –

the first point of sale - and could set the scene for the whole of their stay. Asking if an arriving couple had had a good journey and knowing they had been before meant they would be welcomed back in a different manner to people visiting for the first time. Get that wrong and you are off to a poor start. Everybody wants the check-in procedure to be as quick and as efficient as possible allowing them to settle into their hotel room or lodge with as little inconvenience as possible.

Observing arrivals and checking-in procedures on one occasion, I noticed one of the receptionists was rather grumpy and taking her to one side later, I discovered she had had a bust up with her boy friend, so I went easy on her. Aiming to boost her confidence, I remarked a few days later how well she looked. Rather than accept the compliment she replied: *'Are you implying that I don't always look good?'* Ho, hum.

There were often serious billing problems when guests were checking out, as when someone was being charged for a bottle of wine they said they had not ordered. Most people would be quick to draw attention to such an error; conversely, many would keep quiet if they were not billed for a bottle of wine they had downed the night before. Testing the system, I found it happened to me as well. This was all due to a lack of training and unless sorted, would lead to a continuing loss of revenue. To exacerbate the problem, Front of

House staff had not been permitted to adjust a bill, but would have to tell departing guests a cheque would be forwarded to them, because the Accounts Office was located in Kendal, some twenty miles away. That made no sense at all but the problem was quickly resolved by closing down the office in Kendal and moving the whole Accounts Department onto the Estate. As a result, Front of House staff were authorised to make bill adjustments at their own discretion without reference to anyone.

Every Monday evening, owners were invited to a bucks fizz and canopies reception. This was an opportunity for everyone to meet and for us to explain what was happening on the Estate. There would usually be a good turnout and it was always a pleasure to greet owners and visitors alike. What would annoy me considerably was a guest, with a long-standing grudge, whinging on about some nebulous impossibility, which they clung to as an orangutang baby clings to its mother. This was never the time to bring it up, the grouse not the orangutang that is. My reply invariably was to suggest a short get-together after the meeting. One such was a complaint about me, when I was accused of badly handling a baby crying incident. The baby was bawling its head off so much that no one could hear what I was saying. I politely asked the mother to take the baby out to avoid disruption. There were lots of nods of approval, but, someone reported me, suggesting I was intolerant towards families. A similar incident occurred at a later date. But I had learnt my lesson and said nothing and carried on until some of the audience shouted out for the mother to take the baby out so they could hear what Mr Fairs had to say. Touché.

We dealt with issues outside of the buildings and the Estate itself. One of our initiatives was to bring support in preserving the Fells. We called it *'Our Man at the Top'*, inviting Langdale visitors to contribute to the payment of wages for an additional member of staff as part of the footpath repair team. Staff were employed by the National Trust. This was hugely popular and well supported by lodge owners and hotel guests alike and continues to be a great success today. It now goes under a different name and is supported by most leisure resorts in The Lake District. We suggested adding £1.00 to their bills, a modest amount to begin with. Our man was kitted out in a Langdale sweatshirt and, to further the link between the Estate and *'Our Man at the Top'* we encouraged visitors to go and see him at work. Not a good idea as it turned out because the number of visitors was overwhelming and with so much chatting, it stopped him working. We quietly dropped the idea by not telling guests where he was working.

Muncaster Castle came into our frame, in particular their owl programme. The castle opened in AD1258, so before my time, so to speak. Whenever they found the time, they would bring some of their birds of prey over to us to give a presentation to lodge owners. During one visit, I was asked if we could look after some orphan barn owl chicks, provided we could offer the right sort of habitat for them. This included an area of uncut grass, which is the habitat of voles, and a suitable tree for a nesting box. The field in front of Elterwater Hall was ideal and our Ground staff were delighted in not having to cut the grass and were agreeable to feeding them frozen day-old chicks imported from Holland. The castle owners fixed the large nesting box at the appropriate level and it was a great delight watching the four chicks develop until they were big enough to fly away. We were all set to repeat the exercise the following year until discovering the European Union had brought in all sorts of new rules that made it untenable. The word 'bonkers' comes to mind very clearly.

As a distraction from my work, which proved a complete waste of time, the Chairman of S & N discovered that the title: "The Lord of the Manor of Langdale" was to be auctioned off in London. His secretary rang asking me to go and bid for it. Carrying out research on the matter, I discovered Feudal

Lordships of the Manor are, today in English property law, legal titles historically dating back to the Norman invasion of 1066. They are incorporated into law and can be bought and sold as historic artifacts just like washing up liquid or Rich Tea biscuits. They have no connection to the House of Lords or British peerages. The purchaser has the legal right to use the honorific title of Lord or Lady of the Manor. Arriving for the auction, I checked the map and discovered, this' Lordship' was in a different place and completely unconnected with The Langdale Valley, some twenty miles away. It seemed pointless to bid, but thought it prudent before making my departure to advise the secretary. She consulted the Chairman and the message was to bid for in anyway. For £10.000, I received a worthless piece of paper in my name thus entitling me to be called Lord of the Manor. What a complete waste of time and money. The document, known as a *Deed of Entitlement* is probably squirreled away in some long-forgotten file, gathering dust. What took the biscuit, was, not once in my life have I been addressed, correctly, as: 'My Lord.' It's the staff, you know.

The Estate bubbled with the news when, one New Year, we received a request from the Hollywood actor, Tom Cruise, and his followers to join us in the hotel for our New Year's Eve Party. The restaurant was fully booked but, pleading with us to help, the hotel staff managed to move things around to fit in an extra table. These actions taken, it almost guaranteed he would not turn up. No, they did not turn up!

Designed to neutralise the excesses of the previous night's party, a New Year's Day, Fell walk with, no less than the General Manager, for hotel guests and lodge owners, was introduced. We would meet on the car park and set off, supported by several leisure club staff with rucksacks full of mince pies, and thermos flasks full of glühwein to celebrate the New Year on top of one of the nearby Fells. New Year's Day had a tendency for the weather to be foul with heavy rain. This time it was no different. Foul, that is and heavy rain with it. I did the sensible thing and went back to sleep. My slumber was interrupted by a frantic call from leisure club staff to say, miraculously the weather had suddenly changed. Something like a hundred keen walkers were waiting in the car park pawing the ground with their boots, ready to start the walk. Like greased lightning, I was out of bed, feeling very guilty, but, eventually forgiven when we reached the top to witness the wonderful view from the top of Loughrigg Fell where we scoffed the mince pies and quaffed the warming glühwein. Before setting off, everyone had had to check in at the club desk to enter their names and, on return, sign out to confirm their safe return. It was normal, sensible procedure which was copied throughout the Lakes. One year there were four missing names and we began to get worried. A search party was despatched, but without success, and after several hours of anxiety, we rang their lodge as a last resort only to discover they had peeled off at Wainwrights Inn, preferring a morning, drinking beer rather than continuing with the walk. No need to ask how we felt about that. And, what happened to the back marker?

•••

Two years after arriving at Langdale, the business had returned to profitability and, in a way, my work was complete. But I had no desire to leave. I had sold my house in East Sussex, had a new home in Kendal, and had been appointed a Director for the Organisation for Timeshare in Europe. Add to all this, I was now a Founder of The Lake District Tourism and Conservation Partnership and I could not think of a better place to live. Contrast this statement to that I made on my arrival two years earlier.

The business was running smoothly, so I turned my attention to new ideas. One involved planning overseas walking holidays for Langdale Owners dove-tailing the two together to provide a unique service. The opportunity presented itself when an Army colleague,

Robin, set up a trekking business in Kathmandu and invited me on a visit. During my stay we developed ideas for taking a group to Annapurna on a trekking holiday. This was an exciting prospect and I could not wait to get involved. Robin had been a Squadron Commander in my Regiment and had decided to take early release from the Army about the same time as me. He had served in a Gurkha unit and spoke good Nepalese and had recently said goodbye to his first group of satisfied customers. He told me how he had been invited by Colonel Jimmy Roberts to operate the hotel and trekking business for him. Jimmy was the pioneer of group trekking in Nepal, and much admired in the trekking fraternity. He had settled in Nepal, taken out Nepalese citizenship and bought a house in *Pokhara*. A confirmed bachelor, he even brought his bearer with him from his old regiment.

It had become something of a tradition to invite clients to the Colonel's house for drinks on his terrace to watch the sun setting over Annapurna. Robin mentioned he had just one rather awkward client who had been complaining about everything and this was having an unsettling effect on the others. The Colonel invited this client into his office and asked him if there was anything he could do to help. The man repeated all the complaints Robin had already told him about. The Colonel said he: '*... already knew all that,*' and asked how much he had paid for the holiday and then wrote out a cheque for the full amount, telling him: *'We clearly cannot meet your expectations and your presence on the tour is terminated. You can leave in the morning and make your own way back to Kathmandu and the UK.'* The guest left the office with his tail between his legs, carried on with the holiday and never uttered a word of complaint again. It was guests like this which greatly complicated our lives in this industry. There was always one and the Colonel's way of dealing with a complaint almost always showed up the flimsiness of the complaint.

The Chairman of S & N was approached by one of the Ministers in the Irish Government seeking advice on a proposed major leisure development including timeshare on the east coast of Ireland. I was flattered to be asked to investigate and report my recommendations. Arriving at Dublin Airport I was greeted by a government Minister and several representatives from interested businesses. A helicopter was placed at our disposal and passing over the Republic of Ireland's Aviva Stadium, famed as a venue for international rugby matches, we set off to carry out a detailed reconnaissance of the site. I quickly came to the conclusion there was little likelihood of the area being sufficiently attractive for such a major investment, but, as a guest in their country, diplomacy prevented me from mentioning this at the time. We dropped down to one of Ireland's best golf clubs and enjoyed a gourmet lunch before returning to Dublin where I was booked into a luxury hotel for the night. Accompanied by some of my helicopter companions, we enjoyed an exceptional dinner in one of Dublin's best restaurants, all at the expense of the Irish government. The hospitality was impressive. I completed a detailed report on the visit and as far as I know nothing was heard of the proposed development again. Determined to return to Ireland, I planned several walking holidays to Ireland including the Dingle Peninsula, the Ring of Kerry and the rocky islands of Skellig.

•••

But, I was becoming complacent. Dark, complicated clouds were boiling up on the horizon yet again. I was asked to host several visits from anonymous people and to show them over the Estate but had no idea who they were until the penny dropped. Complacency vanished. They were commercial land agents operating on behalf of large hotel groups, clearly interested in purchasing Langdale Leisure. What particularly annoyed me was the brewery did not have the courtesy to take me into their confidence, and I was left to figure it out for myself which was difficult and I quickly became aware, one well known hotel group had already put in a bid. It was time for me to change my loyalty from my employer, and confide in Fred, Chairman of the Owners Committee and tell him what was about to happen to their second homes. Fred shared the same concerns, as it was clearly not in the best interest of Langdale Owners for the Estate to be taken over by a bunch of hoteliers. It was essential every effort to control our own destiny be made. A meeting was arranged with the brewery and, without going into a lot of detail, well, let's skip the detail all together, we were given time to consult with the owners with the aim of clubbing together enough money to purchase the Estate.

The bank agreed a loan up to fifty percent of the asking price, provided at least half of the owners were willing to purchase one share each at one thousand pounds. No one could own more than one share for each lodge week they owned. After many months of hard negotiations and, yes, anxiety, on 17 November 1996, the inaugural Annual General Meeting of Langdale Owners plc elected a first chairman. There was delight and considerable gratification from everyone in the room celebrating the success of the buyout. Thousands of timeshare owners had purchased, what was arguably, the finest timeshare development in Europe and the future was now in their hands.

CHAPTER 11

Planning to Walk the World

'First stop, Himalaya'

It was the right time for me to develop Langdale Walking Holidays. It was as though all of my life had been directed towards this point. I had collected together all of the skills I would need for manoeuvring guests – was that a term I was going to use for them – around our planet and return them back safely to their homes. As such, my plans for their involvement in slightly risky ventures were as yet, unformed, or rather, formed in my mind with the proviso :'I can't possibly do this, or that, with them'. This changed to: 'Well, why not, with a bit of care?'

At the buy-out, the Directors had questioned a possible conflict of interest. The Board was understandably concerned about using the word 'Langdale' in the title. This was run across the desk of lawyers who advised it was a generic name not specifically confined to Langdale Leisure. As seen in the Langdale Pikes, and Langdale Valley. The deal was settled when I offered to pay them a percentage of any profit made. It was never the intention for LWH to have profit as a priority; it was to be more of a Travel club, giving Langdale owners the opportunity to travel together to different parts of the world. The theory behind it was associated with Langdale owners' preference for high quality accommodation and service, what we would call the best available, in the areas we were to visit, from 5-star boutique hotels to "rustic lodges" off the beaten track. If you do not know what "rustic lodges" might be I explain this a little further along in the book when I walked through Rajasthan. Best to keep you on tenterhooks for the time being. This, combined with their love of walking and a bit of adventure thrown in, brought together all the ingredients for a successful undertaking. As the business developed, more and more non-Langdale owners joined us, mainly by word of mouth. We never had to resort to advertising.

I was a house guest of Robin, the MD of Summit Trekking and his wife Wendy at their colonial style home in Kathmandu. That's in Nepal, its capital, and sits at 1,300 metres. It was exciting to discuss the prospect of Summit Trekking hosting the first LWH group to Nepal and for me to join one of the regular treks to Annapurna, the tenth highest mountain in the world at 8,091 metres, that is a lung-sucking 26,550 feet, a few days later.

Exploring Kathmandu for the first time, showed up a whole new world in relationships. I should explain. I was introduced to the pet chicken and duck belonging to Robin and Wendy, who were inseparable. The duck with the chicken that is. I am sure Robin and Wendy were also tied together with lasting love. This duck followed the chicken everywhere. Evenings, just at dusk, would find the two waiting patiently at the front door, queuing quietly to be taken up to their hutch on the roof terrace, safe from any attack from a mongoose during the night. The chicken, once inside the door, then became difficult and had to be chased until caught, with feathers flying everywhere, accompanied by a cacophony of quacking and clucking, continuing as they proceeded up the stairs, with the duck dutifully following right behind as it jumped up the risers one by one. Safe for the night, the next morning they would be let out to make their own way back down the stairs without prompting, and returned into the garden for breakfast.

They had a good night's sleep, which is more than could be said of me. It was the Festival of Diwali and the Hindu neighbours celebrated from their roof terraces throughout the day and night. This is one of the most popular festivals in Hinduism and symbolizes the spiritual victory of light over darkness, good over wrong and knowledge over evil. The reason, however, I could not sleep was not because of the Festival but due to the inconvenient fact I shared a room with another house guest who snored his head off all night..

Eventually, I joined the chicken and duck up on the roof terrace, preferring to listen to the relaxing Hindu music echoing over the neighbourhood. The chicken and the duck who were sharing the same experience were unperturbed, and slept through the whole night.

I was both delighted and disturbed the day before setting off for Annapurna. Delighted by my introduction to trekking in the Himalaya but distraught because of the thought of continuing to share a tent with the snorer. After a couple of nights of this I had had enough as his loud and persistent snoring was driving me insane. In a fit of frustration, I gave him a good kick. He shot up out of his sleeping bag and started scratching his head, apologising profusely. But the snoring continued and he pleaded it was not him, but the guy in the next tent. To cover my error, if there was one, I said he was snoring as well. Not to remain down-hearted, I devised a solution. A single lady in our group appeared to take a fancy to him. Naughtily, but determinedly, I actively encouraged the budding relationship until he asked me if I would mind if he moved into her tent. Would I mind? Would I hell! What a piece of good luck but little did she know what she was letting herself in for, not that I cared because there is a limit to the amount of sleep one can be deprived of. You might recall the Stasi were experts in depriving one of sleep as well. Perhaps she was immune to snoring, because they stayed together for the rest of the trip. Alleluia came to mind as I drifted off.

We were off to a racing start with the first Walking tour to Nepal diary marked for November 1991. Ten clients were needed for it be viable and I was overwhelmed to discover that thirty had signed up. This was to be the first of several, unforgettable visits to the Himalaya, and the beginning of twenty-eight years of walking and exploring in seventy different countries, the bonus being the company of like-minded people, all seeking a taste of adventure.

Selecting an airline to take us to Nepal was a new experience. Tempted by the price and the offer of complimentary overnight accommodation in Karachi by Pakistan International Airways, seemed to be a good choice. Had the early research been better, we could have avoided the curfew that greeted us, due to a general strike and political problems on our arrival in the most populous city in Pakistan. We had to be escorted to our hotel by the Armed Forces. Were we entering a war zone I asked myself? Am I back in the Armed Forces? Taking notice of the machine gun posts at every intersection along our route manned by the Pakistani Armed Forces, (an automatic reaction dating back to my early years), we made our way to the hotel where we, surprisingly, received a warm welcome. Before dinner, quietly enjoying a soak in the bath while reflecting on my responsibility towards my clients, I wondered if I had inadvertently exposed them to unexpected dangers. I had to set these thoughts aside when there came a plaintive knock on my door as I was planning to go down to dinner. It was a single lady member of our group seeking advice on the antics of a uniformed concierge. He had knocked on her bedroom door. Having just got out of the bath, and still with a towel wrapped around her, she was met by the concierge enquiring if she needed anything. He entered in the room uninvited and started to dry her in a rather over familiar way. Yes, that was one way of putting it madam, but there were others as well. He was asked to leave and not surprisingly she was more than a little concerned. Reluctantly he left. Having broken up with her husband and embarking on her first holiday without him, I suspect she had acted rather naively earlier on. Rather than complaining to the hotel and putting the concierge attendant at risk of losing his job, I dealt with him myself by *'putting him in the picture'*. Apart from the smell of tear gas smelling something like vinegar, infiltrating the hotel, the remaining time in Karachi was uneventful, but we needed to move on. We were excited to continue our journey to Kathmandu.

It was a delight to be greeted by our hosts at Summit Trekking with a traditional Hindu greeting. Seeing a large banner at the entrance of the hotel proclaiming

'*Welcome to Langdale Walking Holidays to the Summit Hotel*' we began to feel we had made a good choice in coming to Nepal.

Anyone who has ever been trekking in Nepal will understand the importance of spending a few nights in Kathmandu, both at the beginning and at the end of the holiday. At the beginning, to initiate the acclimatisation period and, at the end, to allow for delays on the trek which could result in missing the international flight home. While there, I had agreed to host a joint welcome party with the hotel. Our contribution was to ask all guests to purchase a bottle of duty-free spirits which cost a tenth of the local market price. These were handed over to the hotel as our contribution to the party. The hotel organised the entertainment, music and invitations, and added the floral decorations and lighting to make sure it looked like a party. The invitation list included the Commanding Officer of the Nepalese Royal Guards Regiment, the British Ambassador, several United Nations officials and the head of the British Gurkha Unit responsible for the recruitment for the Brigade of Gurkhas. The next night we were all invited to the British Gurkha Unit where we were welcomed by a pipe band and traditional Gurkha rum. Gurkha rum is kept in a bottle shaped like their traditional kukri dagger and holds 375 ml of the liquid. We were also privileged to listen to a presentation given to the British Foreign Secretary a few days earlier. Maybe he was made the guinea pig in rehearsal for our visit?

The maximum safe size of a group was reckoned to be around ten, so we needed to be split into three groups for the ten-day trek. I had previously discussed with Robin the possibility of visiting Tibet and re-joining the group back in Kathmandu. Accompanied by Wendy, a fluent Nepali and Tibetan speaker, we enjoyed a spectacular flight over the Himalaya with South China Airways, to Lhasa. We checked in at the hotel and wondered why everyone was wearing arctic clothing. It was still November and the Chinese authorities did not allow any form of heating until 1st December, regardless of temperature, which was well below zero. Added to that, Lhasa is one of the highest elevation cities in the world at three thousand seven hundred metres. (12,000 feet). The combination of the freezing cold temperature and altitude resulted, for some, in altitude sickness and a couple of sleepless nights.

It was worth making the journey to Lhasa just to see the Potala Palace. Formerly the seat of the Tibetan government and winter palace of the Dalai Lama, lost in the invasion from China in 1949, this immense religious structure and masterpiece of Tibetan architecture, has changed little since we were there but, is now a major tourist attraction. When we visited, it was comparatively unknown to the outside world except as a destination for pilgrims from all over Tibet. Wendy managed to wangle our way into the kitchens where monks were preparing the evening meal. We were offered tea with yaks' milk, an acquired taste to say the least. It has a fragrant, sweetish smell and because of its sugar content, sugar is not added to tea made with this milk.

As there was no prospect of hiring a car, the plan was to drive back to the Tibetan/Nepal border over the Tibetan Plateau in a jeep and driver provided by the Chinese Tourist Authorities. Our first stop was Shigatse, the second city of the Tibetan Autonomous Region of the People's Republic of China. It sits at about 3,860 metres above sea level and, more importantly to many, is the gateway to Everest. The unmetalled snow-covered road was challenging but the views of the high Himalaya, with Everest always in view in the distance, was unforgettable. Not so memorable were the hotels, probably rated less than half a star by UK standards. They had no heating, no hot water, and only a single fifteen watt ceiling light. Frugal is a good and accurate word which better describes these properties. The elevation was even greater than Lhasa, so there was no question of wearing nice silk pyjamas to bed, not that I possessed any, and the only thing I took off were my boots, taken to bed with me like any lover, in case they froze overnight if left outside. A typical dinner was a bowl of rice, a tin of shrimps and tea. I could not wait to go back! But the bazaar was interesting, also Tashi Lhunpo Monastery, the traditional seat of the Panchen Lamas, the second most important Lama in Tibet. Things have probably improved now but at the time, and based on what I had experienced, Tibet was not a destination at the top of my list for future walking holidays. But it proved to be a fascinating one off journey and I was able to add it to my store of stories.

When we reached the border with Nepal, Wendy related to me an astonishing story about an American couple she was accompanying a few months earlier. Where the Tibetan and Nepalese borders come together, there is an area of "no man's land" stretching several hundreds of metres down a steep hill. Half way down this slope the husband collapsed and died on the spot. Wendy raced back up the hill to the Tibetan customs post but was turned away and told the area was part of Nepal, not Tibet. Rushing back down the hill again to talk briefly to the distraught lady, she carried on to the Nepalese customs post, only to be told it was nothing to do with them as they had no control over the area. There were no mobile phones in those days but in an effort to avoid a diplomatic incident she managed to persuade Nepalese customs to allow her to call the American Embassy in Kathmandu. They agreed to send a car the following morning. Wendy managed to employ a couple of porters to carry the body to the border and, from there, to a primitive hotel. They shared a room with the body until the car turned up the following morning but with nowhere to stack a body easily as rigor mortis had set in, Wendy had to use her initiative – not airborne initiative perhaps but good enough – by going to the local market where she bought some rope to tie the body on top of the car.

All was well until a rather stiff hand slipped down from the roof and swung through the open window to hit her in the face. This is quite true. The two of them, one quite a bit warmer than the other, continued on to Kathmandu where better help was at last, forthcoming with the American Embassy arranging for the repatriation of the body to the United States. What a very sad and disturbing story. It accounted, in part, to our quickened pace to get out of Tibet.

Travelling in the Himalaya is seldom without incident. Many people arrive, not prepared for the effects of the altitude, nor with the right level of fitness. *Summit* had to deal with a typical problem with an American couple after only one day on the Annapurna trek. Arriving at the camp site well after everyone else, they complained the walk was all uphill and they could not continue! Hullo? They were overweight and totally unfit. Maybe they thought they were going for a walk in the park? The next day one of the Sherpas took them back to the airport at *Pokhara* and we never heard from them again.

The aerial aerobatics of several *Lammergeier* (bearded vultures) soaring below us on a high mountain pass on the Khumbu trail distracted one lady, momentarily, committing the cardinal sin of ignoring Wainwright's doctrine of always looking where one is going. She was looking down onto the Lammergeiers at the same time as continuing to attempt to walk along the trail. She stumbled and fell, narrowly avoiding a thousand foot drop but, nonetheless, tumbling down the side of the trail for twenty or thirty feet. Covered in cuts and bruises, but fortunately no broken bones, we managed to half carry her to a tea house where we were to spend the night, recognising the trek was over for her. I managed to sort out a helicopter to *casevac* (casualty evacuation) her back to Kathmandu. I had been advised before the trip always to carry a good reserve of dollars in US currency as private helicopter companies had learnt by experience only to carry casualties with advance payment. Some disreputable tourists had previously called in helicopter support and then departed Nepal without paying. When we returned a few days later, our client was looking fit and well, apart from a profusion of plasters and bandages.

Conundrum. What do you do when one of your clients refuses to cross a mountain river in full spate along an admittedly, spindly, under motion, suspension bridge several hundred feet up in the air? There was no option for us but to cross it, but she was terrified. The Sirdar, our head guide, had the solution which, possibly had arisen before. He blindfold her and guided her across. 'What the eye does not see the heart does not grieve' Success was assured from that moment on.

Leaving Kathmandu airport on our first visit proved to be something of a problem. As we were a large group, the airline, PIA, wanted us to check-in as a group, lumping all luggage together to save time. Several members in the group had purchased carpets with the result we were overweight and expecting me to pay an excess luggage charge of a couple of thousand US dollars. I refused to pay and the only solution was to recover all the luggage already being loaded on to the waiting aircraft. There was a great fuss and everyone reverted to checking in individually, which is what we wanted to do in the first place. On my next visit to Nepal, and again travelling with PIA, I naturally wanted to avoid the same problem and was advised to visit the airline manager in his office in Kathmandu the day before our departure. I was told he only saw people by appointment. But I could see him sitting in his office reading a magazine, so found it difficult to understand why he would not see me. After a bit of a stand-off, he grudgingly agreed to see me but was off-hand and unhelpful. I decided to leave and not waste any more of his precious time. As I did so, leaving his office, I accidentally dropped a fifty US dollar note on his desk. So clumsy of me. He didn't seem to notice. Nothing was said, but the following day, arriving at the airport, I was greeted like his long-lost friend. He had arranged vouchers for us all to have refreshments in the restaurant while airport staff ran around collecting all our luggage. Amazing, having lost fifty dollars what a rainbow it created for our departure?

Summit Trekking had arranged a trek for the British Ambassador and, coincidentally, one morning we found we were camping in a village not far from the party. I was invited to join them for breakfast. It was like something out of Rudyard Kipling and the British Raj all mixed up together. A small field close to the village had been cleared of cattle, sheep and goats, tents were all in a dead straight line, something which gladdened my heart. British, Nepalese and Gurkha flags were flying in the wind, and a breakfast table meticulously prepared with napkins, table cloth and the smell of fresh coffee in the air, we were all set for a breakfast to be etched upon one's mind for a very long time. British government officials and Gurkhas were all expected to set an example and maintain the highest of standards when visiting an area where Gurkhas are recruited to join the Brigade and where numerous Gurkha pensioners lived. As a nice touch, the British Ambassador was wearing a pith helmet. Now, that's style.

We slept in village tea houses or in tents transported by the ubiquitous yak. The tent was the more popular as it kept us away from villages which were always noisy. However, one night, obliged to be staying in a village tea house, I was awakened by the surprise visit of several cows who had entered our room and could not find a way out. Being cowful, sorry, careful, not to offend the cows, due to their Holy status, it became more stressful when one of the uninvited visitors delivered, four times masticated grass, straight onto the floor about twenty centimetres from my camp bed. That is eight inches by the way. It put me in quite a moo-d.

Each village offered us a different experience. We shared a room with six other male fellow travellers. It had now become de rigeur there would be another sleepless night due to snoring. To escape, I asked the Sherpas to pitch a tent for me outside the village. The ladies, envying my exclusive and noiseless relocation, joined me the following night. I was in good company, much to the envy of the snorers.

Although porters carry one's luggage, we always tried to travel with as little kit as possible. On a ten day trek, for example, one change of clothes should be sufficient. After five days, I put on a clean shirt, my favourite, for the rest of the trek. It was much admired by the Sirdar who made no secret that it would look good on him. He had his reward when I presented it to him at the end of the trek and he promptly put it on, even though it was well overdue for a visit to the laundry. It is the custom to present unwanted clothing, and even not so unwanted clothing, to the Sherpa and Guides at the end of a trek, along with a gratuity. Everyone was encouraged to be as generous as possible. That we did.

It was a way of life, ground into them by generations of shortages, that the Nepalese never wasted any food. Curry was on the menu most nights and when we had finished, anything left on our plates, including bones, would be swept back into the pot and shared by the sherpas. No one stepped back on learning they could be eating someone else's discarded parson's nose.

On earlier treks, we had enjoyed sitting around a campfire after supper, but we were advised that some do-gooders from the UK had complained to Robin about the ethics of using timber which was in short supply and contributing to de-forestation, so it was stopped. Environmentalism perhaps at its most frank, but it was no problem to us because we were able to drift down to the Sherpa camp to share in their camp fire.

After several tours to Nepal, we received an invitation to attend the 25th anniversary of Summit Trekking and the Summit Hotel over a weekend in Kathmandu. No one in his right mind travels to Nepal just for a weekend. But, you only live once, so we did take it on while adding an extra day for a trek around the Kathmandu Valley. Satisfied, slaked, soothed and sated, we left for home realising we had seen sights, climbed mountains and met people which few Europeans had even witnessed. We were extremely lucky. More, privileged is the right word.

As an end piece and, reminded of the snow, the ice and the altitude, brought me back to a visit to Norway. We were probably some of the first tourists to visit the mountain goat farm at Akrafjord. The only way to get there was by boat across a fjord to the farm jetty followed by an uphill climb along a track to a traditional Norwegian farm, isolated from modern day impact on their lives. Time had stood still, well, pretty still, for the last century or so, where the locals continued to enjoy living and working as their forefathers had done. This further manifested itself when I made a call of nature following a track to the 'loo' which was separated from the other buildings. I noticed the toilet paper was not a neat roll of 'Cushelle' but consisted of cut pieces of newspaper hanging on a piece of string. The picture on the top piece of paper exposed to all eyes, ready to be ripped away at anytime, was of Liverpool Football team. While I studied my bare knees, I pondered on what the team would have thought of their picture ending in the High Pasture of Norway twelve hundred miles away on the end of a piece of sisal string. Funny how these small images stick in your mind to be retrieved years later.

CHAPTER 12

Trials, Tribulations and Tours in Europe

'Some clients can be a bit....difficult.'

A considerable part of my time on tour had to be taken up ensuring every member trekking with me was happy, relaxed and enjoying themselves. Sometimes, it could be quite...difficult. Trials and tribulations would arise due to groups of discerning clients wishing to travel to distant and often remote parts of the world not quite understanding what they were taking on. We had to learn, quite quickly, how to deal with what could turn out to be interludes, intrusions and intervals to the fixed plan, which could spread like a cancer to others in the same group. Incidents including an airline going into liquidation, a general strike, floods, earth tremors, volcanic eruption, accidents, break downs in the middle of a desert, unreliable local guides, hotel reservations going wrong, medical emergencies, cancellations, and... the occasional whingeing client. All of the above happened at one time or another and every single one had to be dealt with on the spot. It was fortunate for me to be tour leader on most of the holidays, although I was supported by several others who had excellent leadership qualities. They were totally reliable and could solve most issues when the best of plans went askew. As it was crucial to deal with any issues arising and, regardless of cost, I differed with the larger travel companies where their tour leader often had little authority over funds to sort an issue. It would have to be referred back to Head Office with a consequent built-in delay.

Covering twenty-eight years, we visited over seventy different countries, many of them several times, all of them unique in some way. Rather than plough through them from A to Z, a number of these destinations have been picked out as very special and, possibly where you have not been (yet), as a way in which to wet your appetite for more.

Recalling how, at Pontins, we managed to eliminate unpunctuality by using the well tested Army system of pointing to the floor and making the culprit do press ups, tongue in cheek, I introduced the same system for clients who were persistently late for a walk. Nothing annoyed my groups more than for one or two unthinking clients to be late and keep the whole party waiting as they stabbed dead leaves into puddles with their walking poles in their frustration. But told to do a thousand press ups, and, only excused after one or two, they took it in the spirit intended. It became a bit of a standing joke, but it was rare, after a few demonstrations, for anyone to be late after that.

Payment of single supplements are often contentious. These days hotels rarely have single rooms, resulting in single travellers having to use a double room for single occupancy, thus attracting payment of the single supplement. The cost of a room is the same whether it is to be occupied by one or two guests. Our Booking Conditions required one to conform, sharing or otherwise in a room. Asked if one would like to share with someone else, it was clear we had got the wording wrong on the document when someone replied '…yes, but preferably with my wife.'

Advising clients what to bring with them was made simple by sending out a Kit List. One guest wrote to say we had omitted to include underwear. It was left out because we thought it was obvious, but, to please everyone, it was then added back in under K for knickers. Of course, it could have been under B for Brassieres or, excitingly V for vests, but there were quite a lot of men on each tour so we could have just left it as U for underwear.

One of the features of our holidays was to seek out interesting places for dinner. The Azores enabled us to eat at the private home of a titled lady, known to our Agents. Following a tour of her substantial wine cellar, our party very much resembled a regimental dinner in the Army. We toasted our Queen and then the President of Portugal with some excellent local vintage port. Portugal is Britain's oldest ally, seemingly sharing many similar traditions. As a point of interest the alliance was formed in May 1386 and has lasted ever since.

There were more royalty filling the corridors, when we visited Vietnam where we took dinner in the home of the former Queen Mother of the Vietnamese Royal family. We enjoyed exclusive use of her private dining room, entertained by musicians, where our group wore theatrical dress extracted from a substantial wardrobe kept in the house. (Rather like one's dressing up box at home). We had to elect a King and a Queen for the evening where they sat enthroned on a raised platform at the head of the table, looking down on the rest of us mere minions. The power went unfortunately, to the King's head as it does so often, I have observed. I was, naturally and very sensibly, cast in the role of Head of the Armed Forces but had to chew my fingers watching the man relishing his power for the evening, I was beckoned to his side on several occasions during the meal where he demanded more wine. Finally, getting fed up with his demands, I threatened a *coup d'état* unless he promoted me to be Minister of Defence. I won the round by blackmailing him, saying that the next day he would have to be back marker …all day!

•••

Flipping through my well-filled diaries to Fiji, I recalled there was a request for lobster one evening. I hired a bike and went off searching in the off- the-beaten track local villages until, discovering a local lobster fisherman whose family arranged a memorable barbeque where the barbecue grill was overloaded with lobster, one of seventeen species in Fiji apparently, including the well-known green lobster. Such is life today one can buy Fijian green lobsters in the post these days providing it is in season.

At the end of each tour, it became the custom to hold an Honours and Awards ceremony, giving recognition to anyone who had distinguished themselves on the holiday. There was usually one who had gone the extra mile such as the doctor on one of our New Zealand visits who was presented with an award for being the best doctor on the tour. Yes, quite. Understood. Having enthusiastically accepted, he was returning to his seat when, suddenly, he stopped in his tracks, turned around and exclaimed 'But I'm the only doctor on the holiday'. One presentation was in the form of a lady guest's banana holder due to her preference for bananas with her picnic lunch.

Who could tell the best joke was always worthy of recognition and one lady guest received an award for always asking questions (she never bloody stopped); another for being the best dressed – he carried an umbrella and wore plus-fours and a tie. One client distinguished himself by insisting on having his photograph taken with no clothes on during the Routeburn Track in New Zealand. Well not quite naked because he continued to wear his hat and boots, but this still qualified him to be the most naked man on the holiday. (Interesting phrase don't you think? 'Most naked.' This implies there could be a 'just naked' and a 'more naked 'gentleman).

One soon came to appreciate people who found it easy to relax, identify the company of like-minded people, the companionship and the wish to let the tour leader deal with every aspect of their holiday. We had many clients in top jobs – CEOs, doctors, accountants, bankers, leaders of industry and entrepreneurs, who all enjoyed allowing their day-to-day decisions to be made for them, the complete opposite, in fact, of their everyday lives. They did not have to think or calculate; this was the appeal for many. Nonetheless, in return they expected the highest standards. Others were like hens, always appearing anxious about something or other unspecified, and were easily identified clucking through the chaff on the floor. Trying to persuade them not to think ahead, but to enjoy one day at a time, came hard to this group. These were the guests eternally wondering what time the lunch stop would be instead of absorbing the scenery around them. At its worst, we would find a guest querying if there would be an early breakfast provided on the last day of the holiday This would be made on the first day of the holiday! But it is the way some are programmed, and must be told: *'You really have not come here to enjoy yourself'.*

After a delayed return from North America due to 9/11, we had slipped behind with planning for the next holiday which was to Jordan. Several of the clients booked onto the holiday were concerned about travelling to the Middle East because of the current, security situation which was, to say the least, muddled. One couple had already cancelled. I wrote to the CEO of our Agents in Amman asking for some reassurance. Not only did I receive a positive reply, but also a letter from the Minister of Tourism himself saying:

'We in the Hashemite Kingdom of Jordon totally disassociate ourselves from terrorism and violence and always treat our visitors with courtesy and with the greatest respect. You will always receive a warm welcome, an exceptional level of service and guarantees to take great care of all our guests. Jordan has some of the most spectacular scenery in the Middle East; the people are known for their hospitality and you can expect to be warmly welcomed and assured of a safe and relaxing experience in our amazing and unspoilt country.'

This was reassuring and most welcome. I copied it to everyone and the tour went ahead as planned. There was an almost total absence of other tourists, which was surprising in view of the Minister of Tourism's assurances but, maybe they did not receive the same letter?

On arrival, we were upgraded to the very best hotels in each of the areas we visited: not surprising as many of the hotels were, otherwise, empty. But good for us. Recalling my last visit to Petra with the Paras, where we slept in sleeping bags as guests of the Arab Legion in a 12th Century Crusader Fort, this came as quite a contrast. Reflecting on my changed circumstances from our delightful 5-star hotel bedroom window, I counted myself lucky and certainly appreciated the upgrade from a sleeping bag on sand to a goose down pillow…on another goose down pillow.

The next two days were spent exploring the mysteries of the Nabatean capital of rose-red stone. Petra. An astonishing place to visit by even those not interested in that particular slice of history. A bonus, no doubt, was the absence of other tourists who, usually, dominated and clogged every step of the way down the red sandstone ravine.

Two guests wanted to join us on the Jordan trip but one was anxious about spending the night under canvas in Wadi Rum. Unfamiliar with camping and concerned that there would be no hair dryer, I gave her a call to say that would not be a problem and a hair dryer would be provided. Reassured, they joined the trip and when we arrived in Wadi Rum, I presented her with a hair dryer. *'There is nowhere to plug it in,'* she observed, quite shrewdly. Ah, but I had only offered to provide a hair dryer, with no mention of power supply or anything else! As it turned out, she became captivated with *Wadi Rum* which T. H. Lawrence had described as *'...vast and god-like, and echoing',* having made his base there during the Arab Revolt of 1917-1918. I was soon forgiven.

When guests began to stir in their desert camp the next morning, it was cold enough to bring up the goose flesh. It was, in fact, freezing cold and it can drop to minus four at times and snow has been known. And this in the desert! There were the few usual whingers, as we required them to go out and collect as much firewood as possible. This was added to the nearly dormant embers of the fire from the night before and spirits rose as the cold group began to crowd round as if a baron of beef on a spit had been enjoying the flames warmth, while our Bedouin hosts prepared an Arab breakfast. Morale lifted further as if it were mist on a lake with the sun breaking through and we found we were on our way to Al-Aqaba, Jordan's only sea port. It lies just east of the Jordan-Israel frontier on the Gulf of Aqaba. Having chartered a boat to explore the harbour we came across Bill Gates' enormous luxury yacht anchored in the harbour. Pulling alongside and talking to a couple of his British crew, we suggested they may like to invite us on board for coffee. They did not share the same enthusiasm. Strange?

An event from the past, surfaced at this time and brought to light an embarrassing incident which occurred on a return visit to Jordan. Camping facilities in Wadi Rum had been much improved and after an evening dinner and entertainment by Bedouin musicians, the guide and I enjoyed a few beers around the campfire after everyone else had retired to their tents. I had forgotten to bring a torch with me, so the guide made up a desert lamp for my use. This consisted of a brown paper bag half-filled with sand, with a candle stuck in the middle. The candle was lit to light my way and off I went to find my tent. I had taken the precaution of laying all my kit out on the spare single bed in typical Army fashion, only to stumble / stagger / sway over one of the guy ropes as I entered the tent. The candle set the brown paper bag on fire scattering my kit all over the place. There was nothing else to do but get undressed with plans to sort everything out in morning. I should, perhaps not have consumed the extra bottles of beer, because in the middle of the night the call of nature was compelling. Without any clothes on, and now an absence of any form of lighting, I considered there was little to worry about as I did not expect to find anyone else going my way, so to speak, so I took the chance of heading towards the lavatory well, hole in the ground. It was when I was returning, a smidgin of a problem arose. I was quick to realise I had entered the wrong tent – those gottles of geer - when the lady inside the tent, now close-by, started screaming. I beat a hasty retreat (possibly where the well-known phrase: 'beating the retreat' had come from) and managed, eventually, to locate my own tent. Next morning, I listened in absolute horror as one of my couples reported that a wild Bedouin raiding party had attempted to storm their tent in the middle of the night. I apologised for the unruliness of the country and told them to stay close to me for a couple of days until we had cleared this part of our trip! Goodness me. The things one has to accept being abroad.

•••

During all the years of travel I received many, strange, curious and weird hazards, which included my second death threat. Our Agent had chartered a boat for us to travel to Dugi Otok (Long Island) on the Adriatic Sea to explore several small islands, much as we had done on a previous visit. Our backdrop was magical, and freshly caught fish served to us at a fisherman's home for lunch. Arriving at the harbour at Zadar a city on the Dalmatian coast, filled with Roman artefacts, this time there was no connecting boat, leaving us with the only choice of a huge tourist ferry with several hundred tourists on board. There had been a mistake, but without an alternative, we had to endure karaoke and for eats, a cold fish was slapped down with a smack onto a plastic plate; altogether an awful experience. As soon as we disembarked, I sent an email to the Agent expressing my disappointment. He was out of his office and his assistant, without thinking, copied my message direct to the owner of the boat company. He replied with a death threat, no doubt the usual response in this part of the world? I never did go back to Croatia.

Rafting had been tabled for the River Zrmanja, with its clear, warm waters, but to get to the starting point we had to pass through a mine field, and a Serbian village totally destroyed by small arms fire and explosives. The river rafting was exhilarating, but the evidence still on show from the Balkans War was a very real reminder of the war which had struck in Europe even in the late twentieth century.

This sort of tragedy could be found in so many parts of the world. It is a regrettable fact of man's continuing insanities. It raised its head on one of our visits to Madeira. Walking along the northern coastal footpath, one of our client's disappeared, like Houdini, over a grass covered cliff. The guide, who was leading the way, and myself, as back marker, immediately climbed down and discovered the man unconscious and enough blood clinging to the torn grass, to make the incident serious; to make things worse, he was precariously wedged against a bush with an interesting straight-down drop below him.

I climbed back up to the footpath, my Army training beginning to be exhumed from long ago, and asked all the men to remove their belts. Tied together, they were used to secure the casualty to the bush, preventing him falling any further. While this was going on, one of the ladies was screeching (possibly the same lady as we had had in Wadi Rum) at us, not to touch his head. At the same time, and following the mens' example, and my urgent command, the ladies all took off their bras (yes, I know but it was all I could think of at the time), and started tying them together in belt and braces fashion (sorry), to ensure we would not lose our casualty who was also, more importantly, my fee-paying client.

They were quite useless – the bras that is – but during the undressing process, a group of German walkers passed us by, and, mystified by this performance being shown as a matinée that day, remarked: *'wot is dies'*. Difficult to explain with half a dozen topless ladies armed with walking sticks and men with their trousers wrapped around their knees. What was going on, indeed?

Following correct procedures, the guide climbed back up to the foot path and called emergency services on his mobile phone, while I stayed with the casualty. His wife told me he was diabetic and had omitted to take his medicine that morning and, while admiring the view, he had blacked out and fallen. Help came quickly and with great difficulty the casualty was loaded onto a stretcher and hauled back up to the foot path. He was taken to a waiting ambulance about a mile away. I climbed in the back with him before it took off, hurtling around hairpin bends at great speed, clanging away joyously, as if it was the Lutine Bell announcing a major wreck. We arrived at the hospital in one piece. The guide stayed with the group and took them back to the hotel in a line of waiting taxis. Fortunately, the injuries were mainly superficial and he was released the following day. Arriving back at the hotel, my first task was to reassure his wife, who was much relieved. One of the members of our group, meanwhile, gave me the good news, he had taken it upon himself to cancel our dinner reservation at a local hotel for that evening. *"Why the f*** did you do that"* I asked politely? He had considered it bad form to go out to dinner while one of the group was lying injured in hospital. Marvellous. Just marvellous, Mike. Bloody well done. Oh, just great. Frantically trying to find an alternative restaurant for a large group on a Saturday night, proved to be a real test, until one the best restaurants in Funchal, also one of the most expensive, came to our rescue, blowing my budget to pieces. Apart from the casualty and the ensuing damage to my wallet because of the huge extra cost of dinner, everyone was happy.

While all this excitement continued, there was a lady guest who was clearly not enjoying herself. Seeking to establish the reason, I asked what was bothering her. Her opening salvo was that she did not like walking! Secondly, she said, pursing her lips up as if about to suck a Sicilian lemon, she could not sleep as the bed was uncomfortable, and so she went droning on and on. I was relieved when her friend helped me out by asking her if she had read the Booking Conditions. She had not, but had she done so, as her friend mentioned to her, she would not have found any reference to enjoying herself, but had she paid the supplement, she might have, otherwise, had a lot of fun. 'You haven't Come to Enjoy Yourself', she said to her friend. Useful phrase after all. That helped me out and the dear lady began to see the funny side of it. I omitted to say to her, if she joined us again, and because she could not sleep, a room without a bed could be arranged for a small additional fee. What is the sense of having a bed if you cannot sleep in it! I made a point of trying to encourage her to enjoy the rest of the holiday by getting her to talk about herself. She revealed she did not like her husband, nor her neighbours. I never did discover what she did actually like which is a shame as it might have been quite illuminating.

I had a disagreement with a guide. Everyone knows how to respect the environment, including the need to ensure all rubbish is picked up and taken back to base. One day, someone chucked banana peel into a bush which hung there like a used contraceptive. Rather than draw attention to it, I surreptitiously plucked it off the bush and wrapped it up before putting it in my rucksack. The guilty person observed this and apologised. The local guide piped in to say bananas grew everywhere in his country and leaving it lying around was perfectly acceptable. We did not use him again for his attitude was so far removed from our own it was not worth the bother of trying to bring him into our own circle of thinking.

A similar incident occurred in the Pyrenees. Included in our picnic lunch, were cherries. One of our clients, not unreasonably, removed the pips from his mouth by spitting them out. Before leaving, the guide picked them up one by one and put them in his rucksack, much like I had done in Madeira. The guide explained there were wild goats in the area and it was important for them not to become dependent on the human food trail. Additionally, cherries were not indigenous to the area. It was an innocent mistake but the guide was correct - leave no trace. Better still, leave it cleaner than when you arrived.

My mantra, *'You haven't Come Here to Enjoy Yourself'* repeated here, regretfully, *ad nauseam* became adopted as a catchphrase. Thereafter, everyone began to use the refrain and my intonation whenever something came off the rails, often with someone helpfully backing me up with the expected follow up - *'you should have paid the supplement'*. If someone was overheard telling me they were having a great time the response from several would be *'careful now, you haven't come here to enjoy yourself'*.

An accomplished walking guide and a lover of the Lake District, and author, regularly came on our walking holidays and offered to plan a holiday in Ireland. Shortly before the holiday was due to take place, his wife rang me to say he was in hospital. With the holiday sold out, but planning incomplete, I had to drop what I was doing and get over to Ireland to sort things out. The selected new guide had the unlikely name of Bernie Goggin, well known locally as a natural history expert and an experienced walking guide for the Dingle Peninsula. Difficult to get hold of, I finally managed to speak to him later on in the day at the Dingle Hotel. It was late afternoon and he was still in bed. (Where else?) He came down to the hotel bar eventually but I found it almost impossible to understand anything he said due to his rough-hewn Irish accent, charming though he was in other ways.

But, we got there. What a wonderful place; the people, the food, the landscapes carpeted in twenty different greens, the winding lanes, the horses and carts. Next time you go to Ireland make sure you include Dingle in your itinerary. During the day it is much like any other small Irish town; at night time there is a huge transformation. Every other building seems to convert into a pub and what, in the daytime is a chemist or hardware shop, at night becomes a fully-stocked tavern, all playing live Irish music and all packed to the rafters with laughter and music and happy customers. It was always difficult to get to a bar. Even the church turns itself into a music hall, with traditional Irish ceilidh dancing in the aisles. What would the Vicar say if that happened in leafy Surrey or the Welsh Baptist chapel in Blaenau Ffestiniog?

A site full of dramatic backdrops and the continual screech of thousands of gulls is to visit one of the two rocky Skellig Islands. One is inhabited by a large colony of gannets (35,000 pairs of nesting birds), the other is known for its well preserved early Christian monastery, dating back to the sixth century with its beehive-shaped huts, oratories and crosses. Situated off the southwestern coast of Ireland, the island is difficult to get to, but well worth the effort. Climbing the six hundred steep steps carved from the rock, to get to the top, we were amazed by the hundreds of puffins nesting in what looked like enlarged rabbit holes, the birds all paying us the courtesy of coming out of their nests to nod us on with their colourful beaks, as we struggled towards our goal. We had arrived earlier at a little wooden dock, where we had to cope with an eight-foot swell and had to leap onto the dock as the boat rose up like a lift, when, at the exact moment, the deck hands commanded us to jump aided by an outstretched hand. On the return journey the wind had risen and the Atlantic swell increased so much, it was touch and go whether we would be able to get off the island. Persuasive as it might have been to some, it would have been an inhospitable place to spend the night. Ghouls, ghosts, presences, were all well-documented, with the island becoming the ideal location for one of the scenes from the Star Wars movie which made me wonder what the early monks would have made of that equipment being lugged up the steep hill.

•••

Cork to Wengen is about 1,600 miles, revealing, at the end of the flight, a typical alpine village in the Bernese Oberland region, famous for its wooden houses, skiing in winter and breath-taking mountain walks in the summer. Accompanied by Urs, our local guide, we spent many a happy day yodelling our way through the mountains, all the more interesting because of the well-planned locations of ski lifts and gondolas, the best mode of transport being the cog railway to the top of the *Jungfrau,* height 3,454 metres, that's 11,300 feet, looking down on the magnificent Aletsch glacier. *Jungfrau* translates into virgin or maiden. It is like travelling from summer to winter in less than an hour. One can marvel at the transformation from the flower filled meadows of the lower valley to below zero temperatures at the top, where you can ski or tramp around in deep snow throughout the year.

The journeys are not always the best part of a holiday, but, in Switzerland it is quite different. Their integrated transport system where airport, coaches, railways and river travel are all synchronized and inter-operate in one place, provide seamless travel. Our group arrived at Geneva in good time to connect with the rail connection to Lauterbrunnen and then taking the cog railway to Wengen. We had plenty of time to walk the short distance from the airport to the rail station and everyone knew the departure time. Once the train arrived, it waited for what appeared to be seconds, before departing at speed, on the dot. There were no excuses about the wrong type of snow or leaves on the line. Once aboard, we thoroughly enjoyed the scenic journey to Lauterbrunnen. All except one couple, that is, who had mysteriously disappeared. There was nothing we could do but carry on without them. Later that night we found out what had happened. They had got off at the wrong station and boarded another train not realising it was only going to a siding several miles away. And there it stayed. This couple, with their luggage trundling along the railway track for what must have seemed ages, eventually arrived at the hotel in time for dinner.

It is said Swiss hotels have a reputation for providing the best hospitality in the world. That has not always been my experience. At dinner one night, one of our clients asked for a description of the dessert, which none of us had ever heard of. The waiter tried to explain, but we were none the wiser, so he was invited by the waiter into the kitchen to see for himself. The manager, outraged by this intrusion into his kitchen, asked him if, as well as inspecting his kitchen, maybe he would like to inspect the rooms and the leisure areas as well. We thought about it but, instead, decided not to go back.

Departing from an hotel is an important time of the tour. Checking out of the hotel on one of the trips, the owner of the hotel asked if we had enjoyed everything. Truthfully, I mentioned some shortcomings in the dinner menu, so next time we would book only for B & B and use local restaurants. He assured me the next time would be better. The following year we were given a warm welcome and given the good news. Remembering comments made the year before, he had arranged a very special menu for us on the first night. I asked him what it was. 'Braised horse', he whinnied. We stuck to the local restaurants. It wasn't the idea of horse, *per se,* it was more the thought of those lovely long eyelashes staring up from the plate that put us off.

Although I have pointed out we did have difficult clients from time to time, this should not be seen as the norm. Most of our guests went out of their way to smooth the cracks and crevices and lancing the boils of the one or two guests who wanted to make a fuss about, usually, nothing. They did, invariably, like to be the centre of attention. Often, these guests began to come round to our way of thinking and would join in the laughter at some silly event which had taken place. Looking back, which I do often enough as I grow older, we were so lucky in the decency of our tour parties despite the trials and tribulations which can and will, inevitably happen on the best planned holidays. We, in the Army, called it the *Fog of War* and a similar situation, without the bangs and explosions, happened from time to time in my well-ordered schedules.

CHAPTER 13 (PART ONE)

Converting Clients Into Friends

Repeat bookings

As time passed, and we travelled to many more countries, our clients, companions-in-arms, enjoyed themselves to the extent where they were insisting on becoming repeat travellers. Most would book themselves, joyfully, into the next, advertised holiday, with the absolute determination they would contribute to ensuring the holiday would be a roaring success. This mood accelerated, bonding, that awful word of modern life, ensured we all became friends sharing the difficulties and the triumphs together.

Brothers in arms, bands of brothers were clichés but they were also true with our tours and reflected the mood each day as we set out with our rucksacks, blister packs and 'interesting' packed lunches. Each country had a different idea of what constituted our take-away meal. It all added to the 'off-piste' attraction away from the Torremolinos discounted package holiday syndrome or the Short City break in Madrid.

I believe one of our successes was the wide choice, almost limitless of destination. Choose, if you will, between Antarctica, the wilder parts of the Himalaya, the end of the world in Patagonia or a dense jungle in Rajasthan. The food would change just like the scenery or the people's dress – one day, hot chilli, the next it would be raw fish. One holiday would be at high latitudes, the next would be the heaving ice floes at water level watching Chinstrap or Gentoo penguins leap into the cold water as though it were a warm bath.

Each tour would be a one-off; none of us would quite know what to expect after I had made a recce to iron out the largest problems likely to raise their heads though even with careful checks, they would never be able to cover a rogue hippopotamus climbing into our swimming pool as it did one day. (As it was already in our pool when we arrived for an evening dip we did not know if it had dived in or slid into the water with a toe test first.)

•••

Flying into the Buddhist kingdom of Bhutan to explore its monasteries, fortresses and to trek through its dramatic mountains and valleys is an experience of a lifetime. The group was totally amazed by the panoramas of the high Himalaya and Everest itself at 8,849 metres – that is 29,035 feet in old money, as the aircraft approached Thimphu, Bhutan's capital. Does anyone know where Bhutan is before trying to get there? It has a romantic flavour, redolent of Ali Babar and eastern spice markets but is placed exactly due north of Bangladesh, say six hundred and twenty kilometres, capital to capital. A Buddhist nation with a King, its language is *Dzonkha.* It was fortunate we had Lesley as our tour leader and her exceptional leadership qualities proved to be of great value having to deal with several issues along the way, with one of these "odd couples" who insisted on making their own arrangements. This turned out to be yet another example of the trials and tribulations of running a travel company. I had not met the couple before, nor ever heard from them since. The gentleman concerned booked the holiday by telephone on the condition he did not want me to contact him other than through his office, explaining he wanted it to be a surprise for his wife. He also wanted to make his own flight arrangements as he had lots of accumulated air miles to use up. Adding to these complications he said he was also to be routed via Kathmandu. As our holidays were protected by the Civil Aviation Authority through our Air Travel Operator's Licence, ATOL, this was complicated for us because he also wanted the protection of our ATOL licence, which was not possible. Eventually he had reluctantly accepted they would not be covered. When the group arrived at *Thimphu,* Lesley sent me a message to say this couple had not turned up. I discovered why when awakened by a telephone call in the middle of the night from this gentleman explaining they were fogbound in Kathmandu and angrily demanded to know what I was going to do about it. Well, I suppose I could have asked a thousand women armed with silk butterfly wings strapped to their backs to waft hot air from five hundred coke brasiers, towards the mountains, as they do in Spain for the orange trees caught in the frost. Such selfish attitudes luckily occupy the time of a very small percentage of our travellers.

We move on. There was nothing I could do about it except to say I would let Lesley know. The fog eventually lifted and they arrived in Thimphu a day late, by which time the group had already moved forward to our next destination, but our agents greeted them very efficiently at the airport and transferred them to the next hotel to join the group. That was not the end of their frostiness as they were not happy with their room, which was identical for the whole party. There were several other issues that were beginning to have a dampening effect on the rest of the group, who were all having a great time. Lesley learned Mr. Awkward's wife had never had any desire to go to Bhutan on this 'special' holiday in the first place, did not enjoy walking, anywhere, let alone out in the wilds of a foreign country in the east of the world, nor did she like group holidays. One might have thought he would have known his wife rather better than that. When they got back to the UK, I rang the gentleman twice at his office. He said he was in a meeting and would get back to me. He never did.

The purpose of drawing attention to the few things that do go wrong is to understand the responsibility which goes hand in hand with operating a travel business. And from learning about what goes wrong, means you have a chance in the future, of putting it to bed before it collides with the group.

At the end of the first tour to Nepal, several clients asked where we were going next; I knew then we were moving in the right direction. I use the word 'client' for lack of a better description in those early days, but realistically, a better label would be 'friends' because that is what most of them became, meeting time and time again at reunions. It was so nice to meet and talk, with gross exaggeration, of the mishaps now translated into catastrophes.

•••

At the very bottom of our world lies Antarctica. Arriving there, would have made our group upside-down as it were, to the rest of us up here, reminding me of a memorable time, also upside down over RAF Abingdon airfield in somewhat more difficult circumstances. The Antarctic had its own snags and obstacles, of course. Captain Falcon Scott wrote in his diary in January 1912 upon his arrival in the Antarctic.

'Great God, this is an awful place and terrible enough for us to have laboured to it without the reward of priority.'

This seemed to match Daniel Defoe's comments on the Lakes though it was pushing luck to make too close a comparison between the two.

One of our groups flew off to this benighted land led by our intrepid tour leader, Geoff, famed for being photographed naked (almost) in New Zealand. The group, having flown from Buenos Aires to Ushuaia spent two confused days attempting to determine the 'real' most southerly post box. Depending upon one's point of view, one could choose Detaille Island or Isla Redondo, then along came a third on Port Lockroy. Nothing changes with upmanship even when one is this far south - in the biting cold.

The MV Ushuaia, a sturdy, eighty-five metre long expedition ship carried the group across Drake's Passage in relatively calm seas; they estimated the wave heights at a few metres when they could have been twelve metres, that's close to the forty foot high mark. The weather and sea conditions are particularly bad in this area due to the currents at this latitude meeting no resistance from any land mass. It is famously known to mariners as "The Roaring Forties".

The voyage took forty hours. Our Tour arrived at midday in reasonable weather as Antarctica proper, hove in sight. The excitement was tangible as the group loaded themselves into their inflatable Zodiacs which grounded with care on the beach. The idea of being stuck on the Continent without a paddle as it were, made each landing that much more careful.

Crunchy, dry snow stretched out into the far distance in all directions, the temperature about nought degrees, the sky clear. The whole party was told that they were not to leave any litter behind, AT ALL. Strangely, a loophole appeared for there were no 'facilities,' so we did manage to leave something behind when we left.

We were, of course, expecting to see snow and knew all about its properties, but this was the same stuff under our feet which had coated Captain Falcon Scott's tent and wrapped Captain Lawrence Oates gently in his eternal blanket. His body was never found and lies somewhere below the icy surface. Now, the whaling stations were rusting away, beached boats lay like flensed whales, their exposed ribs very similar to those enormous mammals who had died over a hundred years earlier.

Cameras came out in force when Gentoo and Chinstrap penguins appeared, as delightful in real life as on the screen with David Attenborough. The Gentoo is no more than ninety centimetres in height with a distinctive orange beak and a brilliantly white chest. It was as if an army of Maître d's' were lining up to take lessons on how to be good butlers The Chinstrap is a smaller animal, about seventy-five centimetres in height with no colour, just black and white. It is thus easy to distinguish it from its bigger cousin.

Cameras came out a second time, bigger lenses this time as the group's leader, the indomitable Geoff made an executive – read crazy – decision to take an Australian group on at skinny-dipping. Advised the sea temperature was actually -2 degrees; the Australian chickened out at the last moment. Geoff jumped in nonetheless and amazingly, after careful examination under zoom lenses, nothing was found to have dropped off. Score one to the Poms. This was better than cricket.

The journey took the group through the islands filled with whales of an unspecified type, but as there were at least nine types of whale, they could have been any one of them so we were excused from naming them with certainty. Elephant seals so aptly named by their elongated nose and their deep trumpeting call were everywhere, while the air above our excited group was filled with the screeching, shrieking, squawking, screaming of skuas, kelp gulls, blue-eyed cormorants and the classic stormy petrels. Mary Stewart's *The Stormy Petrel* was a good read in its day. These were the images everyone wanted to see – and hear – with the mass of wild life, backgrounded with the barrenness of the ice desert. Below our feet were two and three-quarter miles of ice sitting on liquid lakes, kept liquid by the pressure of the ice upon them. The highest mountains in the world merely poke their snouts out of the snow some occasionally throwing out volcanic ash as dirty marks on the pristine whiteness. The highest is Mount Vinson at 4,892 metres, a cool 16,050 feet.

There were a few buildings. On Deception Island (that's too romantic a name for the place) the British had once run a Research Station there, finally abandoned when it suffered from three volcanic eruptions nearby, the last in 1970. On Detaille Island the British Antarctic Base was also derelict, forlorn, its windows gazing sightlessly out to the icy inlet though still managing to stand firm on a bare craggy rock base for its foundation. It will be still there, I am sure, long after I have shuffled off this mortal coil.

Where ever one looked, there were signs of how the end of whaling had seen off this once profitable industry. The cold would ensure the timber would never rot, leaving only the iron and steel fittings to disintegrate into peeled orange, gracefully easing the frames down as lightly as surgeons would to their patient onto their operating table.

There is, today, a sombre contrast between the demands of the legally binding agreements which determine the conditions for existence on Antarctica – which those countries, party to the agreement, have ratified – to control the absolute purity of the Continent and the bleak, barren, utterly forbidding landscapes where God seems to have gone home to tea a long time ago.

On the return to Ushuaia the boat took an additional ten hours to return to base with "interestingly" high waves and a good place for the crew to sell *Kwells* in advance. The group was followed all the way by swirls and curls of albatrosses circling the ship confirming to the crew and the group, if one wanted to believe the ancient rhyme of having good luck all the way home.

After fifty hours of a heaving world, where the horizon was in constant, violent motion, the terra firma of Ushuaia did not feel as *firma* as the *terra* they had left two days earlier – the distance is about eleven hundred kilometres. Otherwise, the transition our group made leaving Deception Island, was as if they had left the moon to return to earth. Antarctica was so unique from any other tour made. There was not a single element which could be compared with the rest of the world which made any sense save for the wooden huts staring out to sea looking at...what? Perhaps they too had had yearnings to see that other world filled with green and to feel its warmth?

But, what an experience.

•••

There have to be favourites. Everyone draws differing pleasures from a holiday. Some memories embed themselves deeper than others. So it was, the love affair between myself and Oregon, Known as the Beaver State with Salem as its capital it has a strange motto: *'She flies with her own wings.'* Oregon is situated way out west between the states of Washington and California on the American Pacific Coast. I am often asked which of all the countries we visited was my favourite. You've guessed it, Oregon. We went there four times. It should have been forty, or forever, as it was such a great place, but unfortunately Covid-19 cancelled our last planned visit. Coronavirus has a lot to answer for.

One of Oregon's many attractions was Sunriver Resort. Unlike other holidays where we would be travelling throughout the country, here we stayed for a full two weeks. This 5-star 'spirit of the great outdoors' had the whole enchilada: three thousand acres of recreational paradise, luxury where ever one placed a foot, privately owned ranch style homes, swimming pools, tennis, golf, fishing on the Deschutes River, kayaking, horse-riding, forest, cycle paths and a country club. To make it even more attractive, it had its own airfield for private aircraft. Close to the Cascade Mountains, we absorbed the magnificent serenity of Crater Lake National Park, the Oregon Trail and the Deschutes National Forest.

Dave of Wanderlust Tours proved to be an outstanding guide. Together with his wife, Alita, and the other guides, we were introduced to the dramatic natural landscapes and the geological phenomena of Central Oregon, known as High Desert Country.

Denise and I would travel to Oregon in advance of a group to check out our arrangements. Arriving at Redmond Airport we would be greeted by the wonderful aroma of juniper and sage. Smelling the scents we knew we were back.

We would just have enough time for a few games of tennis and exploring the many trails that form part of the Sunriver Resort, before Dave and his wife would invite us around for a barbeque in his desert garden where we would sit around his fire pit while we finalised the programme for the next two weeks.

After a desert guided walk, our tour would arrive at our evening rendezvous as the sun was setting, at a place known as Chuck Wagon. This was a remote eating house, famous from the days of the great cattle drives into California. Drovers between the 1850's and 1900's would often pause here having ridden fifteen to twenty miles in a day, and enjoy a better meal than could be provided by their own cooks. To this day the eatery produces a menu much as the ravenous cowboys used to enjoy. The choice now, as then is either steak or chicken, with no quarter given to vegetarian or vegan menus, or for that matter, nut free, milk free…I could go on, as we have today. As we sat down we found we were in for a surprise. We were naturally, all hungry after a full day's hike in the desert, but nothing like as hungry as the cowboys would have been in the saddle from sun up to dusk. Unaware we had not been on a cattle drive that day, even though we had no chaps on, and with no regard for portion control, we were each served either a whole large chicken or a twenty-eight ounce steak, along with beans and a baked potato. There was no waste as we were all given boxes to take away anything not eaten, which was most of it, and used for picnic lunch sandwiches spread over the next week. I'm not sure about a week-old baked potato sandwich but we all need to try things at least once.

One of the rewards after a hard day's walk was to relax in the outdoor jacuzzi with a glass of wine and watch deer and coyotes wandering around in the forest, which was our garden. There were other great restaurants, but the most popular dinner parties were our own barbeques. Denise and I would go to the supermarket and load up with seafood, steaks, salmon and anything else we could think of to make for a successful evening, which would always include some fine wines from California. The group, as one man, would muck in and these evenings were repeated several times during the holiday rather than going to one of the local restaurants.

•••

We had built in an optional extension to Vancouver Island, which lies off Canada's Pacific coast We travelled by Alaska Airways to Seattle, then took the catamaran to Victoria. With the help of our friends, Brian and Pennie who lived in Victoria, British Columbia's capital, we had planned an interesting programme, including a visit to Tofino, the most westerly small town on the Pacific coast of Canada, famed for its hot springs, bears and whale watching. A day with a First Nation tribe had been planned which involved a boat ride across the Sound to look for whale and bear and end up having fresh salmon for lunch in their village.

Remembering, in the United States, it was correct to refer to Indians as Native Americans and in Canada, as First Nation, I searched for their office in Tofino and had to ask a local if he could point us in the direction of the First Nation office. He had no idea what I was talking about until it clicked. *'Oh, you mean the Indians,'* he said.

Arriving on the island, scrambling ashore on rocks covered in slippery seaweed and negotiating the strong Pacific swell which almost swamped one or two of us until we were able to judge the rise and fall of the water to struggle ashore, we felt a little like Captain James Cook who went ashore here in 1718, the first Europeans. We set off on what was described as a two hour walk through the forest, until I realised our First Nation guides had no notion of time. Asking how far we had to go after three hours, the reply would be *'soon'*. Useful grunt? Soon this turned out to be nearly six hours, by which time we were all starving, well, not quite starving in Biafran terms, but bloody hungry nonetheless. We saw blackberries growing in profusion along the trail so we helped ourselves to stave off the pains. Asking one of the guides if they liked blackberries, he replied: *'Yes, but we can get them in tins'*. It was not surprising by the time we arrived at the village, the salmon had that grey, flabby look, being over cooked and, this time, not surprisingly, cold.

The Canadian Government had been assisting the First Nations in developing tourism and I suspect we were the first to take part in their plan, but what the hell, we had a great day out, arriving back at the hotel ravenous, (again) to be able to crack crab claws liberally coated in garlic butter running down one's fingers transferring the grease onto our wine glasses which required constant attention.

On the day of our departure, I was called early morning, telling me to turn on the TV. The caller mentioned we would not be going anywhere today. We were watching 9/11 live from New York. We, like the world, were horrified. What to do now? I gathered everyone together to discuss the plan for our extended stay. As it was a terrorist incident, most travel insurance policies would not cover this kind of extremist event. I had to do some fast thinking. My first approach was to ask the hotel manager if he would consider a reduction in the tariff for us to stay on. The reply was negative. Spending the morning searching around, we managed to find another 5–star hotel prepared to negotiate a better rate, realising there were not going to be any more tourists for some time. Back at our hotel the manager had had time to reconsider his own position and generously offered us a better rate which persuaded us to stay. Sensible man. Explaining this to everyone, no one complained when I invited them to pay the reduced accommodation costs and they should try to re-claim this from their insurance company. We held twice-daily emergency meetings while I spent hours on the 'phone trying to get through to British Airways in London, without success. One of our client's kindly allowed me to use his satellite 'phone, which was a great help. In any case there were no aircraft movements across the whole of the American continent. When flights did start up again, I decided to move the group to Vancouver to be close to the airport. Some passengers were getting away, but not us. There were long queues at the airport, which resembled a refugee camp with emergency marquees and soup kitchens everywhere as if we were in the poorest part of Chicago in the Depression. Why is it always soup rather than a steak sandwich for example?

Each day I joined the British Airways queue and could not help but wonder at the attitude of some passengers bringing up all sorts of reasons why they should be given priority treatment, and, simultaneously, abusing the staff. Those people were not going anywhere. Patiently waiting and not making a fuss, there was success at last and, with very little notice, we were on our way, with upgraded flights back to the UK. Not once did anyone complain after a week of anxiety. But, did I forget to say, we were British?

It was agreed to share our respective experiences of our attempts to claim on our travel insurance policies. All of us, except one, drew a blank because terrorism was not covered. But one lady came up with the answer. She explained to her insurers, the event had caused her deep distress. This, apparently, was the line to have taken, though not one of us had any stress at all. It worked.

•••

The Army teaches you *'time spent in reconnaissance is seldom wasted'*. It meant I would be off to South Africa to plan the next holiday. Arriving at the resort and expecting to be met by my Agent, I was concerned there was nobody waiting patiently at my arrival gate armed with a cardboard sheet with my name in scribbled black ink writ large upon it. When my contact eventually turned up, he appeared to be in a bit of a state. The day I arrived an hippopotamus had been an uninvited guest in the resort's swimming pool, causing much alarm amongst guests and staff. Someone had the bright idea of throwing a thunder flash into the pool. Much to my surprise, skilled as I had been in ordnance, although not attacking hippopotamuses (I am assured this is one of two correct ways to spell the animal's name) it worked, solving the problem as the enormous animal galloped, or rather, trundled, off into the night with everyone much relieved.

I continued my reconnaissance to the Northern Drakensburg the main mountain range of South Africa with some quite high mountains reaching 3,500 metres, that is 11,400 feet. Driving along, after passing through Pietermaritzburg, I could see hundreds of Zulus loping along in that characteristic striding run and coming straight towards me in the middle of the road. Remembering the movie 'Zulu', and being a Welshman, I considered it a possibility to sing my way out of this small issue, but how would the Zulus know I was a Welshman? I suppose I could try, just as Ivor Emanuel had sung: *'Men of Harlech'* in the film? Later I discovered they were going to Pietermaritzburg to demonstrate, as one does in this part of the country.

I arrived at the Little Switzerland Resort but, forgoing lunch, I joined several staff members who were in a rush to set off to rescue a cow, as one does, stuck in a deep hole and not feeling very happy with life. The Land Rover was fitted with chains and the cow was eventually rescued. He 'mooed' away to express his thanks before scampering off to re-join her herd. This was the first of many visits to this mountain resort, much enjoyed by everyone over many years. I relished the company of the owners who became good friends. They always took a close personal interest in our group and arranged all sorts of extras for us, such as Zulu dancers entertaining us after dinner most nights and joined us on several of our walks in the Royal Natal National Park twenty-five kilometres away.

Enjoying a cup of tea on the balcony one evening, I was blown away with the sheer beauty of the nearby hills called the *Thaba Bosin* plateau or *'barrier of spears,'* which sounds a good bit more dramatic than *Thaba Bosin.* If you have seen this movie 'Zulu' already mentioned, I can tell you the same hills in the long shots are the ones I was looking at while sipping my tea. Such a sublime moment for me, separated by almost one hundred and fifty years from those darkest of times in the Zulu wars yet with so many memories of eleven V.C.s' being awarded at Rouke's Drift in 1879.

Getting to the top of the plateau involved climbing a chain ladder up a vertical rock face, which some of our group found challenging. One or two became, what is called, *'cragfast'*, meaning half way up they could neither continue or go back down again. I call it the *Grand Ole Duke of York* syndrome. But with the help of our guides, everyone made it and were exhilarated by the experience. Arriving on the top we were in Lesotho, a high-altitude, 3,482 metres of landlocked kingdom encircled by South Africa. There was a police post situated right at the top for no reason I could deduce but found out later it was to discourage local tribesmen from pushing isolated tourists over the cliff to steal their gear, as had happened the year before. So, good reason for the post to be there really.

Horse riding was included in our itinerary so we divided up into two groups; experienced and novices. Although I had been taught to ride as a junior officer in the Army, that was a long time ago, so I made the decision that my best place would be with the novices. You will, surely recall my account at the Big Horn mountain, Algonquin Provincial Park, which was, not to put too fine a point on it, not too successful. And, here again, there were not enough horses for the novices so, heroically, like Captain Oates for the second time, I joined the experienced riders. What a mistake. Stupid! Silly! Crass!, brainless and dumb are useful adjectives at this time. Surely I had learned my lesson? We took off – good description - across the African veldt with me holding on for dear life, all the time scared sh**less I was about to fall off with my foot caught up in the stirrup and dragged along to certain doom. Surprising myself I remained upright, panting but able to stroke my horse's mane1 when we eventually arrived back, never to mount a horse again.

Every night, before dusk, the herd of horses belonging to the resort made their way from the veldt into the corral. I was surprised to see a zebra accompanying them. Christopher told me the zebra, although still untamed, had sensed a better quality of life, with plenty of hay, and realising he was safe from roaming lions by joining the horses incognito. At first, the horses tried to kick him out and would have nothing to do with him, until eventually they accepted him as a member of the herd. He had become a horse, although no one attempted to ride him. They have an exceptional bite I am told.

Departing after one particularly enjoyable visit to Little Switzerland, Christopher said he was about to employ a general manager, so next time he would be able to spend more time with us. He took on a former South African police inspector as General Manager who set about his duties with great promise and enthusiasm. One of the Zulu security guards had been in the habit of not turning up for work so the new Manager put him on a disciplinary warning, followed by dismissal. The Zulu quite obviously did not like this treatment and stole back to the resort one dark night and shot the General Manager, killing him. The police investigation concluded there was no evidence, despite everyone knowing who the killer was. While the investigation was continuing, the Zulu died of AIDS. Probably a just end to the saga.

Some of my ideas worked; some not so well. It was not a very bright idea to lumber our clients with a lecture on dinosaurs by a well-known local archaeologist on the first night of a holiday, particularly when everyone was jet lagged after a long flight. I recognised my mistake as soon as one of my guests started snoring and fell off his chair. Undeterred, the archaeologist droned on until he was interrupted and told dinner was ready.

The only thing I did not like were the *Hadeda Ibis* birds. Why? Because one always knew when they were around due to their piercing, screeching calls. They favoured perching on the thatch roof of my bungalow – shades of Kuching - and started their daily routine of shrieking and screaming just before dawn, clearly to draw attention to themselves and to make sure we were not going to miss one moment of daylight. *'Slap some bacon on a biscuit and let's go, we're burning daylight'* as John Wayne used to say.

A storm had blown some Ibis chicks out of their nest. The Owners, anxious for their safety, particularly from mongooses roaming around, built them a nest under some bushes and detailed their Zulu staff to keep a twenty-four hour watch over them. They survived to squawk away assuring other guests unwanted early morning calls. No need for an alarm clock.

•••

Let me write about the end of the world. Most have heard of the region, not many could slide a finger down a map of the Andes to point it out. If you try and go further you will get fairly wet, and cold as you drop into the Strait of Magellan or Drake's Passage. Fewer still, have ever visited, so, of course, we had to go there and gathered together an interested group.

Patagonia is, confusingly a geographical region and not a country in its own right. The area is governed, jointly by Argentina and Chile. All was going well so far, having arrived on time and, loaded up, we headed off to cross six hundred kilometres of Patagonian Desert on the way to the remote outpost right under the foothills of the Andes and close to the border with Chile. We were booked into *Hosteria Lagos del Furioso* and marvelled at its location on a curious strip of land between two lakes under the shadow of *Cerro San Lorenzo,* the second highest peak in the Patagonian Andes rising to 3,706 metres. No need to work it out here if you do not want to. My calculation is 12,200 feet.

The long drive gave me a welcome if overdue time to reflect on how far I had gone since my days – years – in the Army which I had loved. At the point where I had made the decision to leave the forces, I thought, at times, I might have gone off my head. Now, alone in this remote land, I realised those years had all been part of building and storing knowledge which was now being deployed to great value. It made me realise I had indeed, made the right decision to leave when I did, and in my way, was able to pass on many of those skills to my guests.

We really were in a breathtakingly, remote, wilderness with no other humans in sight for miles in either direction. Our only companions were wild duck, flamingos, rhea, guanacos, foxes, pumas and condors. Writing this it seems like a zoo had escaped. Clients who joined us on that trip will never forget it, particularly the two-day journey on dirt roads across the desert. Along the way we noticed a guanaco tangled up in a wire fence running alongside the dirt road. Being half asleep at the time, it took some time for it to register, but, after several miles, we turned, because we were British, and loved our animals, and thus had to do something about it. We drew up alongside to discover the guanaco, a female, well and truly caught up in the wire with her partner running back and forth in a great state of alarm on the other side of the fence. We all got out with several guests suggesting different ways of tackling the problem which was becoming more complicated by the moment. Comments such as: *'David you take the back legs and I'll direct operations from over here,'* were not helpful at all. Despite the male's attempts to fight us off, we managed to untangle the animal after taking half an hour out of our precious time needed to arrive at our destination before nightfall, only for the female, now freed, to run off on the wrong side of the wire whereupon her partner became even more agitated. But, eyeing up the height, drawing back with its long legs, squinting a bit, it roared off towards the wire which it cleared in a magnificent leap of freedom. The last we saw was the two of them racing off at great speed into the desert. Turning back was the right thing to do and we continued the journey feeling rather satisfied with ourselves. If we had not come along, the poor animal might well have died at the jaws of the pumas and foxes. As it turned out the couple had a new life in front of them.

Our first guided walk was to a nearby lagoon. Covered in water in winter and leaving strange shapes when it evaporated in the summer, it looked to us like a lunar landscape, with the soil turning chalk white as it dried out in the sun. We passed several bleached animal skeletons, half buried in the earth as if they were props for a western film, and wondered how they had met their end. Our next trek was to Monte San Lorenzo via a huge granite massif with blue-tinted glaciers in the distance creeping down the heart of the highest mountains in the Southern Andes. Our only companions that day were the ten foot wing span Condors soaring high above us keeping a close eye in case we were tempted to climb up to their nests perched hundreds of feet on vertical cliffs. Just as well we had forgotten to bring any ropes with us! Our guide was hoping to show us a puma but the nearest we got was its den with many animal bones scattered around and a distinctive big cat smell.

The hosteria was simple, but comfortable, but on the last night the Manager approached me with obvious concern showing on his face. He was also wringing his hands. Prone to enjoying an occasional glass of wine, our thirsty group had nearly cleared his wine cellar. The nearest store where he stocked up on everything was a six-hour drive away. All he had to offer was his most expensive wines. By the end of the evening, he was planning an early departure to re-stock his, by now, totally empty wine cellar.

Trouble began to raise its head on the return drive to El Chaltén, in the Glaciares National Park, a distance of some five hundred and sixty kilometres. One could describe it as a sort of frontier town and the gateway to Monte Fitz Roy not climbed until 1952 by two French alpinists. Halfway down the road, we had reached a small settlement with a few rundown houses, a police post, a garage and café, when one of our two minibuses broke down. It took six hours to fix it. To pass the time we filled up our petrol tanks and jerrycans and managed to get back on our way. It was a long journey to El Chaltén and I asked the guide, riding in the first vehicle, to make sure both vehicles stayed together and with full jerrycans of petrol distributed between both vehicles as it was touch and go whether we could get to our destination on a full tank. In the Army the man would have been on a charge because his daft driver, showing off in the front car, went racing off leaving us well behind in the dust. Getting close to El Chaltén, the petrol gauge was showing nearly empty. I asked the driver to pull over to top up from our jerrycan. He looked at me blankly. *'All the jerrycans are in the other vehicle, senor.'* There is a word for it in the Army but I won't use it here. But we made it, arriving at the hosteria in the middle of the night.

But, there was worse to come. I had booked en-suite accommodation for the group, but what we were given was backpacker accommodation with bunk beds and one bathroom between six people. One of the ladies we shared a room with, insisted I left the room until she got into bed. Making myself scarce until she was asleep, we were told no other accommodation was available. Finding it difficult to sleep, I got up early - also to provide the lady with a bit of space - and did a bit of scouting around. Close-by I found a half-decent development still being constructed and asked the owner if he had enough rooms completed to take us all. We were his first guests. Problem solved.

Sitting on the edge of the Southern Icefield, El Chaltén and El Calafate, the latter on the edge of the ice-field, just a stone's throw away from the Perito Moreno Glacier and close to Monte Fitz Roy and Cerro Torres, two of Patagonia's most impressive mountains; they stick up like rotten bats teeth, spiky and sharp.

We visited Fitz Roy on Valentine's Day quite special to be there when, on a normal day in England we might have taken one's spouse out of a pub lunch. Here, arriving at Base Camp we found an honesty letter box. Opening it up, one guest placed a Valentine card from me addressed to Denise, inside the box. Asking her to have a look inside, she was surprised (probably not so surprised actually) to find the Valentine card addressed to her.

Sitting with our picnic lunch overlooking Monte Fitz Roy's 3.400 metre cap we were enchanted by the amazing view over the lake and glacier which sat in front of us as if it were a West End stage. We marvelled at the thunderous roar as tons of ice calved off the glacier to disappear into the lake. Meanwhile, Denise had, finally, opened her card and remarked it was the most perfect Valentine Day imaginable.

From the sublime to the ridiculous one lady had a serious accident requiring surgery. We had four doctors on the trip so I asked one of them for advice and assistance. *'No good asking me, I'm a brain surgeon'.* Fortunately, one of them was a GP.

When we reached Chile's Torres del Paine National Park more trouble began to start up, difficult stuff, out of our control. The guide, listening to the local news, believed he had heard something concerning one of the domestic airlines going into liquidation. It had to be, of course, the airline which was to take us to Ushuaia on Tierra Del Fuego, the southernmost tip of the American continent shared with Chile and known for its spectacular landscapes, snow-capped mountains and glaciers. The highest peak, Nevado Ojos del Salado at 6,893 metres is the highest volcano in the world and that is at 22,615 feet. Within the timescale of our itinerary, there was no other way to get there except by air. From Ushuaia we were booked to fly back to the UK via Buenos Aires, but if we could not get to Ushuaia, neither would we be able to get to Buenos Aires for the return flight to the UK. That would have required additional hotel accommodation and re-booked seats on another airline. After many calls to the airline but without anyone answering, it was time to use what was left of my *'airborne initiative'*. Departing the National Park a day earlier, our coach took us to *Rio Gallegos* where we managed to find hotel accommodation for the group, while the guide and I made our way to the airport to see what chance there was of booking an alternative flight to get to *Ushuaia* the following day, only to find the airline's check-in desk locked up. Hundreds of would-be passengers were stranded, some without sufficient funds to book alternative flights, even if any were available, which was unlikely. Some were visibly distressed seeing no help forthcoming; there was no one in the vicinity willing to help them. It was late on a Saturday and things were looking desperate when an idea came to me. Entering one of the offices uninvited, we managed to speak to a member of staff who spoke English. He examined our tickets which are known as consolidated tickets, meaning the international carrier was contractually responsible for domestic flights and requiring them to find alternative flights. After a great deal of hassle, Buenos Aires arranged for an unscheduled aircraft to pick us up to continue our journey to *Ushuaia* the following morning.

The return flight from Buenos Aires to the UK via Madrid was several hours late in departing. It arrived in Paris too late for our connecting flight to the UK. It meant we all had to queue up in line, as if been loaded onto cattle trucks heading for Auschwitz where, after several hours, we were told no more aircraft would be available as they were about to close for the night. We were advised to return to the airport the following day and try again. In the meantime, our luggage had been going dizzy as it completed the hundredth circuit of the carousel until some of our clients went to check it out, only to find their luggage had been transferred to a huge storage hangar at the far end of the airport. Showing great initiative, they flagged down a van and instructed the driver to take them to the hangar where they were able to identify and collect all our luggage.

The airline did manage to book hotel rooms in Madrid for all of us, and, reunited with our luggage, we made our way to the nominated hotel while I attempted to find alternative flights home. Frustrated with the whole level of incompetence, and with the airport about to close, I noticed a British Airways desk and asked if they could help. As cool as you like, they understood the responsibility associated with consolidated tickets and booked us all on flights home the following morning. The world's favourite airline. Back at the hotel, everyone was in high spirits on hearing the good news. It was drinks all round. Perhaps then, I felt it was worth remaining a tour leader.

CHAPTER 13 (PART TWO)

More Slices of the World

It was to be South America again. The country drew us in as if it were Evita and her cohorts themselves, to the land she so loved. I began to plan the tour which would be led by one of my expedition leaders – we had grown in size by this time – when two days before the departure of the group to Peru and Bolivia, this tour leader was rushed into hospital and was going nowhere further for some time. I was committed to another trip and up the creek without any paddles, with no tour leader. I rang Elwyn a regular tour traveller and already booked onto the holiday, asking if he would take over. He was delighted to help and I was in my car with all the files within half an hour and greatly relieved the tour could go ahead.

Little did Elwyn know of the problems ahead.

As far as I am aware, I do not believe Elwyn ever served in Airborne Forces, but he certainly had to deploy his *'noggin'* when confronted with a problem trying get the group across Lake Titicaca from Peru into Bolivia during a national strike. To beat the striking pickets, he arranged with the guide to cross the lake in the middle of the night. I was reminded of George Patton with his 5th US Division crossing the Rhine at night. Despite moans and groans about losing a night's sleep, the group, now feeling like a commando raiding party, set off carrying their luggage to the edge of the lake after crawling through the undergrowth. The larger boat waiting to take them to Bolivia was anchored offshore but could not get in any closer for fear of being attacked by demonstrators. Climbing aboard the small boat with the weight of the group plus luggage threatening to overload and sink us, some thought it was their final journey. Everyone managed to embark safely onto the impatiently waiting boat, allowing them to be on their way across the lake.

Arriving in Bolivia the group was greeted by demonstrators trying to climb aboard our coach while others succeeded in smashing a few windows. The group spent the journey sitting on the floor of the coach amongst broken glass, but thankfully making it to the hotel without any injuries. Elwyn should have received the Order of the Coach (OOC) but did collect a pile of brownie points. He was pleased to settle for a banana. There was no chance of getting out of the hotel the following day, due to angry demonstrations, marches through the town and armed forces patrolling everywhere. They were quite a volatile nation.

One of the most important issues when planning a tour to Peru and Bolivia is to ensure the group was properly acclimatised. Every traveller worth his salt, wants to go Machu Picchu, the Incan citadel high up in the Andes – at 2,430 metres, that's around 8,000 feet - constructed in the fifteenth century. The flight route took the group to Lima and then on to Cusco, where many walkers spend a couple of days working off their altitude sickness. This can be easily avoided by leaving Cusco on the same day, making for the Sacred Valley over two thousand feet lower. In such a way Machu Picchu becomes more enjoyable and by the time Cusco is reached on the return journey, everyone is fully adjusted to the altitude. One other way, I was told, was to suck cocaine sweets made from the leaves of the cocoa plant, a species native to South America. Cocaine tea was also suggested as a palliative, all perfectly legal in South America. None of us suffered from altitude sickness. Read into that what you want.

•••

Almost at the bottom of the world, our Antipodes, New Zealand visits were the most challenging to arrange, but, in a strange reversal always turned out to be hugely enjoyable. Two activities always included on each of our visits were heli-hikes and the four-night Abel Tasman Track near Nelson on the South Island. Both were outstanding.

Everyone was aware, Border Control on arrival in Auckland was liable to search luggage for fruit, which was forbidden, and dirty boots which could introduce contamination into the country. One lady was fined one hundred New Zealand dollars because a sniffer dog had detected an orange in her bag. She complained bitterly but she should have known better.'... *Rules is rules, Dirty boots is dirty boots madam.'*

At a harbourside dinner in Auckland, one of the group wanted to see her brother, a purser on a Saga cruise ship docked nearby. The ship was due to sail at midnight but as no one was permitted on board, we all waited on the dock with her to see the ship set sail. The only other humans in sight had gathered on the harbour to give her a good send-off was a brass band. Taking it turns to ask the band to play our favourite tunes, I was surprised and delighted they knew *'Hen Wlad Fy Nhadau'* the Welsh national anthem. ('Old Land of my Fathers'). When we asked her brother, waving to us from the deck, where all the passengers were, because we thought they would want to bid farewell to Auckland and appreciate the send-off by the band he replied: *'The old farts have all gone to bed.'* Quite so.

Peter, our guide in Queenstown for the remarkable heli-hike, came limping to the heliport in agony. He had fallen over his dog's lead that morning, but bravely attempted to carry on. When he was getting out of the helicopter, he collapsed with a dislocated knee. We were high up on a mountain with little or no tracks, and now without a guide. He clearly could not continue. He handed me the map, and after a quick briefing, he was off on the same helicopter back to Queenstown. We were on our own and had to find our way to the pick-up point in six hours' time. – shades of the Army? at which time I would have called it the RV point. The problem with off-trail hiking is the 'going' can be very slow, having to beat one's way through long grass and side-stepping inconvenient bushes. It does not help if you take the wrong route… as I managed to do, but when we approached a sheer drop, we realised we had gone the wrong way and carefully retraced our steps before starting out again. Keeping cool heads we made it back to the helicopter pick-up point for the flight back to Queenstown.

When making our way to the Franz Josef Glacier, our guide was notable for his looks, a bit like John Sullivan, the bare-knuckle fighter in 1889, distinguishable that is, by the large number of cuts and bruises all over his body. He had fallen head first into a crevasse a few weeks earlier and had been stuck fifty feet down, unable to move. It must have been a terrifying experience waiting for the ice to move again more than hopefully in an outward direction. Probably still dining out on it. He described the rescue before being quite ready to face the challenge again. We took extra care crossing a couple of crevasses by fixed ladder, but were rewarded later with a heli-hike up to the top of the glacier. Heli-hiking is, basically, employing a helicopter to take one up to the top where there is no other way to approach the summit.

•••

Coach travel is a quite different form of holiday to anything else. Well, of course it is, you say. A charabanc is not an airplane is it? Coaches not only provide the ability to gaze out of a wide window half-asleep while someone prattles on, but is more a feeling of '…we are on our way,' which brings to many a comfortable feeling of security. The gentle shake of the seat, I am sure, reminds one of the days when one was shaken similarly in one's mother's womb. When travelling by coach with a group, one of the features to look out for are passengers who return to the same seats each day. Always make a point at the beginning of a tour of asking clients not to sit in the same seat each day, particularly the more popular front seats. One couple who joined the tour late and missed the briefing, made it to the front seats every day, much to the irritation of everyone else. Taking them to one side to explain, everything was fine again. It was my fault for not giving them the full briefing. Pay attention to detail.

Journeying long distances by coach in New Zealand as we did, demanded I give careful attention to our drivers who doubled as guides at times. Many travellers will have experienced the too-long blather of an enthusiastic driver talking to jet-lagged travellers quite uninterested in the fact the largest whale in the world had been caught three hundred miles from where the coach was at this moment.

Commentaries from the driver/guide can be difficult, so discussing this with him or her on the first day is essential. It is commonly known as NZDVD – or even more commonly, New Zealand Drivers Verbal Diarrhoea. On one trip, the driver never stopped talking, not only about the areas we were passing through, but droning on as a continuity man, incessantly about himself, that no one had the slightest interest in listening to. The man had a captive audience. How to deal with it? No matter how diplomatic one is in requesting less verbosity, drivers can easily be offended. On this occasion, he was not only offended but did not utter another word for the rest of the day. I called the Agent the following day and we were assigned a replacement driver for the rest of the trip. There was one, though, a co-operative driver whose company I enjoyed. When making suggestions, his reply was either *'fluffy duck'* or *'good as gold, Dave'*. We were attempting to explore the west coast on the North Island one day when it was pouring with rain. Our cooperative driver said it would be sunny on the Pacific East coast and we could visit Napier. He knew an excellent vineyard that served a good lunch. When we arrived, the sun was shining, as he had predicted, and we had a great day. I thanked him for his initiative and a great day out, but do not recall him thanking me when I was helping him to reverse out and managed to direct his coach back into the hotel's smart new entrance porch!

Checking in for the second time at the Heritage Hotel in Christchurch, the Receptionist, having checked her computer, and realising we had stayed before, greeted us with *'Welcome back Mr Fairs and I thought you might like to know we have upgraded everyone to Junior Suites'*. There was a bottle of champagne in my room. It always pays to look after your customers and, since then, the hotel has several times been, unsurprisingly, winner of *'World Luxury Hotel'* for the Australasia and Oceania region.

Wandering, later, a trifle unsteadily across the square from the hotel, having finished the bottle, we visited the impressive Christchurch Cathedral where the famous Christchurch Boys School Choir was rehearsing for the evening service. We met the Bishop who was wandering up and down the aisles at the time, although not as unevenly as myself, where he made us feel very welcome, even persuading us to come to the evening service. Before starting his sermon, he made a point of welcoming our group, even remembering some of our names and where we came from. I wish we had a few more Bishops like him in the old country. Or one?

Same group, different town, Queenstown. We arrived at the same time as a large Japanese group. Knowing we would have to wait a long time, I leaped off our coach like a Thompson's gazelle, and got in before them to collect our keys We left passports and form filling until later. Once the keys had been distributed, I joined the group only to discover our four single clients had accidentally been up-graded to junior suites with lounge, lake view and kitchen with a washing machine. We were booked in for three nights so this was a bonus for our single clients, who often got a rough deal when it comes to room allocation. Instead of keeping quiet about their good luck, one of them wound up some of the team by showing them around, '...come and look at my wonderful washing machine,' resulting in dissatisfaction because the usual grousers had not been allocated similar accommodation. '...And I haven't even got a washing machine in my room.' Trying to keep everybody happy, I managed to sort everything out, except for one couple, the "odd couple again." Always a wife and husband banding together for additional strength, the wife goading on her husband as if she was an Omani camel driver prodding its camel up a steep sand dune. To save any problems, I gave them my room. Returning to the Front of House after the Japanese group had been sorted out, it was left for Reception to find a room for me. As luck would have it, and surely because I was the tour leader on our third visit to the hotel, I was upgraded to a VIP Suite? With plenty of room in my suite, the following evening everyone was invited around for a pre-dinner drinks party. The same couple who had been given my room immediately observed they did not have a room like that, implying it was unfair. They sounded like some members of a particular political party!

'Perhaps Madam, Sir, you would like to go and play on the motorway for half an hour? No, no. Not the A1. The M1. It's busier.'

An added dimension to the New Zealand holidays was achieved by breaking the twenty-four hour flight from UK half way, stopping overnight outbound and inbound, choosing variously from Los Angeles, Kuala Lumpur, Singapore, Sydney and Bangkok. In Los Angeles we stayed at Marina Del Ray to enjoy a day on nearby quirky Venice Beach. It broke the jet-lag and enabled us to arrive at our destination far more refreshed than we might otherwise have been and strength enough to allow the wife to carry the suitcases inside and up the stairs to the bedroom.

We chartered an America's Cup, Grand Prix Racing yacht for a hands-on sail around Auckland harbour. Hands on was, in fact, hang on…tightly…for dear life when we had strong winds which seemed intent on capsizing our craft at every tightening of a halyard.

One cannot travel to New Zealand without experiencing one or other of the famous walking tracks on South Island. Three to four days wilderness walking with a choice of the Milford, Hollyford or Routeburn Tracks. The Routeburn, for example rises up thirteen hundred metres with some steep sections, and is often in competition with the Milford for the best walk. Another, the Abel Tasman Coastal Track, sixty kilometres in length, is a four-night affair where one spends two nights each at rustic homesteads sitting on the beach at Torrent Bay and Meadowbank, Awaroa. Guided walks are along beaches, estuaries and creeks on the Abel Tasman Sea. If the tide is out, one can avoid the longer route by wading across the estuaries. When the tide is right out, crossing can be made by walking along the sand. On the day we were there, we hurried to one crossing point to beat the incoming tide only to arrive too late. The guide was sceptical about risking crossing the estuary but, faced with a ninety minute detour and taking a democratic vote on it, I decided to take the risk. The tide was coming in fast and the distance to the other side about three hundred metres.

Everybody turned up their shorts and anxious to avoid any further delay, we were all set to go. (shades of Morecambe Bay?) All except one lady who was concerned she might not make it due to the speed of the rapidly advancing tide.

'Madam. The longer we wait here discussing it, the less chance we have of any of us making it. And if we go on talking like this we are all going to drown.' That sort of painted a clear picture for her and she proved eventually she was game enough to agree to come with us. The water was, though, by the time we had reached the halfway mark, up to our waists. I was surprised that the New Zealand equivalent of the RNLI – I believe it is called Coastguard New Zealand – was not called out, but we all made it back safely ensuring that at the Honours and Awards ceremony at the end of the holiday this distinguished lady was, to her amusement and pleasure, awarded the title of 'Estuary Queen'.

•••

India was always going to pull us back again and again. It was in our DNA, born out of generations of British Civil Servants. At its height, just 1,200 civil servants and support staff numbering a total of 4,000 British administered to 300 million Indians over four million square kilometres. They managed to hold down this extraordinarily exciting, yet chaotic world by rule of law. Bedlam was born here and visits to Rajasthan were designed to get us off the beaten track to explore ethnic tribal areas and remote villages. At night we would stay in old forts and palaces turned into hotels. We would also include several nights of indulgence in some of the best hotels in India. The contrast worked well and repeat visit requests came continually through my letter box. India was always on the agenda. One example of the type of places we stayed were "rustic palaces", one such being the Ghanerao Royal Palace, in Ranakpur, Western Rajasthan, a rather faded, rambling old fort built in 1606 (just six years after the opening of the East India Company) now struggling to catch up with standards expected of western visitors, but rather wonderful for all its shortcomings.

The owner, Thakur Sajjan Singh, was also the hands-on manager. As tour leader, Mr Singh graciously allocated me the best room in the hotel, and after unpacking for our three-night stay, laying out my kit Army style, I was off to check everyone was settled in. One couple were not happy with their room, but our group had occupied all available rooms, so I felt obliged to let them have my room. Next there was another couple also unhappy with their room and for the second time of packing and unpacking I was like a refugee searching for a bed for the night at the Sally Army. Mr Singh offered me a room behind the kitchen that was actually some sort of tower and not normally used by guests. With no windows or electricity and a ceiling fifty feet high, it was unappealing, to say the least and made me feel quite claustrophobic. Sleeping was difficult but on the maxim: *'I have not come here to enjoy myself,'* I remained mum.

At long last, Mr Singh and I were quietly enjoying a cup of tea together when the same couple complained they only had one bedside light. I was tempted to say they were lucky because I only had a bloody candle, but thought that would not help matters much. Instead, Mr Singh said he would find a light for them. Half an hour later the couple approached us again to say the light had still not yet been delivered and it was getting dark. After another half an hour or so they came rushing over for the third time to say they did have a light but it had the wrong plug and the *'boy'* had connected it with bare wires and matches. '...yes, but what is your point madam?' They considered it a health and safety problem. When they left expressing their dissatisfaction, Mr Singh said they did not have any more bedside lights and the *'boy'* had run all the way to Mr Singh's house half a mile away and taken his wife's bedside light. His house had different plugs to the hotel.

Mr Singh invited me to the quadrangle after dinner to listen to the music of a Hindu festival that could be heard outside the hotel. The same couple came over to ask if we could stop the noise as they could not sleep. 'Stop the noise of a nationwide religious festival Colonel Fairs…please.' I was told the Festival was scheduled to stop in ten minutes and the following morning the couple thanked me for stopping all that *noise* the night before. Amazing what you can do with sleight of hand.

Such guests would be so much happier if they avoided group holidays or staying at home and certainly not the interesting countries such as India with all its chaotic glories. Surely, it is why we wish to visit, to get away from the strictures of Britain or Europe?

Rajasthan meant ending our holiday at the internationally known Lake Palace Hotel, beautifully positioned in the middle of a lake in Udaipur. Knowing the Chairman of the UK Timeshare Council, was a friend of His Highness the Maharana of Udaipur, and had been invited on elephant safaris with him in the foothills of the Himalaya, I asked him to write to His Royal Highness by way of introduction. The Maharana's P.A. called me to arrange a visit to the Palace. When I told her there were twenty of us in the group, it must have surprised her but the message came back with a request for the names of everyone in our group including rank, title and decorations!

Before departing for India, a bundle of gold crested pasteboard arrived, inviting us all to go to his Palace on the day we arrived at the Lake Palace Hotel for a cocktail party. I had booked and paid extra for rooms with a lake view. While everyone else had a lake view, I was allocated a rather tatty, single room, without a lake view, but decided not to make a fuss. In any case, I was assured no other rooms were available. Half unpacked, I suddenly thought it prudent to enquire how to get to the Palace. 'Why did I want to know that?' requested the receptionist. 'Because we were invited by His Royal Highness (that's the correct way to address him) to a cocktail party and we have no idea how to get there.' A private boat was sent to collect us and everyone, impressed with the Royal Palace and its hospitality, were transported back to the grand days of the British Raj.

The general manager also appeared on the scene asking if there was anything he could do to help. I mentioned a room with a lake view. *'Absolutely no problem at all Mr David'* I was offered tea and biscuits in his office but declined as I had to re-pack everything. (again). *'The boy will do that'.*

The P.A. took me to one side after an hour or so suggesting I should thank His Royal Highness and be on our way as he had another engagement. Following her instructions and extending my thanks for his hospitality, he replied, *'Where the bloody hell do you think you are going?'* There were many interesting and intelligent people in our group and he was clearly enjoying our company. I mentioned our delayed departure to the P.A. and expressed concern that we could be late for dinner. *'That will not be a problem, Mr David, His Royal Highness owns the hotel'*.

The manager arranged for us to attend a Beating Retreat at another converted palace. We were served tea on the balcony while waiting for the tattoo to start. It consisted of one camel, one drummer, one trumpeter and a flautist. They marched up and down with precision reminding me in a small cameo of the past what it had once been in the Raj days when it would have drawn crowds to the massed bands.

The memories of India go on and on. Tented accommodation in an old hunting lodge in Samode was luxurious and the service impeccable. A member of staff was allocated to look after our group and soon after we had unpacked, he asked if there was anything we needed. I requested a fire be prepared for after dinner. Nothing was too much of a problem. While the flames crackled and crisped the grass at the edges, we spent the evening around the huge fire listening to stories of the old hunting days and the British Raj. The first person I saw the next morning was our man who came running over requesting: *'Bed, tea, Sahib?'* Beyond the call of duty.

The streets in the small village of Deogarh were too narrow to accommodate our coach so we were transferred by jeep to arrive at our hotel, Deogarh Mahal, nestling in the Aravalli Hills. Dinner, was a romantic experience, served in the open air on the battlements of the hotel. It did not give us any clue at all as to what was about to happen next.

Our rooms were found with great difficulty within a labyrinth of corridors where muddle and confusion came before logic. Rooms 1-15, 27 and 101? This would not have been a problem at any other time but in the middle of the night there came an enormous explosion of noise caused by a volcanic tremor shaking the hotel as if it were a pepper pot. At first, there was absolute silence, not a pin was dropped, or so it seemed; then the animals started up with camels, elephants, donkeys, cows, monkeys and buffalo to name but a few of the menagerie, all began, in unison, to screech their heads off in alarm. Eventually, I found my way to the Front of House after several wrong turns along the warren, to find staff had gathered also wondering what had happened. While I worried and fretted trying to plan how to get through the narrow streets with all our luggage, if they were blocked with debris, the entire cast of our group slept through the screeching, the roaring and the ee-yoring while I worried how we were going to escape. Bless them! You haven't etc.etc...

Tucked in with the other messages of thanks received after our visit to Rajasthan, there was one rather special one worth drawing attention to at this time. From that couple without a bedside light, it recommended the group should use hotels that did not serve Indian food. They preferred English food. Bless, two!

Should have gone to Blackpool.

•••

The Galapagos Islands have always held a deeply romantic cachet to travellers and a difficult one for a school boy to get his tongue around, yet, in the hands of a good geography teacher he or she could paint a picture of mystery, a sealed book, a riddle even, as one listened to Darwin preaching all those years ago.

Travelling to the Galapagos Islands is usually a once in a life-time opportunity. The four visits the groups made began to feel like a commute. Four visits equalled four, enchanting experiences. Each guest was briefed by two naturalists who accompanied each tour on the need to keep the impact of the visit to the islands to a minimum. It was just as if we were being briefed to land on Antarctica. Their advice was worth its weight in gold. The Galapagos Archipelago is a unique ecosystem which provided the clues for Charles Darwin to expound his ground-breaking Theory of Evolution following his landing there in 1835. It is now, very sensibly, a world heritage site.

The thirteen islets lie six hundred miles, that's one thousand kilometres almost exactly due west of Ecuador's coast and belong to that country with dozens of smaller islets dotted in the Pacific, all volcanic in nature.

Following a visit to Quito, Ecuador's capital lying at 9,000 feet above sea level (don't run for a taxi at this level) the first tour took a flight to Baltra, home to one of two airports on the islands and from there we boarded the new, expanded exhibition boat the M/V Coral II now a third bigger having completed an extension upgrade in a dry dock in Guayaquil. It had been a worry. Repeated requests to our Agent for information had thrown up muddle and confusion. I had been more than anxious about the readiness of the boat we had charted for our first visit. Flights had been booked and could not be cancelled and the whole trip was in jeopardy causing me sleepless nights. So I booked a flight to Guayaquil to determine what, exactly was the position. As I have always said, learned the hard way in the Army: 'Time spent in reconnaissance is seldom wasted'. I found out that the boat had been literally sawn in two with replating going on to lengthen the whole craft. That is, to provide more cabins. Business in the Galapagos was good. The boat was supported by masses of bamboo scaffolding with hundreds of ant-like labourers swarming all over the place attempting to get the ship ready for the Captain, Patrick. He reassured me everything was on target and nothing to worry about. I returned home my mind soothed. Patrick proved he was right so off we sailed on the time agreed, each day landing ashore at a different island, transferred by small, motorised dinghies known as zodiacs.

Some of us might have been more ardent naturalists than others, some had extensive knowledge of the bird life, but none of us could keep pace with the huge range of flora and fauna including boobies, albatrosses, finches, gulls, red-billed tropical birds along with the reptiles endemic to the islands and a hundred more before walking among the sea lions and mocking birds.

As the Coral II was sailing one day to its planned destination, the Captain came over breathless with excitement asking us to look towards the island of Fernandina. A plume of smoke several miles high was clearly visible as if castaways had, at last, seen our boat. We were, somewhat more eloquently, but just as exciting, witnessing a huge, new eruption. The Captain agreed to alter course for a closer look. Everyone gathered on the weather rail and were asked if the tour should abandon the fixed programme to head off to Fernandina to take a closer look at this phenomenon. The decision was unanimous. Arriving after dark, it was fascinating to see enormous streams of magma spewing out of the volcano in colossal bursts of energy before making up its mind to head for the sea in a four mile long trail or orange and yellow glowing in the night sky. The heat was intense, demonstrating the awesome, unstoppable power of the volcano. We anchored off the island for the night and next day boarded the zodiacs to study the red hot magma closer up as it flowed in total silence to the water.

We later learned the eruption had become world news. We were the first to witness it close up, the tour recognising they had been spectators to a singular occurrence they would never forget. The government of Ecuador, put it this way: 'The eruption occurred along circumferential fissures, parallel to the caldera rim (I'm sure some of you will understand) which fed the lava flows down the steep south-west slope of the volcano. The activity continued for several weeks before, exhausted it burnt itself out'.

We came across a post box on one of the islands built of drift wood and old brandy casks made by ancient whaling men in years gone by. Their ships would stop off in the Galapagos to fill their water barrels and collect turtles, cruelly stored alive in the hold, as fresh meat. Another reason for stopping there was to visit the post office where it was the custom to leave letters addressed to families all over the world or to be collected and delivered to ships bound for any of the ports shown on the envelopes. A bit hit or miss and a crude method of keeping in touch with loved ones but, I suppose, not unlike our own postal service in some ways! One of our more thoughtful clients found a letter addressed to a house not too far from where they lived in London. They made a point of delivering it when they got back. Someone opened the door, took the letter and closed it again. Extraordinary. Perhaps, next time, the letter should be left in the box to mature – say for a hundred years?

Some of the other memorable events covered unplanned visitations by hundreds of dolphins all arriving to say good morning to us. They followed our boat for mile after mile between the islands. At night we would gaze heavenward at the stars from the upper deck, where, without any light pollution, we were given a journey to the heavens by our naturalists. Amongst other things of note, we learned if we ever had an issue on desalination we were told to talk to the local iguanas. They have evolved from land animals back into amphibians and, uniquely, are only found on the Galapagos islands. They have learnt how to drink the salty water, removing the salt – don't ask me how – before spitting out the residue before each one then attempts to outspit the others. The minimum, we observed, was at least several metres though we didn't, in fact have a tape measure with us for further accuracy.

We had to take great care while tramping through the nesting grounds of the albatross nesting grounds for there were thousands of them, in fact between fifty and seventy thousand birds. Their nests were crude but sensibly positioned close to the high cliffs, well placed by mothers teaching their chicks how to fly once they had decided to leave the home. It was explained that, if there were two chicks in one nest, it would be rare for more than one to survive, as the stronger of the two would push its brother or sister over the edge. It is a tough start in life for an albatross, tougher still for its brother…or sister.

•••

One of our guests, John Harris, bumped into a colleague at Baltra airport. He had been visiting the Charles Darwin Station on Santa Cruz Island which received funds from the Galapagos Conservation Trust based in London. Knowing John's background in banking, and being something of a 'turnaround' wizard in industry, he confided in John that the Trust needed an interim Chief Executive Officer as the previous incumbent had left at short notice. John was so impressed with the Galapagos in general he wanted to help in any way he could. He learnt the aim of the Trust was to help protect vulnerable ecosystems found on the islands with pioneering conservation projects while raising awareness of the islands for future generations. Typical of John, he jumped at the opportunity. The challenge was to re-align the approach of the great and the good trustees with the small executive team and the large number of willing volunteers. At the time he took the venture on he discovered that too high a proportion of donations were being absorbed by administration and costly projects. He streamlined the administration operation and simply scrapped some of the more expensive fund raising initiatives. John also introduced many improvements, skilfully re-arranging the operation and became Chief Executive Officer for the Trust before managing the recruitment of a full-time CEO.

The Galapagos Conservation Trust (www.galapagosconservation.org.uk) is the only UK charity working solely for the conservation and sustainability of the islands. It now raises over £1million annually. Two members of the Darwin family continue as Ambassadors for the charity.

This is a nice story brought about by a chance meeting at Baltra Airport on our arrival in Galapagos. John remains a life member of the Trust.

•••

After the Galapagos the tour turned to exploring a more remote part of Ecuador staying at the exclusive EcoAmazonia lodge *La Casa del Suizo* which sat on the banks of the Napo river, a tributary of the Amazon. (All tributaries seem to end up flowing into the Amazon). To get to it, there was a six hour drive along a dirt road through the Andean Highlands to the tiny port of *Punta Ahuano* where everything stops. We were thus obliged to take canoes to get to our destination. In and out the water was part of life including floating down the river on inflatable inner tubes, idly wondering, well, all the time in fact, whether our swimming costumes would stand up to possible interest from piranhas, the freshwater fish known to ambush prey in groups. It was with considerable interest, we learned happily, these fish did not like fast-flowing water preferring to lurk in the undergrowth and weeds along the banks. As they have, apparently, the strongest bite known to man, that is 'quite strong' when considering the bite of, say, a great white?' We were able to arrive back each time, *omnes in una*.

Just as interesting to me were the three hour guided walks through primary rainforest, the sort of jungle one reads about all the time but never really understands its density and depth. Guests freaked out at tarantulas, some with eleven inch legs – well I would too – and 'picnics' on the river banks before visiting a Quichua village opened our eyes further. If everyone had to visit such places perhaps more would stand up and fight for the planet.

A useful trait we picked up to take home was being taught how to use a blow pipe by the villagers and discovered the group had found a star, an ex-Hong Kong policewoman who won our prize for the best blow pipe shot, even beating the locals for accuracy. Arrow tips were without poison at the time but they could have proved useful when we returned if we had trouble on a Saturday night in down town Kendal.

There are seventeen million square kilometres of land in South America, seemingly, as one drove south, everyone of them totally diverse from its neighbour; everyone fascinating in its peoples and animals with some of the most valuable ecosystems in the world. We mustn't let this slip.

CHAPTER 14

Marcus

I had an amazing, clever, talented son. His name was Marcus. All fathers use adjectives as I have listed, and more, but in this case I have hundreds and hundreds of independent letters, emails, public comment and personal briefs to support my claim. Marcus was known world-wide through the astonishing success of his on-line Architectural and Design magazine, *'Dezeen'*. He created it, built it up through being a gifted journalist, until one day it became the most popular design website in the world. He had a wonderful family and now he is gone. Marcus died on 30th June 2022 at the age of 54.

This book is thus dedicated to him, to all the talents I was not aware of, and of the many talents I knew he retained and used daily. To come to terms with this tragedy – it is still hard to believe he has gone from our lives – I have included the day in February 2023 when *'Dezeen'* gathered the Architectural and Design world around it to demonstrate to me beyond any doubt at all, how talented and loved he was by so many people. He made *'Dezeen'* the indispensable site for design news and when it came to the latest product, interior or building, if one wanted to be seen, one had to be in *'Dezeen'*. One can only speculate what his next project would have been, but it is taken for granted there was another chapter yet to come.

It is rare that an individual can be so gifted yet so admired – genuinely – at the same time. I have taken the liberty of adding some of Marcus's friends 'goodbyes' together with my own personal speech at the memorial service.

Before 'Dezeen' arrived, Marcus and I worked together as Partners with our own company Langdale Walking Holidays, and he is remembered with affection by the clients he led to different parts of the world.

I hope this short chapter fills a gap in my story. Marcus is described here at the end of my book, appropriate perhaps, for these words also define the final chapter in his life but he will be remembered for the way he led in his life, and achieved so much in that short time.

Marcus sent me an email one day in May 2022 two months before he died.

Dad,
It makes me very proud of you to read your story. You've had an incredible life and have overcome difficult circumstances to achieve so much. You're amazing. I love you very much. Marcus.

Marcus 2022

CHAPTER 15

Retirement

At the end of the day…

I have no idea what retirement is because now, in my 80's, I am fortunate to continue to retain my health, remain fit and active and enjoy an excellent quality of life. I walk the Lakeland Fells which remain a delight and can still thrash a tennis ball across a net. Then, there is the garden, always needing attention not to say organising the walking tour reunions. Thus, my mind and body remain committed to the future.

Writing this book adds to my fulfilment particularly as I recall all the amazing events and places my work has taken me, to sharing it with so many decent people who have added to a tour's success. I would like to believe, by getting people to accept challenges seemingly beyond them, and for them to achieve the difficult objective, it has made them better people. To leap into freezing turbulent waters on Dartmoor; to climbing vertical chain ladders in South Africa, going the extra mile on long walks, keeping going when one's mind is saying there's nothing left, or shooting the rapids in the Grand Canyon. That's when they can walk tall and be very proud of themselves.

Then, there are the altitude problems, scary suspension bridges in the Himalaya, negotiating one's way through steep canyons in Utah, parachute jumping in New Zealand – it all adds up to quite a ball. Having travelled to so many places around the world, I have woken up to the realisation of the wonderful places here in Britain still waiting to be explored. It is the next stage for me.

I used to be a very fit man, by necessity I might mention but though I retain a taste for adventure, my fitness is no longer as it had been. My new mantra for the next few years or so is to try to prove to oneself anything is possible if one believes in it.

Out of all this, I have deduced, the best things in life are the people we love, the places we've been and the memories made along the way. I live with Denise my wife, my rock, in a converted farm cottage in the Lake District. A mountain stream, clear as crystal runs through the garden while Kendal lies on the edge of the Fells close by. We often sit in the garden gathered, and wrapped within our memories retracing in our minds the thousands of miles we have travelled together. But, we cannot hang around too long, so much more to visit and explore. Retirement sounds good to me when it does come eventually, as it will give me time to plan the next big adventure.

Nile 1961. *'Negotiating for a donkey to take me to the dentist.'*

Egypt. Pyramids. 2009
'David and Denise. 'Taking the hump.'

New Zealand. 2009. Abel Tasman….
'Can't keep the author out of a canoe.'

Patagonia. 2005. *'250 sq.km and 30km long. That is a lot of ice.'*

Dolomites. 2018. The author.
'You can see he needs two sticks to hold himself up.'

Colorado river, Grand Canyon 2013
'This is sometimes known as rafting though here…?'

POSTSCRIPT

The Army opened my eyes to a wide, challenging yet exciting world which I knew, one day, would need to be explored in detail. Military training brought me the discipline and the skills needed to run a successful holiday company for like-minded, curious wanderers following close in my footsteps, while sharing in the camaraderie which adventure brings.

It taught me to use my *'airborne initiative'* – to use my own abilities, to think things through or, as they say in the north, 'use my noggin'. It also coached me, that, when things got tough or out of kilter with my carefully laid plans: *'I was not always there to enjoy myself'*.

Leaving the Army at the peak of my military career after 25 years was a difficult decision for me to make, but in the end it turned out to be the right decision and a second career in the leisure industry has been enjoyable beyond my wildest dreams, particularly the privilege of managing the spectacular Langdale Estate in the English Lake District. Also, and more importantly, had I remained in the Army, I would not have met my wonderful wife.

When I hung, upside down in my harness, hurtling towards solid ground at a rate of knots, I only had myself to get me out of the scrape. These two axioms, in italics, have been part of me all my life, though now, my boots remain longer on their hook than they did when I was visiting seventy countries more than once. But what I have learned over the many years, is how good and reliable my clients were, always wanting to help each other, aiding friends across an ice-field, a steamy jungle or into a flimsy canoe, at odds with a rough sea. Clients turned into friends as if they had metamorphosed from one material state to another, to surround me today like a warm cloak.

Another axiom which has become part of my beliefs is: *'Life doesn't have to be perfect to be beautiful.'* When one has looked upon the world as I have had the privilege to do, experienced its afflictions as well as its values, I have learned, where ever I see people living together, in what ever country I travel, they all aspire to the same things: Education for their children; enough food on the table and peace in their country.

On such a note, I believe this is as good a place as any to end my story.

Carry on. David Fairs

APPENDIX 1

WALKING THE WORLD

David wrote a section for the Appendix on what he described as statistics, proudly lining up in rather boring columns, not only every country and capital city he had visited but the number of times he had returned to the same place. While perhaps, there is some merit in letting a reader know of all the places he went, David is a modest man beneath that Para. Smock and, he felt, in the end, there was little point in continuing in this style. In typical fashion, he began to tackle the issue from another direction. He asked me to suggest a format!

David's many groups did travel to over seventy countries, from the frozen Antarctic to the lofty heights of the Himalaya, the sweaty jungles of India to the barren Steppe of Patagonia. Countries were not chosen because they might be 'nice to visit' but because the group could find something new to learn. It was always going to be a challenge. His travels took him over old battlefields such as Borneo, Northern Ireland and Cyprus familiar to him with his former life, or switching him radically to the lushness of Switzerland and South Africa.

He often went back, pressed to do so by his many fellow colleagues – no longer clients but close friends - all bound by the fascination of the birdlife in the Galapagos or the teeming chaos of Rajasthan. When ever the next destination had been highlighted under David's review of all six continents in turn, and made his decision, he would always find a willingness to fill the plane and the hotels with eager participants. Over fifty percent of his travels were long-haul, indicating the wish to explore further afield, flying to lands familiar to them through television documentaries but needing the scent of spices in the Souq to make it all real and believable. It would often bring them into close contact with the more basic of living, the dung, both animal and human, the filth of the streets, the madness of traffic where no rules seemed to be adhered to, and the vivid contrasts between European 'sanity' and the youth and eagerness of Africa and Asia.

It was Alan Whicker in 1965 who declared his 'First 'Million Miles'. His wide-ranging T.V. programmes which began in 1959 (with Cliff Michelmore in the long-running *'Tonight'*) and ending in 1993 with his own travel programme. David Fairs can probably match Alan in his own travels in length although it would never occur to him to tot up all the miles and show it off as some sort of *Signa Romanum,* the Centurion's Standard.. That is not his style. To him it was the successful completion of another tour, bringing everyone home safely while, each year his store of knowledge of the world increased to become that more valuable for future tours. It would be interesting to ask him now: 'Where haven't you been?' East Cheam perhaps?

Whether or not David planned his venture in part two of his life, to be as far-flung or as successful, is not something he talks about, though one imagines him quietly pleased at the way his Army career gave him the skills to plan, organise and lead his groups. We, as a nation, could learn a lot from the way in which the Army trains its men. His fingers must have often strayed to the far side of the world on his Atlas, as he sought new, strange, mysterious countries to explore - a far cry from the days when he would take a picnic down to the Gower Peninsular on a warm, sunny afternoon.

It was the Army which remains inured into his very psyche. When one is climbing a vertical metal ladder up a cliff, disappearing into the mist (or clouds?) it is reassuring to know David's sharply acerbic comments from far below, are making sure they are supporting your buttocks, because he believes you can get to the top. And, so you do, emerging on the top ledge where you can see to the end of the world.

Richard Newman

APPENDIX 2

COMMENTS FROM CLIENTS

Here are a few comments from clients:

'I remember a magical holiday in India where David steered us through jungles (and a rogue guide who he dealt with as if he were still wearing a green beret) and that self-confidence which has become one of his hallmarks. It is the sheer professionalism of his organisation, even down to the comfort stops where 'gentlemen' had to 'lighten their load' using an opened-up oil drum (probably with a can opener) at the back of a filling station. Unfortunately, it was too high for me but, enough said. David's command to me when we reached our hotel in the deepest and darkest of jungle was "go man the Gatling gun Richard" whereupon we were allocated a tower room in this 'fort' with a panoramic view over Rajasthan. Cool gin and tonic before dinner with ice sourced from some hut in the wilderness, under a shaded veranda with the best crowd of travelling companions one could meet and, as I said, all under the careful eye of this experienced man who, inter alia, has made 80 jumps out of airplanes travelling at 120m.p.h. for some extraordinary reason.

Richard Newman

'I had just retired in 1998 from a 36 year career in banking and was spending New Year at the Langdale Hotel. I noticed a display cabinet for Langdale Walking Holidays in the hotel including a forthcoming trip to Nepal. In order to assess whether we would book the holiday, Netta and I joined a LWH Reunion at the hotel.

We had no hesitation in booking on to the trip to Annapurna Base Camp, which I was keen to do and Netta was keen not to miss (a subtle difference), so she handed in her notice as a teacher. Nepal was an amazing adventure and cultural experience to a third-world country which had a profound impact on us both. On return, Netta took up supply teaching and raised significant funds for Nepalese schools, having been shocked at how little material was available in the hill schools.

That is how we came to join LWH, booking many equally memorable trips over 28 years including New Zealand (twice), Oregon, Galapagos, Peru, Bolivia, Jordan, Madeira (twice), Tuscany, Crete, Pyrenees, Isles of Scilly, the Dolomites and Venice, together with numerous reunions.

Why did we keep booking holidays with LWH? Firstly, they were always extremely well organised by David Fairs and included an element of adventure which added an extra dimension to visiting faraway places. Indeed, David could always be relied upon to sort out any problems that occurred on the holiday. One example was when our hotel reservation in Queenstown was cancelled because of the worst floods in New Zealand for 100 years. Our route to Queenstown was also blocked due to a bridge being washed away. His advice was not to worry and to let him do the worrying and for us to enjoy the holiday, as everything would be sorted out, as indeed it was. By the time we reached the South Island the New Zealand Government had installed a Bailey Bridge and we had been upgraded to a wonderful hotel. His personal involvement was of immense value and re-assurance.

We met delightful like-minded people on each of the holidays with many becoming lifelong friends. This has been particularly valuable for me as I still feel comfortable joining the holidays despite my wife passing away several years ago.

I think that the secret to David's success is that he has an incredible appetite for travel to new and faraway places where he himself wants to visit and experience. He has taken us to places and experiences to which we might not otherwise have travelled and would not have been delivered in the same way by other larger tour operators.

John Harris

Dear David- many thanks to you and Denise for our wonderful holiday in Oregon. It was excellent from beginning to end and one of our best holidays ever. Crater Lake, Fort Rock and the High Desert stand out as totally new experiences, but the whole package from beginning to end was hugely enjoyable. We were much impressed with the pace of life in Oregon – relaxed and laid-back in the glorious summer climate, but with a challenging environment to provide excitement. Sunriver lived up to its reputation, and you looked after us so well and made our enjoyment complete. Thank so much for that.

Andrew and Jill

'My Aunty Nan used to send me back copies of Readers Digest in an attempt to improve my English. It didn't help but it introduced me to the regular article called "The Most Unforgettable Character I Ever Met". Well, there you have it – David Fairs.

We met him through Langdale Estate Lodge Owning. Our first "David" holiday was to Jordan – somewhere we probably wouldn't have gone on our own initiative. We were immediately hooked by the quality of the experience and so started a long and firm relationship leading us to rebook over and over. Typically, we met similarly hooked adventurers and a growing set of friends.

Why so addicted? The extensive research, the careful design and planning, the scrupulous attention to detail and the instantaneous troubleshooting did it for us. Any problem had either been anticipated or solved without anybody realising. Then, of course, the engaging personality of Mr. Fairs himself could keep us spellbound as we were regaled with his comprehensive store of jokes and stories, beautifully recounted.

Thus evolved our wonderful memories of Rajasthan, Tuscany, The Cotswolds, Montana, Wyoming, Arizona, New Mexico, Nevada, Utah, Oman, The Seychelles, Madeira, Egypt, Tatra Mountains (Poland), Borrowdale, Pembrokeshire, Llanbedr Pont Steffan. Experiencing Petra almost empty due to 9/11.

Turning the coach back to Jaipur to retrieve a bag containing passports, tickets, money, cards – forgotten in a daze of gastroenteritis. Wondering if the caldera would blow whilst we were standing there in Yellowstone. Meeting survivors of pirating in Mahé. Bewitched by Bird Island in the Seychelles. Negotiating post hurricane hazards in Madeira. Astonished at the fossils in the desert Ancient Ocean in Giza. Noting Cardiovascular symptoms and disintegrating boots in Zakopane and the horror of Auschwitz-Birkenau. Feeling hiraeth sparked by telynores and penillion in Falcondale.

All this Memory Bank, a lifetime of pleasures, excitement and camaraderie with very decent people is courtesy of knowing David Fairs. The most unforgettable character I ever met.

Christine and John Williams

David Fairs

David Fairs was born in Wales shortly before the outbreak of WW2 into a family with little spare cash. Scrambling with difficulty through the first 18 years of life, he was drawn to the Army and commissioned in 1953, the year of the Coronation. Nothing stopped him from achieving his goals, first as a Paratrooper, then a Royal Marine Commando; canoeing 1,000 miles down the Nile, ending up with his own Regiment. He saw active service four times before leaving the Army he loved to develop long-held ideas in travel.

Life became difficult. Doubts arose, dark days came, but 25 years of steadfastness in the Army enabled him to change to a completely new life. He managed a Pontins Holiday camp with eye-opening commentary, before setting up his own Tour company, its aim to walk round the world accompanied by clients seeking a taste of adventure always linked to the best possibly quality. His careful planning took him from the ice of Antarctica to the heights of the Himalaya, from the steamy jungles of India to the barren Steppe of Patagonia. A million miles.

His Army training never left him, it is part of his psyche, which enabled his many fellow travellers, now friends, to attain goals they never thought they were capable of achieving. David's book is an inspiration on how to lead one's life. It will continue to do so.

David and his wife Denise remain living in the English Lake District, still planning reunions and meeting up with past travel companions.

Milton Keynes UK
Ingram Content Group UK Ltd.
UKHW020942290823
427668UK00008B/26

9 781805 412571